# SINS OF THE FATHERS

James Pope-Hennessy was a writer of unusual range and beguilingly fluent style. He was born in 1916 and educated at Downside and Balliol College, Oxford. From 1947 to 1949 he was literary editor of *The Spectator*. By then, he had already decided that writing was his vocation, and for the rest of his life he earned his living by the pen. He died in 1974.

*Also by James Pope-Hennessy*

Monckton Miles: The Years of Promise

Monckton Miles: The Flight of Youth

Lord Crewe: The Likeness of a Liberal

Queen Mary (Phoenix Press)

Queen Victoria at Windsor and Balmoral

Verandah: Some Episodes in the Crown Colonies 1867–1889

Anthony Trollope

London Fabric

West Indian Summer

History Under Fire (with Cecil Beaton)

The Houses of Parliament

America Is an Atmosphere

The Baths of Absalom

Aspects of Provence

# SINS OF
# THE FATHERS

*The Atlantic Slave Trade*

*1441–1807*

James Pope-Hennessy

CASTLE BOOKS

This edition published in 2004 by
**CASTLE BOOKS** ®
A division of BOOK SALES INC.
114 Northfield Avenue
Edison, NJ 08837

This book is reprinted by arrangement with
Orion Publishing Group Ltd.
Orion House, 5 Upper St. Martin's Lane, London WC2H 9EA

Copyright © 1967 by James Pope-Hennessy

First published in Great Britain by Weidenfeld & Nicolson in 1967
Paperback edition published in 2000 by Phoenix Press

A CIP catalogue record for this book is available from the British Library

ISBN-13: 978-0-7858-1594-5
ISBN-10: 0-7858-1594-5

Printed in the United States of America

FOR
*Irene Worth*

# Contents

# *Illustrations*

Nicholas Owen's house beside the Sherbro River, drawn, *c.* 1755, by himself.

Upper part of an Afro-Portuguese ivory casket, showing a Portuguese caravel (? sixteenth century).

Admiral de Ruyter in the Castle of Elmina. (From a painting by de Witt in the possession of Lord Harlech.)

A view of Cape Coast Castle in 1682 (after Greenhill).

The courtyard of the Castle of Elmina, 1956.

In the Niger Delta, *c.* 1830. (From a lithograph.)

The Benin River, near Benin city.

The overgrown ruins of part of the thirteenth-century fortified walls of Benin city, which were twenty-eight miles round.

Branding irons, fetters, whips and 'iron necklace' used in the slave trade. (Examples from the Wilberforce Museum, Hull.)

'The Myth of the Merry and Contented Slave'; a festival on the island of St Vincent 1794. (From an engraving after A. Brunyas.)

Thumb-screws and mouth-openers from Thomas Clarkson's collection.

Fate of a rebel Negro in Surinam, *c.* 1772 (from an engraving by William Blake).

A West African Slave Market. In the centre a French captain negotiating with caboceers, to the right a French factor. (From the painting by A. F. Biard, Wilberforce Museum, Hull.)

Forests of the Niger Delta.

Efik trader's house, Old Calabar.

Thomas Clarkson (from a portrait by C. F. von Breda in the National Portrait Gallery, London).

Seal of the Committee for the Abolition of the Slave Trade, 1787.

# Maps

Apart from the sources mentioned above, the author and publishers are also grateful to the following for help in obtaining pictures and for permission to reproduce: British Museum; Courtauld Institute of Art; Mr Basil Davidson; Mr Werner Forman; and to Professor A. W. Lawrence, author of *Trade Castles and Forts of West Africa*, and to Jonathan Cape Ltd.

Maps specially drawn by Surrey Art Designs.

'I the Lord thy God
am a jealous God,
and visit
the sins of the fathers
upon the children
unto the third and
fourth generation . . .'

*The Book of Exodus*,
chapter XX, verse 5

# Preface

As the selective bibliography at the end of the book indicates, this study of the Atlantic slave-traders is chiefly based on printed sources. Unpublished Crown Copyright material in the Public Record Office is reproduced by permission of the Controller of Her Majesty's Stationery Office. The only other unpublished material in this country that I have used has been drawn from the archives of the Wilberforce Museum, Kingston-upon-Hull and from the private papers of the Codrington family at Dodington Park.

I wish to record my gratitude for research facilities granted me in the United States of America by Mrs Dorothea Dresser Reeves, Librarian of the Kress Room, Baker Library, Harvard University; by Mr Ray, Librarian of the Schomburg Collection of Negro Literature and History, New York City; by Mr E. Millby Burton, Director of the Charleston Museum, Charleston, South Carolina; and by the Secretary and Librarian of the Massachusetts Historical Society, Boston, Massachusetts. In Jamaica I worked in the library of the Kingston Museum and received much aid and hospitality from the officials of the Jamaica Tourist Board. In West Africa I was allowed to use the library and archives at Fourah Bay College, Sierra Leone and at the University of Ibadan, Ibadan, Nigeria.

Among those who have given me much hospitality during the series of journeys involved in preparing this book I should like warmly to thank Dr J. W. Vinson, of Harvard University; Mr Alan Pryce-Jones who lent me his house at Newport, Rhode Island; Mr Noël Coward, with whom I stayed at Port Maria, Jamaica; Mr Ronald Tree whose guest I was in Barbados; Mr Michael Crowder, of Fourah Bay College, Freetown, Sierra Leone; Miss Lalage Bown, at that time in charge of Extra-Mural Studies at Ibadan University, and Mr John Hunwick of the same university; Mr Robin Atkinson, of Lagos; Mr Edgar F. Shannon, President of the University of Virginia, Charlottesville, and his Special Assistant, Mr Francis Berkeley.

## *Preface*

Lord Harlech has allowed me to reproduce the painting of Admiral de Ruyter in his possession.

Throughout my researches for this book I have been fortunate enough to have had the aid of Mrs Elizabeth Mostyn-Owen, whose intelligence and swift but meticulous eye for detail have proved invaluable. Miss Diana Crawfurd's unflinching interest in, and sustained enthusiasm for, the progress of the work have likewise been of great assistance to me. Mrs Gina Marreco has done research for me in Rio de Janeiro and the slave trade. For typing the manuscript I am indebted to Madame Roger Beau, of Gstaad; and to Jean McDougall, of Church Street, Kensington.

Where necessary I have modernized the spelling in quotations throughout the book.

*Port Hall, co. Donegal*                       JAMES POPE-HENNESSY
*120 Pembroke Street, Boston, Massachusetts*
*Blue Harbour, Port Maria, Jamaica*
*Charly's Tea-rooms, Gstaad*
*9 Ladbroke Grove, London, W11*

# SINS OF THE FATHERS

# Chapter 1

## 'And the candles would not burn'

### I

'I HAVE been on board of Captain Engledo today, where I found him employed in making a curious piece of shell-work in his cabin upon an old picture. Tomorrow I intend to imitate him . . . as we have great numbers of shells upon the beach.'

So wrote, in the hot green winter of 1757, a young man named Nicholas Owen, resident in a whitewashed wattle hut, lined with matting, on the islet of Sherbro, off the Grain Coast of West Africa. By next day his shell-picture was completed: 'I think it's just suitable to my dwelling. It's of a round form with a looking-glass in the middle; I have wrought into it divers figures with various kinds of shell and moss taken from the bark of old trees and shrubs . . . With these and others of the same nature of amusements I pass the tedious hours of my life away.'

Dependent upon passing ships for European company, young Owen had decided that, in his confined 'retreat', he was living 'a very remarkable life', and one surely preferable to his earlier experiences aboard ships on the Africa–New England run. 'And if it wasn't for my woman and four or five people' (he wrote) 'I might very well pass for a hermit. My diet is mean and my clothing not sumptuous.' Owen was persuaded that his solitary life suited him because his temperament was melancholy, and because he was quite contented to gaze out day after day through his window at the same changeless landscape – Kings Town and a part of the Sherbro delta – and to listen to the echo of the Atlantic rollers as they beat over the bars and shoals at the turgid river's mouth. He amused himself by sketching (though he ran out of Indian ink) and by keeping a journal of his daily

I

life, by planting pumpkins and water-melons to supplement his diet of fowls, rice, palm-oil and slobber-sauce, and by hedging in a set of little gardens against the snakes and land-crabs. Two years later, in an even more confined retreat on the banks of the Sherbro River, Nicholas Owen lay dead.

What had impelled this somewhat sensitive and civilized youth to settle on the Grain Coast at all, to brave the fevers, the mosquitoes and a constant, odd sensation which felt like a weakening of his bones? Quite simply that he was a slave-trader – one short-lived Englishman contributing his flash of time and mite of energy to that vast complex of international crime by which, in four centuries, a total of fifteen million men, women and children of African blood were delivered into trans-atlantic slavery, under conditions so hideous that another nine million are estimated to have died during the crossing.

Our chiefest business is in the purchasing of slaves, which is very troublesome. In the first place you are obliged to treat them [i.e. the African middle-men] to liquor before you purchase anything or not . . . You are obliged to take all advantages and leave all bounds of justice when trading with these creatures, as they do by you, otherwise your goods won't fetch their sterling price at home. Some people may think a scruple of conscience in the above trade, but it's very seldom minded by our European merchants.

A few, but very few, of Nicholas Owen's profession did feel a scruple of conscience, but usually later on in life. William Cowper's friend, John Newton,\* who started his career on board a slave ship and made five voyages to the Guinea coast where, like Owen, he lived for months as a slave-factor, was only con-verted to the Abolition movement years after he had left the trade. 'Disagreeable I had long found it,' he writes in his posthumously published *Thoughts upon the African Slave Trade*:

but I think I should have quitted it sooner, had I considered it as I now do, to be unlawful and wrong. But I never had a scruple upon this head at the time; nor was such a thought once suggested to me by a friend. What I did I did ignorantly; considering it as the line of life to which Divine Providence had allotted me, and having no concern, in point of conscience, but to treat the slaves, while under

---

\* Author of the hymn 'How sweet the name of Jesus sounds'.

my care, with as much humanity as a regard to my own safety would admit.

In the same memoir Newton has described the interior of a slave ship, with its five foot headroom below decks divided by ledges for the slaves chained two and two together and laid

in two rows one above the other, on each side of the ship, close to each other, like books upon a shelf. I have known them so close that the shelf would not easily contain one more. And I have known a white man sent down among the men to lay them in these rows to the greatest advantage, so that as little space as possible be lost . . . And every morning perhaps more instances than one are found of the living and the dead, like the captives of Mezentius, fastened together.

An earlier slaver than Newton, James Barbot, has described the difficulties facing ships' surgeons who tried 'to administer proper remedies' to moribund Negroes in the hold. 'This' he remarks 'they cannot do leisurely between decks, because of the great heat that is there continually, which is sometimes so excessive that the surgeons would faint away, and the candles would not burn.'

Newton, James Barbot and Nicholas Owen were near-contemporaries but we cannot just dismiss their callousness as characteristic of their time. More than half a century later, and four years after the British had officially ended the slave trade, another youth, this time a United States citizen of Irish parentage called Richard Drake, was keeping a journal of the slaving voyages he was making from Rio Basso on the Windward Coast to Pensacola Bay in Florida. Leaving the coast on one of these, in October 1812, he found his Captain, Leclerc, reckoning up his anticipated profits. 'I may as well do the same' wrote Drake. 'I have 100 prime blacks – only 20 females – all branded, in good Spanish, with my name "Felippe Draz", and I begin to feel the anxieties of a property owner.' A few days out in the Atlantic, Leclerc spoke to him about the slave trade itself. 'Leclerc and I had a chat about this African business. He says he's repugnant to it, and I confess it's not a thing I like. But, as my uncle argues, slaves must be bought and sold; somebody must do the trading; and why not make hay while the sun shines?' This voyage proved particularly sickly:

3

We had half the gang on deck today for exercise; they danced and sang,* under the driver's whip, but are far from sprightly . . . Last Tuesday the smallpox began to rage, and we hauled 60 corpses out of the hold . . . We stimulated the blacks with rum in order to get their help in removing corpses . . . The sights I witness may I never look on such again. This is a dreadful trade . . . Some of the blacks are raving mad, and screech like wild beasts.

On his return to Africa, this revulsion remained with him:

I am growing sicker every day of this business of buying and selling human beings for beasts of burden . . . On the eighth day [out at sea] I took my round of the half deck, holding a camphor bag in my teeth; for the stench was hideous. The sick and dying were chained together. I saw pregnant women give birth to babies whilst chained to corpses, which our drunken overseers had not removed. The blacks were literally jammed between decks as if in a coffin; and a coffin that dreadful hold became to nearly one half of our cargo before we reached Bahia.

Nauseated Mr Drake continued working in the slave trade for another four and twenty profitable years. In the following pages we shall meet him, and variants upon him, again.

# II

In recent decades much scholarly attention has been devoted to the purely economic, as against the human, aspects of the slave trade to the West. In his calm and mordant book *Capitalism and Slavery*, first published twenty years ago and now re-issued, Dr Eric Williams, the Prime Minister of Trinidad, has clinically explored the vast financial and mercantile ramifications of the British slave trade – the foremost, in its heyday, of the world. Like other pioneers he tends to overstate his case, for he sees the slave trade as the basis of almost every British industry of the

* This compulsory dancing was, as we shall see, 'deemed necessary for the preservation of their health'. Alexander Falconbridge in his *An Account of the Slave Trade* (London, 1788) has recorded that 'if they go about it reluctantly, or do not move with agility, they are flogged; a person standing by them all the time with a cat-o'-nine-tails in his hand for that purpose. Their music, upon these occasions, consists of a drum . . . The poor wretches are frequently compelled to sing also; but when they do so, their songs are generally, as may naturally be expected, melancholy lamentations of their exile from their native land'. Such were the sad origins of the Negro rhythms which have since conquered the Western world.

eighteenth century from shipping to iron, from wool to brass, and as the chief progenitor of the Industrial Revolution. Rejecting as subjective and sentimental the old liberal condemnation of the trade, and spurning the labours of Sir Reginald Coupland, Dr Williams treats Wilberforce and his followers as ignorant hypocrites, and even accuses them of exaggerating the 'horrors of the Middle Passage'. He has, on the other hand, established once and for all the fact that abolition of the slave trade would never have come when it did had the importance of the sugar colonies to Britain's economy not been already on the wane. In his preface to Dr Williams' book, Sir Denis Brogan explains that its author is as 'morally appalled' by his own conclusions as was Karl Marx by his: 'But even better than Marx he makes his point that this is what society is like. The infrastructure is more important than the super-structure, the economic base than the ideologies.' 'Money,' writes Sir Denis, 'not passion, passions of wickedness or passions of goodness, spun the plot.'

But what goad is more potent than money, what passion more ruthless than the passion for it? If we accept that this is what society was like, it does not exonerate us from peering back into a peculiarly sunless and fungoid region of our proud island past. In the nineteen-sixties, when we daily witness or read about the racial violence and resentment which is our direct, our sullen legacy from the Atlantic slave trade, it ill becomes us to take refuge behind the sandbags of economic theory. And what stranger has been able to live in the West Indies, or in the Southern States, or in Brazil without speculating upon the history of Negro slavery – as demoralizing to the slave-owners as it was to the slaves? Who has trodden the stony ramps that lead to the dim, bat-hung slave dungeons of Cape Coast Castle in West Africa, or stood in the haunted slave-yards of nearby Elmina and not pondered on the history of the slave trade? In my own case, convictions seeded during a Washington childhood and developed in later sojourns in the West Indian islands and on visits to the Deep South have been fortified by nights spent upon the battlements of St Iago at Elmina, and by sultry mornings and afternoons in Cape Coast Castle, Shama, Gross Friedrichsburg, Anamabu, and the other old European trading-stations upon what was for centuries

5

known as the Gold Coast. To read about the slave trade began to seem to me a duty – to write about it a compulsion.

Not that the slave trade is easy to write about. A vast quantity of fresh historical, ethnological and statistical matter has lately been unearthed, sifted and published. This invaluable material deals both with the trade's African and with its European aspects. All the same, for most people ethnology remains a dullish subject. Statistics, too, are resolutely unevocative, for figures and percentages do not register upon the mind's inner eye. Unilluminating likewise are ships' books of lading, in which some dead clerk's whorled handwriting has listed gold-dust, male and female slaves, ivory tusks, and other produce of Africa with undiscriminating zeal. It is, therefore, from the more vibrant sources – illiterate journals, dubious records, specious testimonies – that a writer on the trade must strive, with care, to draw.

Further, since the vocabulary of horror is as limited as that of lust, the whole subject of the slave trade has been neutralized by clichés. Slave-traders become 'callous', slaving captains 'brutal', slave-ship sailors 'depraved, drunken and diseased', African chiefs and middle-men 'avid for gain', the enslaved Negroes 'victims of European avarice'. The trade itself becomes 'a monstrous traffic', the transatlantic voyages of the slave ships are summed up as 'the horrors of the Middle Passage'. Originally minted under the auspices of the Clapham sect, these phrases over-simplify the issue, and reduce the vast and reeking panorama of the Atlantic slave trade to the scale of gruesome antics on a puppet stage. Reality has sidled off and sneaked away.

For apologists there are also ready-tailored phrases – 'the brutality of the age', for example, and 'a necessary evil'. And here crops up the problem of being just – which is not at all to be confused with being detached. Even taking human nature at its lowest, a trade in which so many Europeans and Africans indulged for centuries cannot have been run exclusively by money-maniacs and pocket sadists. As an industry the Atlantic slave trade encouraged greed, brutality, hypocrisy and fear. As a profession it was probably more degrading than any other. Its methods were even cruder than its motives. But it was not a simple question of enriching Caribbean nabobs or the great merchants of Liverpool alone. At its height the apprentice carpen-

6

ter in Bristol, the youngest wool-carder in Wakefield, Halifax or Burnley may have depended upon it for his livelihood, just as certain of our great Palladian country houses owe to it the fact that they were built at all. Nevertheless, if we cannot always condemn slavers who were taught to take the trade for granted, this does not mean that we can in any way condone their doings. A trade as widespread and as complex as this involved numberless personalities. A selection of these we shall encounter in this book.

So let us now embark upon a far from pleasant voyage aboard rocking, rancid vessels, in the teeming holds of which no candles burn.

# Chapter 2

# How Curiosity Became Geometry

## I

ALTHOUGH it was the British who perfected slave ship design and slaving instruments and methods, bringing to the trade that efficiency and inventiveness which was once their national hallmark, the European nation which may claim the discredit for initiating the Atlantic slave trade is Portugal. Chronology, like statistics, is a subject dry as hard tack, but we must brace ourselves for a sharp, brief glance at it here.

While there is a valid argument for choosing 1444, historians have generally agreed upon the year 1441 as that in which the modern slave trade was, so to speak, officially declared open. In that year ten Africans from the northern Guinea Coast were shipped to Portugal as a gift to Prince Henry the Navigator. Obtained as ransom for other, superior 'moors' who had been kidnapped after being hunted down like wild animals by the Portuguese sailors, these ten Africans were brought back in triumph by a modest trading expedition commanded by a young protégé of Prince Henry named Antam Gonçalvez. They had not, however, been captured for sale, but simply to be shown to Prince Henry in the same way that rare plants, exotic butterflies or tropical birds might have been shown. By 1444 one of several subsequent expeditions brought back a bumper harvest of two hundred and thirty-five African men, women and children who, landed at the Portuguese port of Lagos, were then disembarked and herded together in a meadow outside the city walls. Here they were parcelled out into lots under the benign eye of the Regent of Portugal who rode out to watch the proceedings mounted on a thoroughbred horse. The Regent's share

of the captives was one fifth of the whole, and these he re-
distributed amongst his retinue. The contemporary chronicler
of the scene records the 'great pleasure' with which the pious
Regent 'reflected . . . upon the salvation of those souls that
before were lost'. The choicest of the Africans were presented as
an offering to the chief church of Lagos, and one little boy was
sent to St Vincent do Cabo to be educated. He grew up a
Franciscan friar.

Except for the fact that families were torn apart, and the
state of terror in which the enslaved Negroes at first gazed upon
this strange white man's country, these early captives were well-
treated, baptized, and absorbed into Portuguese households
where they were petted and educated. So soon as it was realized
that they were a musical people, it became fashionable for some
of the great families of Lisbon to entertain their guests with
African bands. In the later decades of the fifteenth century, the
emphasis seems still to have been upon the saving of black souls
by their conversion to Christianity. Their enslavement was,
moreover, justified by tags from the Bible, most notably the
curse Noah laid upon Canaan after the flood: that his descendants should be eternally subject to all the other races of
the world. But soon this lofty motive, as lofty motives will,
became confused and obscured by others, until in 1518 we find
Charles V granting to the Governor of Bresa the monopoly of
shipping four thousand African slaves a year to the West Indies.
This monopoly, which the Governor sold to some Genoese
merchants, concerned West African Negroes proper, for the
Portuguese had long since penetrated the Gulf of Guinea and
were rifling the 'land of the Negroes'. In 1481 they began to
build their great castle at Elmina on the Gold Coast, a castle
which still stands today upon its black rock promontory above
the grey-green restless sea. Two Papal bulls subsequently gave
them exclusive rights in Africa and sanctioned the enslavement
and baptism of all captive Negroes.

Thus early was the familiar pattern of the Atlantic slave trade
established. The incentives were various: the making of money,
the 'saving' of Africans from 'barbarism', the excitement of
voyages down the Guinea coast and of raiding expeditions up
the rivers, the exertion of a febrile ingenuity in outwitting local
African chiefs and middle-men as, on shipboard or within the

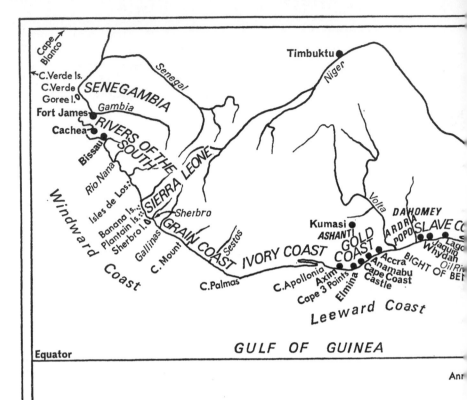

Cape Blanco
C.Verde Is.
C.Verde
Goree I.
Fort James
Cachea
Bissau
Rio Nana
SENEGAMBIA
Senegal
Gambia
RIVERS OF THE SOUTH
Isles de Los:
Banana Is.
Plantain Is.
Sherbro I.
SIERRA LEONE
Sherbro
Gallinas
Sestos
C. Mount
GRAIN COAST
IVORY COAST
C.Palmas
Windward Coast
Timbuktu
Niger
Kumasi
ASHANTI
GOLD COAST
Volta
DAHOMEY
ARDRA
POPO
SLAVE C
Lago
Jaquin
Whydah
Oil Ri
BIGHT OF BEI
Accra
Anamabu
Cape Coast
Castle
C.Apollonia
Axim
Cape 3 Points
Elmina
Leeward Coast
GULF OF GUINEA
Equator
Anr

SOUTH    ATLANTIC    OCEAN

**WEST AFRICA-Eighteenth Century**

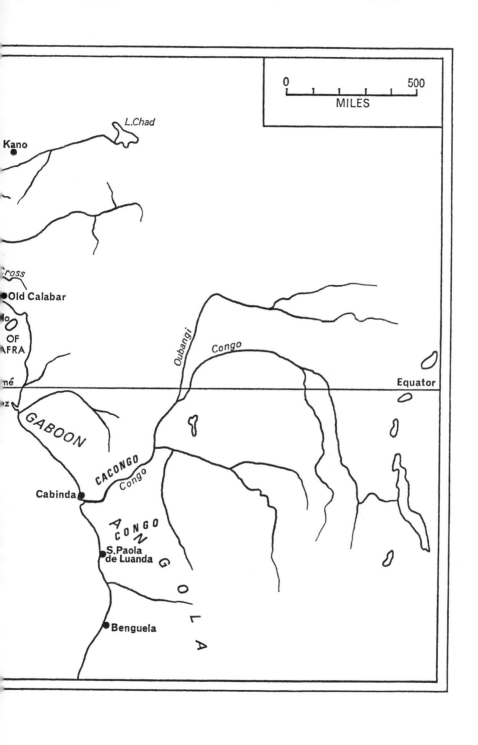

0                    500

MILES

*L.Chad*

Kano

*Cross*

●Old Calabar

Mo

OF

AFRA

né                          Equator

z

*Oubangi*

*Congo*

GABOON

CACONGO

*Congo*

Cabinda●

A
C O N G O
N
G
O
L
A

S.Paola
de Luanda●

Benguela●

dark stone chambers of Elmina, they haggled over the correct price to be paid for a Negro man, a Negro woman, or a Negro child.

But, while the year 1441, or even 1444, may be taken as marking the beginning of the slave trade the most significant year in its history is the year 1492, when Christopher Columbus discovered the New World. For the next three and a half centuries, and at ever-increasing momentum, the development of the new territories across the Atlantic demanded millions upon millions of African slaves. The Americas, and the sugar islands of the Caribbean, became as insatiable as the great god Baal himself. Year after year in quiet, calm office-rooms in a myriad European seaports the thoughtful plans were laid. The aim of these plans was to make money; their result was the stacking of purchased Negroes in the holds of slaving ships, which transported them to a new country. There instead of the happy, limited life of the African villages they found the slave-barracks and the lash. There the sound of drums throbbing nightly in the vast African forests was exchanged for the pre-dawn summons to the cane-fields at the squawk of the conch and for the melancholy tolling of the plantation bell.

## II

Let us now visit one of those quiet, calm rooms in which the fate of so many anonymous Africans was determined. It can be a mid-eighteenth-century office, situated in a sedate stone building on a waterfront – a comfortable, panelled room with a fire of sea-coal flickering blue in the grate. This room might be in any of a number of European ports, and for our immediate purposes it does not matter which. In London or in Lisbon, in Liverpool or Amsterdam, in Bristol, in Nantes, in Lancaster, in Copenhagen the scene would be much the same.

Three or four men, seated round a table, are studying a map spread out before them – one of those meticulous maps with a decorative cartouche in one corner, and a scale of English or Portuguese leagues, or Dutch miles, inset at the bottom. Peering over their shoulders we can see that it is a map of the Atlantic, with the bulging coast of Africa to the right, to the left the conformation of the east American seaboard, and the arc of the sad green Caribbean islands where the sugar fortunes grow: Hispaniola, Jamaica, Barbados, St Lucia and the rest. Between these coastlines stretches a hatched area which represents the Atlantic Ocean with – once again decorative – engravings of miniature ships. But at this very moment, out upon the real Atlantic, ships neither miniature nor decorative are crawling slowly, inexorably westward, their holds swarming with rats and jam-packed with Negro slaves in irons. Other merchant ships on the Atlantic tend to keep to windward of these slave ships, since the salt breeze carries the stench of many of them for several miles.

These men at the table are middle-aged, or elderly, persons of substance soberly dressed, their hair tied at the nape of the neck with a ribbon. Yet because ours is a camera-eye view of them, this does not imply that they are figures from some broad-cloth costume play. They are shrewd and speculative persons, respectable and almost certainly respected, liable to be raised to civic honours, church-going, charitable family men. Merchant shippers, the ships they own are virtually refuelling craft. The fuel these happen to be carrying to feed the machinery of the colonial sugar industry is human fuel, bought or stolen upon the African coast. These shipping merchants are but single examples of the thousands upon thousands of business men who, in all the major and many of the minor seaports of Europe (save only those of Italy*), are committed to that branch of sea-borne commerce known for generations as the Triangular Trade.

Why 'triangular'? Another glance at the map will show. And now, with a liberty which has become the stock in trade of television, we may dissolve to the sailing ships moving merrily southwards down the steamy western coast of Africa, rounding Cape Verde, turning due east at Cape Palmas into the Gulf of Guinea. Here at selected points with names far more romantic than the sordid realities of the mud towns that bear them, a slave ship can cast anchor and stand off. The captain may wait for some European factor or African middle-man to come

---

* The only Italians apparently connected with the slave trade were the Genoese, established in Seville, to whom, for instance, Lorenzo de Gomenot, governor of Bresa and a favourite of Charles V, sold for 25,000 ducats the privilege granted him by the Emperor in 1518, to ship four thousand Negroes to Hispaniola, Cuba, Jamaica and Porto Rico. These Negroes, however, the Genoese had to buy from the Portuguese slave-traders.

aboard with news of the state of the trade, or he may have himself rowed ashore in his pinnace to assess the situation in person. Such news, and a small or large quantity of slaves, may be found at Axim or Takoradi or Commenda or Shama, at Cape Coast Castle itself, at Lagos on the dreaded Bight of Benin, at Bonny or at Old or New Calabar.

At Bonny, for example, the slave ships – often as many as fifteen in number, chiefly British and French – would lie a mile below the town, in seven or eight fathom of river water. Whilst the captains went on shore to announce their arrival, the crew would be busy unbending the sails, striking the yards and topmasts, and beginning to build 'what they denominate "a house" '. This rather complex process, involving the lashing of booms and yards from mast to mast, to form a ridgepole, with spars and rafters laid and tied to this, produced a sort of latticework gazebo, roofed with overlapping mats of loosely woven rushes, and divided by a deal wall, in which was cut a door. This 'house' served several purposes – to protect the crew from the heat of the sun and from the onslaught of wind and rain, to form a pen for the surgical examination and branding of the newly-purchased Negroes, to segregate the men and women slaves, and to prevent any of the captives from trying to leap overboard. The mat roofing was ineffective, and leaked. The heat generated inside the gazebo was intense and unhealthy. Smoke from the fires of green mango-wood stung the sailors' eyes, and had even been known to cause blindness. When the house was completed the 'kings of Bonny' were invited on board, and were given 'dashes' of cloth, cotton, silk handkerchiefs, brandy and beer. In the roof of the house was 'a large trap-door, through which the goods intended for barter, the water casks, etc., are hoisted out or in'.

'The goods intended for barter' – it was these which formed one side of the Triangular Trade: European and even Indian exports, for which the African demand was often as insatiable as its corollary – the western colonies' thirst for Negro slaves. By the random, mid-eighteenth century period we have chosen to consider, the European slavers were long accustomed to the sometimes bizarre needs of the Africans. These ranged from fire-arms, gun-flints and gunpowder to glass beads and to cowrie shells from the Maldive Islands, used in many places along the coast as currency. Then there was brassware, iron bars, bolts of brilliant cottons or of woollen clothes, silks, taffetas, cast-off brocaded coats, cocked hats, sheets of Dutch cotton, knives, kettles, basins, brandy and rum. In the good old early days of the slave trade, ships' captains had been able to pass off any worthless trash on the trusting and inexperienced Africans – but these days were long past. 'The blacks of the Gold Coast' (wrote the French trader and historian, Jean Barbot, in 1682):

> are very skilled in the nature and proper qualities of all the Europeans' wares and merchandise vended there; but in a more particular manner, since they have so often been imposed upon by the Europeans, who in former ages made no scruple to cheat them in the qualities, weight and measure of their goods; which at first they received upon content, because they say it could never enter into their thoughts that white men, as they call the Europeans, were so base as to abuse their credulity and good opinion of us.

But the Africans had soon learned, he tells us, to examine all the merchandise narrowly – to find out whether a cloth had been dyed at Leyden or at Haarlem, to see that the knives were not rusty, the kettles and basins not cracked, to measure iron bars with the soles of their feet, to taste the brandy and rum to make sure that it was not adulterated with fresh, or sea, water. 'In short, they examine everything with as much prudence and ability as any European trader can do.' The ships' surgeons, on the other hand, submitted prospective slaves to an humiliatingly thorough medical inspection to judge their age, their strength, the state of their teeth and of their genitals, and to ensure that they were not suffering from venereal or any other disease. To all the usual dangers and disagreeables of the African end of the slave trade there was thus added a mutual, deep-seated and venomous distrust.

In the slave trade, as in every other, there were good years and lean. Sometimes the ships filled quickly, and the wooden shelves, which the carpenters had erected in the holds now empty of European merchandise, would be crammed with Negroes lying, as we have seen, 'like books upon a shelf'. Then the slave ships, divested of their lattice houses and once more fully rigged, could flee from a coast on which their crews suffered notoriously from often fatal attacks of the fever and the flux, a threat summed up in the seventeenth-century slavers' couplet:

> Beware and take care of the Bight of Benin
> Few come out, though many go in.

At other times the slave ships would lie off the glittering coast of Benin or Biafra for months together, waiting for their full complement of Negroes or, as it was generally called, 'waiting to be slaved'. Such was the scene, for example, in the roads of Anamabu on the Gold Coast, one October day of 1771. Trade at the newly constructed British fort of Anamabu – which still stands today on a hard rock shelf five hundred yards from the low foothills of this portion of the coast, with crimson brick walls coated with white-washed plaster, elegant spiral staircase and cool arcades – was then being undercut by a New England slaver named Richard Brew, who had attracted the trade to his own nearby station, Brew's Castle. Writing to a group of Liverpool merchants Brew explained that at this moment the local Africans would only accept gold dust – which had itself to be purchased elsewhere up the coast for European goods – as payment for slaves. The slave ship captains were querulous and restless, Brew reported. His tone is neither callous nor humane. It is the eternal voice of the middle-man, the level-headed, grating speech of money:

Goods wanted by vessels in this road at present. The *Ingram* wants one hundred and twenty slaves, the *Corsican Hero* fifty or sixty, the *Nancy* [Captain] Cazneau, forty or fifty, the *Greenwich* one hundred and thirty, the *Africa* taken up . . . The *Barbara*, Culshaw; the *Venus*, Goodwin; the *Friendship*, Cummings; the *Hannah*, Hughes; the *Charlotte*, Blundell; all new comers; and the *John*, |Bold; the *Union*, Pole; the *Austin*, Wilcox, and Captain Price soon expected, besides rum vessels;* I therefore leave you to judge of the shocking state of the trade here, and what reason you have to expect any alteration for the better; had the eight hundred slaves that were sent off in the *Peggy*, Captain Mill, and the *Richmond*, chartered ship, circulated

---

* 'Rum vessels' were ships carrying nothing but rum distilled from West Indian molasses. All slaving ships carried a certain quantity of rum to Africa, since it was important to spread alcoholism on the coast, drunken traders being easier to fox. New England, however, had a virtual monopoly of the rum trade to Africa, and distilled West Indian molasses for this purpose.

amongst the shipping, the *Ingram, Corsican Hero, Nancy, Greenwich* and *Africa* would have been off the Coast and would have left a fine opening for these new comers.

Captain Culshaw has had great success in the time he has been down; he tells me, he has purchased fifty-seven slaves; he is a very industrious man, and I dare say, will make a voyage, if any man makes one this year ... I am much mistaken if any ship this year will get interest for her money, except the prices are very high in the West Indies, and little or no mortality amongst the slaves.

Apart from the stimulus provided to European, and most especially British, industry by the export of the manufactured goods in demand on the African coast, the iron-masters also cast and sold vast quantities of manacles, fetters, chains and padlocks, as well as branding irons, for use when the ships were slaved. Dr Williams has pointed out that legal regulations for British ships bound for Africa, the East Indies or the West Indies laid it down that 'three-fourths of their proportion of beer was to be put in iron bound casks, hooped with iron hoops of good substance, and well wrought iron'. This was but one of the many, many ways in which the slave trade nourished the home industries of Europe.

# III

Their merchandise disposed of, their holds packed with what one trader prettily termed 'these valuable people', the slave ships set off on the long Atlantic voyage to the west, skilfully navigated towards some speck in the ocean like Barbados or Martinique. Yet if you picture the ships' officers sighing with relief as they tippled in their mess, you would be spectacularly wrong. To have got a cargo of prime slaves, and to have left the coast without the loss of too many of the crew, was but a preliminary to further and far more traumatic weeks ahead. Even in well-run ships with humane captains (and such there were) the rate of sickness and death amongst the slaves was a source of hourly anxiety. In the worst ships, in which the slave-holds were not properly aired, nor the floors and shelves washed down with pailfuls of vinegar; in which the slaves were not properly fed and exercised; in which the crews were bestial and drunken, the market value of the valuable people declined day after day.

No captain could breathe freely until landfall was made in the West Indies, and one of the oddly-shaped sugar islands, which seem to float like great green sponges on the Spanish Main, hove into view. Even then difficulties teemed ahead. Just as, in some years, the price demanded for slaves on the African coast was abnormally high, so, in the colonies, there might be years in which the price offered for the valuable people was disgracefully low. Prime male slaves could always be counted on to sell well, but what of the weak and infirm, the old who still persisted in looking their age even if you dyed their woolly white hair, the job lot of poor specimens who had been bought cheaply to fill up the shelves at the last moment, and were known in the trade as 'refuse slaves'? Many of those who had not actually expired on ship-board from disease, or who had not committed suicide by jumping overboard or hunger-strike, would arrive at their destination suffering from 'the bloody flux' (a violent form of dysentery); a case is even recorded of a cunning slave-captain who would plug such invalids anally with cotton wool so that they should appear untainted at the auction. Unwelcome letters, such as the following from a West Indian agent to his employer, Mr Benjamin Colman of Boston, Massachusetts, would plop down on the table round which our grave and worried merchants would be seated. This example, of January 1750, concerns a Captain whose name we do not know:

I am now to inform you (and with inexpressible grief) that I have a letter dated at Barbados 2nd December advising that he was under sail for St Kitts (there being no market for slaves at Barbados) with only 43 slaves out of *113*, all the rest being dead, viz. *70*. The few that remained were in health save 2 or 3 of 'em. He had 50 days passage to Barbados owing to calms . . . This makes a great difference to us, and looks to me as if there was no end to our disappointments.

Letters such as this, were, of course, counterbalanced by others in more cheerful vein. In January 1773 the firm of Stevenson and Went wrote from Bridgetown, Barbados, to their Newport counterparts:

Negroes keep up with us and good slaves will command a high price. We sold Captain Wanton's cargo which Captain Rogers brought in a few weeks past at £36 and £35 sterling round, but they were prime, and such slaves will always meet a good and ready market. Slaves have been high at Carolina, but by the last accounts they were fallen, and from the low price of their rice it was the opinion of the Factors that slaves would still fall. We shall be happy if Captain Tuell's slaves arrive in order.

Captain Tuell (who had earlier complained from Anamabu: 'I should do very well if there was any black trade but there is none'), did in fact turn up trumps, reaching Bridgetown, Barbados, in mid-February 'with 94 slaves on board, all well and in good order, which I have sold, the whole of them, all round to Messrs Stevenson and Went . . . for £35 sterling . . . I had seven weeks passage wanting one day'.

The Negroes sold, the slave-shelves dismantled and the fetters stocked away, the ships were first thoroughly cleansed. They were then loaded with sugar and molasses, which were sold in New England or in Europe.* A part of the profit from this was expended on new merchandise, rum and brandy for a fresh voyage to the west coast of Africa to bargain for more slaves.

The third side of the triangle was complete.

---

* In fact, owing to a bad sugar crop, or to the bad management, penury or parsimony of the planters, slave-captains and agents were at times paid off with post-dated Bills of Exchange on European banks. In these cases, when the total worth of the slaves was represented by a sheaf of papers only, there was no money to purchase sugar or molasses, and the ships would return to their ports of origin in ballast.

# Chapter 3

# The Gates of Mercy

## I

AND what, you may well ask, was the attitude of the educated, non-mercantile public to the Triangular Trade when this was at its zenith? By-passing for the moment the active Abolitionists – Clarkson, Newton and Wilberforce in Great Britain, the Neckers, Condorcet, Madame de Lafayette and the other members of the society, *Les Amis des Noirs*, in France – we may take as typical the differing attitudes upon this subject of two men of the highest intelligence: Samuel Johnson and James Boswell. Here a passage from Boswell's *Life of Johnson* is apposite.

Predictably, Dr Johnson was 'against slavery in every form'. Boswell recalls that once, at Oxford, when 'in company with some very grave men', Dr Johnson proposed the irritating toast: 'Here's to the next insurrection of the negroes in the West Indies!' In the autumn of the year 1777, when a Jamaican slave, brought to Scotland as a servant, was suing for his freedom before the Court of Sessions in Edinburgh, Boswell asked Johnson to dictate to him his own views on the case. In this statement, which Boswell recorded word for word, Dr Johnson declared it his conviction that no man has any right to enslave another. He asserted that the plea that, by Jamaican law, the Negro belonged to the planter who had bought him, could not hold. This colonial law he found:

injurious to the rights of mankind, because whoever is exposed to sale is condemned to slavery without appeal, by whatever fraud or violence he might have been originally brought into the merchant's power. In our own time [Johnson continued] Princes have been sold by wretches to whose care they were entrusted, that they might have an European education.* But when once they were brought to a market in the plantations, little would avail either their dignity or their wrongs. The laws of Jamaica afford a negro no redress. His colour is considered as a sufficient testimony against him.

This sane and civilized judgement offended Boswell, who attributed Johnson's notorious loathing for West Indian and American slave-owners to 'a zeal without knowledge'. He quotes, but with disapproval, a sentence from Dr Johnson's *Taxation No Tyranny*, a pamphlet published in 1775 in answer to the Resolutions of the American Congress. 'How is it' Johnson had asked in this pamphlet, 'that we hear the loudest *yelps* for liberty among the drivers of Negroes?' Johnson's views neatly recorded, Boswell begs 'leave to enter my most solemn protest against his general doctrine with respect to the Slave Trade' and adds that he himself was watching 'with wonder and indignation' the thriving philanthropic campaign for the abolition of the trade. It is not surprising to find Boswell, a patrician and a landowner, viewing Abolition as '*robbery* to an innumerable class of our fellow-subjects', but it seems, at first, odd that he should see it also as involving 'extreme cruelty to the African Savages, a portion of whom it saves from massacre, or intolerable bondage in their own country, and introduces them into a much happier state of life'. With recourse to Gray's *Elegy* he goes so far as to declare that 'to abolish that trade would be to:

"... shut the gates of mercy on mankind".'

Though Boswell never apparently changed his mind about the virtues of the slave trade, he does seem latterly to have admitted to some doubts. At a dinner-party given several years later by his friend Mr Langton to enable William Wilberforce to discuss his House of Commons campaign with certain distinguished men he did not at that time know, we find Boswell putting forward the planters' argument that the Negroes were happier in the West Indies than in West Africa. But, having made his point, he added a rider (in words which might well be noted by all political dictators, by many parents and by the

* This is presumably a reference to the fate of two sons of the Chief or King of Anamabu, who had been retrieved from slavery in the nick of time, and had, according to Horace Walpole, made a great stir in fashionable London in 1749.

21

majority of autocratic lovers) : 'Be it so, but we have no right to make people happy against their will.'

Now it was quite natural that plantation-owners should themselves disseminate, and indeed believe, the theory that their Africans had been miserable in Africa. Most people will persuade themselves of anything if there is money in it. Furthermore, many of them were genuinely convinced that slave conditions on a good plantation, with a humane owner and a considerate overseer, were a distinct step up from the 'savagery' in which they had been told that the natives of the Gold Coast or the Slave Coast habitually lived. But here a question rears its head : *who had told them?* Certainly not the slaves themselves, for few owners bothered to follow the example of the Jamaican merchant and planter, Bryan Edwards, who devoted a section of his splendid *History of the British Colonies in the West Indies* (published in 1793) to reports of affable conversations with his own slaves about their early history and their places of origin. No. The vast web of myth and misinformation which for centuries obscured the European vision of West Africa was spun by the slave-traders themselves – the factors in their lonely huts on some spit of sandy land, the officers and men of the slave ships lying off some steamy river-mouth, the sickly garrisons of slaving fortresses perched high on their rocks above the dark green sea. Largely ignorant of even their own country's culture, these men were almost professionally oblivious to that of Africa, and to the West Africans' political structures, social systems, traditions and religious beliefs. The seventeenth-century Dutchman, Willem Bosman, who was factor at the castle of Elmina, and who spent fourteen years along the Guinea Coast, might admire the bronze figures in the palace of the King of Benin, but then he was exceptionally perceptive. The ordinary seamen, telling their travellers' tales in the taverns of Bristol, Nantes or Spanish Town, Jamaica, were of a very different calibre. Already in the plays of Shakespeare's contemporaries, characters with black skins were either villains or clowns; in any case the view was already widespread that to be black was to be inferior. 'So great is our pride' wrote a French contemporary of Bosman 'that the most brutal sailor values himself above the best of those Guinea Kings.'

Seeing has been said to be believing, but these transients on the West African coast-line saw only what they wanted to believe – or, rather, they were incapable of interpreting correctly, or indeed of understanding, what they saw. Nor can we wholly blame them, for it must be granted that what they saw was often rather strange. Yet European nationals, who were still accepting the ferocious pillage of a conquered European city as the legitimate spoil of war, sprang to condemn the minor loss of life involved in the solicitous sacrifice of wives and slaves at the funerals of African grandees. The English, in particular, who accepted it as legal (and, therefore to them, normal) that a child should be hanged in Great Britain for stealing a pocket-handkerchief, vociferously condemned the annual votive offerings of three or four young persons at the mouth of the Niger River – 'votive offerings to the sea' wrote Captain John Adams at the end of the eighteenth century 'to direct vessels to bend their course to this horrid climate'. The English (whose obsessional attitude towards domestic animals, contrasting sharply with that towards their own children, has ever been to continentals a source of hollow mirth) were particularly distressed to find what really amounted to another form of the same fetishism in the Niger Delta – the worship of the sacrosanct monitor lizard, which the African Missionary-Bishop Crowther is credited with having suppressed in the name of Christ only as recently as 1867.

## II

Even today, when air and road travel has made Africa so readily available to Europeans and Americans, there are innumerable aspects of African life which tend to take one unawares. The unfamiliar lurks everywhere, and the presence of western culture seems merely to emphasize this unfamiliarity. Basically the essence of our reaction to the strange, the unfamiliar is a sense of fear. Every country contains landscapes that arouse unease – whether it be some remote Alpine valley, the wild lavender-fields of Upper Provence, a lonely Norwegian fjord at twilight. But in my own experience West Africa contains more weird and eerie regions – rain-forest, mangrove swamp, parched plains of red earth – than any other place that I have seen. It is not only in the foreigner that these landscapes evoke fear. A large part of all old African religions is devoted to placating the unknown and the unseen – evil spirits which live in a particular tree or a particular rock, a thousand varieties of baleful ghosts and witches, the brooding, ever-present spirits of dead ancestors or relatives. I have myself been kept awake at night in Calabar by a friend from Lagos who was convinced that the witches of the east were out to get him, or that he was about to be kidnapped and eaten. During four and a half hours in a canoe along the creeks of the Niger Delta, gliding over the still and colourless water beneath an equally still and colourless but burning sky, I, too, have experienced a sense of fear, or at least a sense of awe. Except for the ticking of the little outboard engine the silence was complete. On either hand stretched the silver-white swamps of mangrove, seeming, with their awkward exposed roots, to be standing knee-deep in the water. Where the creek narrowed you could peer deep into these thickets of mangroves – vistas secret, interminable and somehow meaningless. There was no sign of life save for the shrill screech of some unseen bird.

I was on my way to the ancient slaving port of Bonny, which we reached in late afternoon. Scrambling up some derelict stone steps (slithery with slime and which had successfully managed to detach themselves from the landing-stage so that you had to jump a two-foot gap to reach wet land), I found myself in an area of black mud and tumbled blocks of stone, the latter evidently once destined for some ambitious but abandoned building project. There were a few hovels, and two tiny black and white goats linked to one another by a chain. A group of the inhabitants of Bonny, most notably the children, had assembled to stare at the new arrivals in the observant, assessing yet vaguely derisory way of African crowds. 'Derisory' is perhaps the wrong word; what I mean is the indefatigable African sense of humour, the constant and happy capacity for being amused. In any case, Africans are probably the most watchful people in the world.

That evening, wandering through fetid open spaces, which in old Bonny are designated 'squares', and along the narrow black mud alleys between houses made of rusty corrugated tin, I was interested to find ornate Victorian mausoleums and memorial statuary at the street corners. These turned out to be the tombs of the royal family of Pepple, one of whom, King William Pepple, was the greatest and most amiable of the Bonny sellers of slaves. In the old days of Bonny, the dead were buried beneath their living-room floors; but the Pepples – whose real name, before being corrupted by the European seamen, was Perikale – were too prominent to be so buried, and hence their tombs give a gruesome dignity to Bonny's otherwise dilapidated streets.

As we walked in the closing dusk through this maze of alley-ways, which are watered by black and filthy streams full of refuse, a noise which from the hotel I had heard faintly grew more insistent as we approached. It was a noise of stamping, drumming, clapping and chanting. Rounding a corner we came upon a large number of people standing in a lopsided circle, in the midst of which a stalwart middle-aged woman was performing a curious but frenzied dance, apparently in a semi-hypnotic state. She was dressed in yellow and white, on her head an orange cap bound round with a white cloth, and two more white cloths tied loosely to her arms. The upper part of her face was daubed with white paint, which made her look slightly blind. Her expression was intense, relentless and could, in fact, have been called evil. Her movements as she circled in a diving fashion, had a fierceness about them which I do not believe to be my imagination. Every now and then she would make a rush at the spectators, who backed hastily away. Apart from the band and choir of men and a few women, she had two female acolytes, one of whom represented the waves of the sea, whilst another, with a silver paddle, was presumably a boat. From time to time, exhausted, she would retire into a cabin in the background, where an oil lamp burned. Here she would take a puff or two at a large pipe, whilst one of her assistants got on with the dance. It was an uncanny scene, and made more so by the presence in the centre of the circle of an incongruous occasional table, covered with a doily, on which stood refreshing bottles of whiskey, rum and Gordon's gin. By the sounds which were still reaching the hotel at dawn, this festivity evidently continued far into the night.

Had I been an eighteenth-century English sailor on his first trip to the Slave Coast I should no doubt have called this display of dancing 'savage'. Had I been a nineteenth-century traveller I should no doubt have called it 'quaint'. As it was I found it disquieting in its fervour, and alien because it was full of some purpose that I did not comprehend. Enquiry, however, elicited the general fact that the lady was the Priestess of the local Goddess of the Sea, and that this her annual dance was to placate that Goddess and to ensure that the Priestess would retain her healing powers. I recalled that, in 1872, when my grandfather was administering the West African Settlements, the deposed King Docemo of Lagos would invoke the Goddess of the Lagos Lagoon against the British authorities. In one of her four chapters on fetish in *Travels in West Africa*, Mary Kingsley dilates upon the quantities of sea-gods and sea-spirits that abound along the Guinea Coast. She points out that, since every danger-spot – whirlpool or rock – has a presiding deity, it is natural that the highly perilous surf of this sea-board should have many, too. She found that, among the Twi, children eight days after birth, and widows eight days after their husband's death, were brought ceremonially down to visit the local sea-spirit of any particular patch of shore. There were also witches wandering the sea-shore by night, emitting a brilliant light and eating crabs the while. Like the myriad other minor deities, spirits and witches of West Africa, these marine deities require propitiation and attention, in return for which they will help and protect.

# III

'This country, sir, is run on love', Bernard, a cheerful and friendly driver from the University of Ibadan explained to me one morning, as we were bumping down the Lagos road. Although this remark was made only a few days before the batch of political murders of January 1966, it seems to me broadly true not of Nigeria only, but of West Africa in general. The innate generosity of West Africans and their courtesy to strangers, which made them an easy prey in the first place for the slave-traders and subsequently for the Colonial Powers, are but two of a whole range of characteristics that can be called on to refute the Ignoble Savage theory in which, as we have noticed, even a man as well-read as Boswell honestly believed. Prior to considering in detail the mutual misunderstandings, the ignorance and the cruelty which clouded European-African relations from the very start of the slave-trading days, we must achieve a sharp picture of what Africa was and is, and in which ways its peoples differ from those of the Western world as well as from those of the Orient. If the Europeans engaged in the gold, the ivory and the slave trades misunderstood the nature of Africans, what exactly was the nature which they misunderstood? The poet of Martinique, Aimé Cesaire, coined the now current word *négritude* to express what could more clumsily be termed 'negroness'. First used in relation to all negroid artistic activity, it can conveniently be treated as an umbrella-word to cover native African beliefs, habits, ideals, attitudes and outlook.

What is probably one of the best analyses of negritude ever written was published by the late Mr Dunduzu Chisiza, of Malawi, in the *Journal of Modern African Studies* in 1963. 'It is true' he wrote 'that there is no uniform outlook. But it is possible to single out certain features which are always present in almost every African community.'

Chisiza begins by asserting that Africans are neither of a meditative turn of mind, like orientals, nor inquisitive searchers, like Westerners. He sees them primarily as 'penetrating observers, relying more on intuition than on the process of reasoning', and as excelling in the field of human relations. Whereas Westerners assume that man lives to work, the African, he maintains, works to live, the corollary of this being 'a high preference for leisure', and an emphasis on the pursuit of happiness rather than of beauty or of truth. Spurning isolationism and individualism, the African's ideal way of life is a communal one, starting with strong family relations based on love, and radiating outwards in a general lavish compassion and wish to help. 'I' and 'mine' are used more seldom than 'we' and 'our', and all activities – hunting, draw-net fishing, sewing, harvesting, pounding food, canoeing, playing games, dancing – are group activities. The virtues of generosity and forgiveness are encouraged; malice, hatred and revenge are abhorred. Famous for their sense of humour and dislike of melancholy, Africans wish to enjoy their lives and want other people to do so too. They have also, according to Chisiza, an habitual desire for change, even in religion, which accounts for the ready and enthusiastic conversions which so disturbed Christian missionaries when they found that they were usually unaccompanied by any serious rejection of fundamental African religious beliefs. Light-hearted and well-disposed, they must have struck the early European traders as frivolous and wrong-headed; although most of these agreed upon the prodigal hospitality and the high-bred manners of the African chiefs, their subjects, servants and slaves. In the training of young men great emphasis was laid on restraint, and adultery was punishable by death.

This restraint, product of the inflexible laws which governed social behaviour was, like the propitiatory elements of all African religions, aimed at ensuring a peaceful, orderly and protected life for the members of each community living in the fierce and insecure world of the tropics. Most Europeans saw only the taboos, dismissed them as ignorant superstitions and did not attempt to penetrate their origins or purpose. They were also, perforce, entirely unacquainted with African history, and unaware of the great continental Empires – Songhai, Mali, Ghana and the rest – which had risen and fallen through the centuries. Because there seemed to be no written African history (an assumption now disproved), the foreign myth persisted that there was no history to Africa at all; and a country without a history could not be taken seriously. Language formed another barrier to communication, likewise the Africans' understandable reluctance to reveal the mysteries of their protective ju-ju charms and amulets, or of the fetish houses, to white-skinned sceptics whom they had soon learned that they could not trust.

Again, to the denizens of European ports, with their broad paved streets and brick or stone houses, and even to country youths from Somerset or Zeeland, the West African hamlets and the simple life that went on within their baked mud walls seemed incurably primitive and comic. The freed slave, Olaudah Equiano, alias Gustavus Vasa, who published his memoirs in London in 1789, has described his boyhood in a mid-eighteenth century Ibo community in vivid detail. The son of the Embrenche, or head-man of his village, whose dignity was signified by a lateral cut made in childhood across his forehead, Equiano describes the stern moral code and the pastoral life of his village, with its well-spaced groups of family houses, resembling little villages within the village, its men and women dressed in bright blue cloth ('brighter and richer than any I have seen in Europe'), the grander women wearing fine gold ornaments, the separate establishments for each man's two or three wives, with others for the domestic slaves. He describes the simplicity of the food, the well-known custom of setting some of this aside before each meal, as well as pouring a libation, for the enjoyment of the hovering spirits of the dead. When the women were not employed with the men in tillage they wove and dyed the blue cloth, and made earthen pots and tobacco pipes. It was a simple, contented, self-contained existence, made merry on every seizable occasion by music and dancing. 'We are almost a nation of dancers, musicians and poets' (Equiano explains) 'thus every great event, such as a triumphant return from battle, or other cause of public rejoicing, is celebrated in public dances, which are accompanied with songs and music suited to the occasion.' 'We were totally unacquainted with swearing and all those terms of abuse and reproach which find their way so readily and copiously into the language of more civilized people' (he recalls). 'The only expressions of that kind I remember were "May you rot!", or "May you swell!", or "May a beast take you!" ' This writer emphasizes particularly the universal cleanliness of his people, their constant ablutions and purifications, and the great power of what he calls the priests and magicians, who calculated time and foretold events.

Into this on the whole satisfied and undemanding rural world there crashed the predatory hordes of the slave-traders, the men the scum of European ports, their officers and factors chiefly what were called 'necessitous persons' who could find no employment at home. In fairness to them, though, it must be remembered that the Africans with whom they mostly came into direct contact were greedy, degenerate middle-men, as heartless and as venal as the Europeans to whom they sold stolen youths, women and children. The chiefs or 'kings' as the Europeans termed them were mainly concerned with selling prisoners captured in small tribal wars – forays which the slave-traders encouraged with arms; although cases are recorded of chiefs raiding their own villages at night for slaves to sell. For the African responsibility should never be forgotten; without Africans willing to sell each other there would have been no slaves for the Europeans to buy. It can, and it has, been argued, equally, that without the European traders there would have been no African middle-men at all. Another freed slave, Ottobah Cugoano, who published his reflections on slavery in 1787, told his readers:

> But I must own, to the shame of my own countrymen, that I was first kidnapped and betrayed by my own complexion, who were the first cause of my exile and slavery; but if there were no buyers there would be no sellers. So far as I can remember, some of the Africans in my country kept slaves, which they take in war, or for debt; but those which they keep are well, and good care taken of them, and treated well . . . But I may safely say that all the poverty and misery that any of the inhabitants of Africa meet with among themselves is far inferior to those inhospitable regions of misery which they meet with in the West Indies, where their hard-hearted overseers have neither regard to the laws of God, nor the life of their fellow-men.

In the end, as the corruption spread, the old slaving ports vied with one another as to who had the most slaves to sell. 'Ah the Slave Trade!' a jovial leading citizen of Bonny remarked to me there in 1966: 'The Slave Trade! *Those were the great days of Bonny*, but now we hope, with Shell Oil, to be coming up in the world again!' He slapped his plump thigh as he spoke.

In concluding this attempt to sketch the African character, I do not wish to suggest that Africa, any more than any other portion of the globe, has ever been a continent of saints. The ritual human sacrifices at the burials of important men, the Death Grove of the Asantehene at Kumasi, and many similar practices and places, prove that in Africa, too, human nature had its dark quarter. All that needs stressing is that these millions upon millions of Negroes, bought or stolen, and shipped to perpetual slavery in the Atlantic colonies were in their essence people made for happiness and leisure, a good-natured people gullible to the extent that they knew nothing of the world beyond their deltas and their forests. Most of them had not even seen the sea. It was these people, guileless and pleasure-loving, with their own skills and their own tightly-constructed system for getting through life, who were shovelled into the colonial plantations like coals into a furnace. Once across the Atlantic, they were subjected to murderous working hours in frequently foul conditions, under the hawk-eyes of overseers armed with a leathern lash. Is it any wonder that so many killed themselves both on the Middle Passage or after it, and that the planters lived in dread of yet another slave revolt? It was this fear that had inspired Dr Johnson's Oxford toast.

## IV

In the seventeenth and eighteenth centuries one of the strongest of the mutual delusions held by Europeans and Africans about each other was that of cannibalism. The Frenchman Barbot wrote in the sixteen-eighties that 'some Europeans . . . would also persuade me that the inland blacks of Whydah are man-eaters, and that at a town about a league above Savi, there is a market for slaves, where, at the time of a violent famine, they sold them fatted up, to be slaughtered like beasts and their quarters exposed in the shambles, to be eaten; but I will not answer for the truth of it.' Not all Europeans were as judicial and sceptical as Jean Barbot, and the theory that West Africans were cannibals whenever they could get the chance became an integral part of the slave-traders' mythology. The Fan tribes of the Upper Niger, of whom these slave-traders had never heard, were later indeed proved to be cannibals by Mary Kingsley and other nineteenth-century travellers or merchants, but they were remote and really savage people. The Englishman, Winterbottom, who published an account of Sierra Leone in 1803, went into this cannibal myth thoroughly:

That this horrid practice does not exist in the neighbourhood of Sierra Leone, nor for many hundred leagues along the coast to the northward and southward of that place may be asserted with the utmost confidence, nor is there any tradition among the natives which can prove it ever was the custom; on the contrary they appear struck with horror when they are questioned individually on the subject, though at the same time they make no scruple of accusing other natives at a distance, and whom they barely know by name, of cannibalism.

The famous outbreak of 'human leopardism' in the nineties of the last century in up-country Sierra Leone, publicized during the trials of members of a local Human Leopard Society who, disguised in leopard-skins, would on certain specified nights dismember and eat a young, selected victim, cannot really come under the heading of cannibalism, since the object of the operation was to obtain strength and grace. Even today members of one tribal group will attribute such ritual practices to those of another tribe whom they dislike – the accusation being, so to speak, the very lowest thing you can say about anybody else. Since this is still the case, it seems significant to find it recorded again and again by the old European slave-traders that the cause of half the ship-board slave revolts was the Negroes' total conviction that they were being taken over the sea not to Skye but to be eaten in Barbados.

This belief was ineradicable. Ottobah Cugoano whom we have already met and who was a well-off coast Fantee captured as a boy and taken to Grenada, then liberated and brought to England, where he worked for Cosway the miniaturist and became a leading Abolitionist, writes of his horror on first seeing white men in a town to which he was dragged by his captor : 'Next day we travelled on, and in the evening came to a town where I saw several white people, which made me afraid that they would eat me, according to our notion as children in the inland parts of the country.' This nagging fear of being killed and eaten was, therefore, added to all the other mental and physical discomforts of the Middle Passage.

Even if the European traders had cared to clear up this basic misconception – and there is no reason to suppose that they did – it would have been extremely difficult, owing, as I have suggested earlier, to the lack, or extreme restriction, of the means of oral communication. In his volume on the *Trade Castles and Forts of West Africa* Professor A. W. Lawrence makes the point that 'no European before the nineteenth century is known to have spoken an African language; short vocabularies provided for the simpler needs of trade and person, and there was no lack of interpreters'. He thinks it probable that mulattoes were bilingual; but we can safely assume that there was neither the time, the goodwill nor the means to abate the newly enslaved Negroes' anxieties.

In the seventeenth century ignorant, and even influential Africans who had never seen a white man supposed them to be a species of sea-monster, since they had heard that they came from over the horizon, where no land was, in large ships. When the Danes were rebuilding Christiansborg, the fort at Accra which they had taken from the Dutch in 1661, and which they made into their stately headquarters on the Gold Coast, the Akyem King, Firempong, was made protector of the new fort for thirty-two dollars a month. Firempong had never yet seen a white man and, 'according to the Gold Coast missionary Rheindorf (an African scholar who published his *History of the Gold Coast and Ashanti* in 1895) he accepted the current hearsay that 'the Europeans were a kind of sea-creatures'. Since he wanted to confirm this belief, he asked for a specimen to be sent to his town of Da. A Danish book-keeper, Nicholas Kamp, was despatched and found a formal reception awaiting him. But when he took off his hat and bowed, King Firempong, thinking he was a wild animal about to spring, fell flat on his face and yelled for the assistance of his wives. When the interpreter had explained that Kamp's queue was not a tail growing from his neck, Firempong, still dissatisfied, demanded that Kamp strip naked. This the Danish book-keeper refused to do in public. After a meal watched by all the king's wives – one of whom remarked 'He eats like a man, really he *is* a human being' – Kamp removed his clothes in private before the king. This convinced King Firempong: 'Ah, you really are a human being, but only too white, like a devil.'

For to make things easier, just as the colour black was, for most Europeans, connected with night, witches and the Powers of Darkness, so, to many Africans, white was often the colour of devils, and the smearing of the face with white clay was calculated to inspire terror. At the great Portuguese Castle of the Mine, or Elmina, in the early sixteenth century the priest-in-charge and his two chaplains set out to convert the local Negroes under the patronage of St Francis of Assisi, who had been singled out because the face of his image had turned miraculously and conveniently black on arrival in West Africa – most likely, in reality, the effect of the climate on white lead paint.

This mutual wariness of one another's pigmentation formed yet a further disruptive element in the haggling chaos of the slave trade as it muddled on its evil way in the dripping heat of the West African coast, beneath the mentally-unhinging rays of the tropical sun. The dangers and the enervating effect of the climate impaired (but did not, of course, defeat) the efficiency of European attempts to get the trade in gold, ivory and slaves

33

running smoothly. These attempts are best symbolized by, and were probably most successful in, the serried line of trading forts and castles concentrated on what was for centuries known in Europe as the Gold Coast, and is now the sea-board of modern Ghana. By an anomaly, it was from the presence of these forts, with their slave-dungeons, slave markets and whipping blocks, that there derived one of the few positive benefits contact with the European traders brought to West Africans: new and sufficient forms of food.

*Chapter 4*

# Down the Guinea Coast

## I

BESIDE the scarlet laterite roads of southern Ghana or Nigeria, and on spits of sand at rural landing-stages along the broad, sluggish rivers, merry young Negresses with placid faces but witty eyes are seated on stools, bolt upright. On another, smaller stool before each of them is an enamel basin as vividly coloured as their own headgear. They are usually grouped together under a tree, smiling and chattering as they deftly peel green oranges for sale, using a sharp-bladed knife which leaves the orange ribbed or corrugated at will. These oranges are sold, two for a penny, to thirsty travellers who suck them dry and throw the rest away. Elsewhere along the roads and in the town and village markets lie heaps of coco-nuts, mounds of ugly, tortured-looking yams, paw-paws which taste like wet linen, lemons, limes, hand after hand of bananas. To his first blinding vision of sunlight and of dappled shadowy forests decked out with yellow or crimson plumes of flowering parasite creeper, the newcomer from Europe adds the picture of an infinitely bountiful Nature, of a land of marvellous and prodigal fertility.

No wonder, you think as your car jolts and heaves down the uneven roads, that life here seems so gay and that an atmosphere of *dolce far niente* seems so widespread. Here, at the least, nobody need ever have starved? And reflection on the contrast between this rich, available profusion on the one hand, and the diet of the transatlantic slave plantations (a sticky porridge and dried fish) upon the other, releases yet one more spurt of sharpish indignation. It seems so evident that all any hungry African ever had to do in his natural surroundings was to reach up into the shining foliage of an orange tree and pull down the fruit clustering like pale lamps on the branches. You imagine harvests of ripe maize, yams tended against the Yam Festivals, coco-nut palms scaled with agility, oil-palms tapped for cooking oil. It must all, you think, have resembled the earthly paradise of Rousseau's yearnings, or the gentle, luscious world of *Paul et Virginie*.

In point of fact this was not so. Until the Europeans descended on the coast of Guinea, and indeed for some time after their advent, probably none of these plants, trees and crops existed in West Africa. When the Portuguese first discovered the territories in the fifteenth century 'there is good reason to think that the inhabitants of most areas rarely had enough to eat, unless they were fishermen or lived near enough to the coast to buy smoked fish'.* The Negroes would seem to have lived on game, supplemented by guinea-corn, together with an inferior and uncultivated variety of yam, wild spinach and perhaps certain other wild plants, the value and names of which are long forgotten. Alcohol, that indispensable lubricant to every form of human society, was provided by palm-wine in the moist regions, by a fermented beer elsewhere. All those fruits and vegetables which seem, to the greenhorn visitor, so exotic and so characteristic of the West African scene were actually introduced by the European traders.

Once these traders began to build their forts and to settle in on the coast, the total lack of vegetables, fruits and dependable cereal crops became a natural source of concern. To have strange and inadequate, often repulsive, food added to the other health hazards of a lethal climate was asking too much. So even the tiniest forts and stations planned and developed large nursery gardens, planting European salads, cabbages and cauliflowers from imported seed, starting the cultivation of sugar cane, lemon trees and melons from the Mediterranean, oranges, tamarind and bananas from the East. From across the Atlantic came the pineapple, the guava and the paw-paw. Once it was established that scurvy, universal blight of long sea-voyages, could be prevented by adding citrus-fruit to the diet of the seamen and their slave-cargoes, the demand for oranges, lemons and limes, and for their juice in iron-hooped kegs, spread swiftly

* The words are those of Professor A. W. Lawrence, to whose classic, *Trade Castles and Forts of West Africa* (Jonathan Cape, 1963), I am indebted for much of the information in this chapter.

down the coast. Initiated purely to increase trade efficiency, this raising in the European gardens of foreign fruits and foodstuffs must have been imitated by the Africans themselves, and in that lush climate all these fresh delights proliferated. If we were any of us asked what tree 'West Africa' immediately suggested to our minds, nine out of ten would answer: 'The coco-nut tree.' Yet even this tree, so ubiquitous today, was an European importation from the Indian Ocean. Even as late as the year 1692, the palm-tree was sufficiently rare upon the Guinea coast for sailors to make a landmark of a solitary grove of coco-nuts growing in their ragged, rakish way near the African town and three adjacent European forts at Accra. Colloquially they referred to these coco-nuts as 'the Spanish cavalry'. Such landmarks, with their promise of fresh food and drink, women for hire and slaves for sale, formed a welcome sight to the crews of ships sailing the Gulf of Guinea.

## II

'The Gulf of Guinea', 'the Guinea Coast' – there are certain words or phrases which can not only be heard and seen, but tasted and smelt. I would put those amongst them. The names have sounded down the centuries with the tantalizing ring of the guinea coins of purest yellow gold first minted for the Royal African Company by order of King Charles II. Visually, the words conjure up a low, hot, green shore-line, hazy with vapour, and for ever besieged by the monotonous breakers of the South Atlantic. Taste the words on your palate and you get the pricking of spice, or the cloying flavour of the mango. The scent is that of hibiscus and of the deep mould of tropical forests steaming after rain. Then there is the traditional hint of risk and adventure about almost everything to do with Guinea, whether it be the 'Guineamen', high-masted sailing-ships West Africa bound, or even the 'Guinea merchants' who sped them keeling on their way. Of course the prefix 'guinea' has other more pedestrian connections – guinea-grain or malaguetta, which the Portuguese sought upon the Coast before they had found the true pepper of the East; guinea-grass; and the guinea-fowl, sophisticated cousin of some of the wild fowl of West

Africa. Chaffing Roderigo for his despairing love for Desde-
mona, Iago refers contemptuously to Othello's wife as 'a guinea-
hen'. But from the days of the first Portuguese explorers who
brought back live Negroes and Negresses as trophies for the
Court, Guinea became to the ordinary, stay-at-home people of
Europe an established and persistent myth. Besides the exotic
landscapes and costumes of the West Africans, there was the
added thrill of the 'savage' and the unknown. 'None of us
Europeans ever go to Guinea,' wrote a seventeenth-century
trader 'but we are apt at our return to make horrid pictures of
the manners and vices of the blacks.'

The exact geographical definition of the Gulf of Guinea is,
like all such definitions, bleak but clear: 'A large open arm of
the South Atlantic in the angle of West Africa and including the
Bight of Benin and the Bight of Biafra.' The term 'Guinea
Coast' was customarily applied to the shoreline bordering this
gulf, but the coast itself was considered to begin at the Senegal
River – sixteen degrees north of the Equator – and to curve
down and away to South Angola, sixteen degrees south of the
Equator. 'Upper Guinea' stretched from Senegambia to the
Cross River on the Slave Coast, 'Lower Guinea' from that river
to the Congo and Angola, including the Spanish island of
Fernando Po. By the eighteenth century this coast-line had by
long usage been sub-divided in Europeans' minds. First of all,
running from north to south, came Senegambia, with Cape
Verde and the Gambia River; next came the area known as the
Rivers of the South; then the Grain Coast (where the malaguetta pepper was obtained); the Ivory Coast (source of ele-
phant tusks); the Gold Coast and the adjacent Slave Coast
(both named for obvious reasons); and on down past the lands
bordering the Bight of Biafra to Gabon and Angola. Naturally
enough these European trade appellations did not mean that
the West African shore-line was neatly compartmented in the
fashion of a supermarket and its shelves. Gold could be purchased on the Grain coast, slaves on the Gold Coast, ivory and
pepper on the Slave Coast – although in point of fact slaves
were easily the chief product of the Slave Coast, and of the
marshy regions east of the Volta River.

It may seem odd that, save for one or two Phoenician and
Carthaginian voyages of trade or discovery recorded by Hero-

dotus, it should have taken the rest of the world – or, more correctly, the European portion of it – so long to find West Africa. The explanation lies in the long-accepted European theory that the world was flat. Believing this, mariners would not venture beyond Cape Bojador, for fear that they and their ships would plunge over the edge of the world-platform into oblivion. It took the persistent buzz of rumour that the gold the Arabs sold to Europeans came from a negroid country to the south, as well as Portuguese anxiety to find a direct trading route to India (thus, again, short-circuiting Arab middlemen) to stimulate the Portuguese, at the direction of Prince Henry the Navigator, to push down from Cape Bojador. We have seen that the first ten Africans in Portugal were brought back as a gift to Prince Henry in 1441, but these were probably either moors, or moorish-negroid types. It was not until a subsequent voyage, recorded like this first one by the royal librarian and archivist, de Azurara, whose chronicle of the Guinea journeys covers from 1441–1448* and whose information was based on careful eye-witness accounts, that the Portuguese reached the Land of Guinea proper – that is to say, the mouth of the Senegal River, which they explored in boats lowered from their caravels. In one of these small boats eight men sat. One of these noticed on the river bank a fisherman's hut, which they at once agreed to invest by stealth. As they were creeping up to it, a naked Negro boy, holding a spear, strode nonchalantly out – and straight into their hands. They seized him, and then snatched up his eight-year-old sister, bundling both of them into the boat. Taken back to Portugal, the boy was christened to save his soul and then well educated by royal command. Does not this nude, unsuspecting fisher-boy, stepping, as he had done every day of his short life, from the safety of his thatched family hut into the blinding sun of the river-bank, only to be kidnapped by armed and bearded white-faced strangers, seem in himself a symbol of the serious European start of the slave trade?

* *The Chronicle of the Discovery and Conquest of Guinea* by Gomes Eannes de Azurara, was originally discovered in the Bibliothèque Royale in Paris in 1837. In 1896 and 1897 a translation was published in England by the Hakluyt Society. When quoting from this, I have however taken the liberty of paraphrasing, since the two translators' attempts at an archaic prose style ('let us take such advisement that whosoever putteth himself on his defence shall be slain without pity') is exacerbating today.

As the decade of the fourteen-forties waned, the Portuguese adventurers became bolder, and more ruthless. Africans on the coast were now stalked like wild animals. 'All of you run as fast as you can' was the verbal directive of one Christian captain to his crew, when they had sighted a gathering of harmless Negroes at another point along the coast: '. . . if we can't take the young men prisoner, let's go for the old men, the women and the small children. Be sure that anyone who tries to defend himself is killed without mercy'. In this actual episode most of the panic-stricken but aquatic villagers outwitted their attackers by diving swiftly into the sea, whither the encumbered Portuguese could not pursue them.

## III

However predatory and, indeed, savage the behaviour of his men upon the coast of Guinea, a true crusading zeal ranked as high amongst Prince Henry the Navigator's personal motives for backing these African forays as did thoughts of exploration, trade and settlement. A royal decree of 1448 gave the Prince the right to control trade along the coast. In that same year the Portuguese seem to have begun to build their first African fort, on the island of Arguin, south of Cape Blanco, a suitable site which they had discovered in 1443. Ten years later a religious mission headed by the Abbot Soto de Cassa set sail in a first thankless effort to convert the natives of the Gambia. By 1471 the Portuguese had passed the mouth of the Niger; in 1481 they began to build upon the Gold Coast their famous Castle of the Mine; and in 1485 King John II of Portugal assumed the grandiose but, as it proved, hollow, title, 'Lord of Guinea'.

The crusading aspect of these Portuguese adventures on the coast immediately involved the Papacy, since it was the Pope alone who could grant a Christian kingdom or religious order 'the exclusive right of proselytizing in a particular heathen area'. The next logical step from this theory of a Holy War was that the Pope should place the newly discovered territories under Portuguese jurisdiction. Successive Popes moved gingerly towards this conclusion. In 1454, when the King of Castile protested at the Portuguese seizure of a Spanish vessel Guinea-bound, Lisbon's reply was that Guinea belonged to Portugal.

This statement was soon afterwards officially supported by the Papacy. The attempt to maintain a Portuguese monopoly of the vast potential riches of the Guinea trade could never have been successful, and the very effort to do so probably weakened Portugal's power. All the same, the Papal Bulls ran throughout pre-Reformation Europe. In 1481 the Portuguese court heard tell that a couple of Englishmen, William Fabian and John Tintam, were planning an expedition to trade upon the Guinea Coast. King John II protested that this violated his privileges. The voyage was countermanded. Recognition of the papal right to parcel out the non-Christian world is confirmed by the contemporary request of Edward IV of England to be allowed to share in the African trade. This initiative – in a sense a medieval equivalent of a diplomatic tentative to enter the Common Market – was a failure. In 1493, with the Bulls of the Spanish Pope Alexander VI, the Papacy finally came out into the open and granted Ferdinand and Isabella all the lands already discovered or to be discovered in the New World to the west. After certain adjustments to the demarcation line to satisfy Portugal, and the signature in 1494 of the Spanish-Portuguese Treaty of Tordesillas, the Portuguese ended up with possession of the West African coast-line (giving them unsuspected access to the true route to India) and the lands bordering the South Atlantic which turned out to include Brazil. The discovery and annexation by Spain and Portugal of the Kingdoms of the Sun spelled a terrible and sinister eclipse for the peoples of West Africa who came quickly to be regarded merely as fodder for the mines and plantations of the New World.

While the soldiers and sailors of Portugal were busy making themselves loathed by the Africans for their arrogance, lust and rapacity, their King, John II – 'King John the Perfect', a Renaissance prince and statesman of great erudition and popularity – maintained the old Christian attitude that West Africans were human beings like any others, but just needed converting to the true faith. Early in the fourteen-eighties a king of the Jalofs named Bemoy was dislodged from his position by a popular *coup*. With some of his loyal followers he set off on foot for the Portuguese fort on the island of Arguin, and took ship for Portugal to beg succour from King John. Affectionately received by the royal family, the whole party were promptly started off on a course of religious instruction and subsequently baptized in state with the king and queen as god-parents to Bemoy, whom they re-named John. The Africans were then returned to their country, sailing in a convoy of twenty little caravels, the triangular sails of which bore the sign of the cross, and which were filled with materials to build a fort at the mouth of the Senegal River. The expedition was commanded by one Piero Vas d'Acunha Bisagudo, who soon wearied of the project. His men were dying, the river current was too strong, and he was afraid that the King of Portugal would appoint him life-governor of the new fort. He therefore lured the African Bemoy on board his ship, murdered him and, leaving the fort unfinished, returned to Lisbon to face the wrath (and disappointment) of the King. The interesting point here would seem to be not the treachery of d'Acunha, but the civilized attitude of the Portuguese sovereigns and the fact, latterly exploited by the Europeans on the coast, that African chiefs were ready to appeal to Europeans for aid in civil or local wars.

Despite the obvious impracticability of patrolling the whole West African coast-line and their growing concentration on their new possessions in India and Brazil, the Portuguese dominated the Guinea Coast throughout the sixteenth century. By the fifteen-fifties their slave trade thence was already highly organized on a financial basis, with its chief centres in Senegambia, on the Gold Coast and in Angola and São Tomé. Other European nations still held off, although a good many French, and some English, privateers made unheralded descents upon the coast, proving the military impotence of the Portuguese settlements. In 1553 a group of London merchants sent Captain Thomas Windham, with a Portuguese guide, to Guinea and Benin; the little expedition collected gold at Elmina, but the commanders insisted, against the experts' advice, on going into the dreaded Bight of Benin, where one hundred of the ship's complement of one hundred and forty men, including the leaders, died. All the same another London expedition was prepared in the following year, consisting of three vessels commanded by John Lok. They returned triumphantly with gold and ivory, and also with ten 'black slaves' who were described as tall and strong, and were said to relish European food and drink, but not to care greatly for the damp and cold of Tudor London. These Negroes do not seem to have been regarded literally as slaves (even though Hakluyt calls them so) and they were later returned to their home in Guinea. In the same decade three further English voyages were made to Guinea, each of them in charge of the London merchant, William Towerson. On the first of these, when trading at a village near Elmina, Towerson was accosted by a young Negro who came fearlessly on board ship to demand why he had not brought back five compatriots taken to England the year before. Towerson replied that they were perfectly happy in England, and that they would be brought back once they had learned the language and could be used as interpreters 'to be a help to English-men in this country'. Repatriated on Towerson's second voyage in 1556, these travelled Negroes were welcomed near the Portuguese outpost of Shama : 'the people were very glad of our negroes, specially one of their brothers' wives, and one of their aunts,* who received them with much joy, and so did all the rest of the people, as if they had been their natural brethren'.

These first English visits to the Guinea Coast were inquisitive, amicable and more or less profitable. There had been no attempt to settle on the Coast and until John Hawkins' grue-some escapades in the early years of Queen Elizabeth's reign the English had thus far paid no attention to the slave trade. In the reign of the Catholic Queen Mary Tudor the papal privilege was recognized in theory if not always in fact – at any rate, in 1555, the Portuguese envoy in London managed to get Guinea voyages forbidden. With the accession of the Protestant Queen Elizabeth I this tolerance of a papal dispensation, quite predictably, ceased. Up till then, the handful of English traders who, often in league with French privateers, had swept down upon the Guinea Coast, would seem to have been liked and trusted by the Negroes. The quick-witted Africans had already learned to distinguish between the different nationalities of white men – just as, in succeeding centuries, they used to judge a ship's crew by its port of origin, never, for instance, revenging themselves on a London ship for the depredations or dishonesty of some group of men from Bristol. Their first masters, the

---

* Perhaps the first recorded English statement of that complex problem of African family ties, which has ever baffled and thwarted European travellers and administrators alike?

Portuguese, they always hated, even though that nation had long abandoned the kidnapping tactics of Prince Henry the Navigator's day. Statistics for the Portuguese slave trade in the sixteenth century are virtually impossible to establish. Purchas' *Pilgrims* records one estimate that twenty-eight thousand slaves a year were being shipped out of Angola, but he expresses scholarly doubts: 'This number may perhaps seem incredible and justly . . . but the general report is of divers thousand shipped thence yearly; the Portugals making their gain by the negroes' foolish and spiteful wars upon each other.'

So far as England was concerned, it was reserved for that hero of Victorian story-books and stirring ballads, Sir John Hawkins, to destroy in no more than three slave-raids – in 1562, 1564 and 1567 – his country's mild and tenuous good name along the Coast.*

# IV

The prime modern authority on Atlantic slaving and its documentation† has warned us that 'the exploits of Hawkins are of much greater significance in the history of relations between England and Spain than they are in that of the English slave trade'. For political reasons Hawkins' three marauding voyages (about which he himself lied, and Queen Elizabeth and her Council prevaricated) were not allowed to set an immediate precedent: 'For complete lack of evidence to the contrary,' the same scholar explains 'one must conclude that between 1569 and 1618 England's only connection with the slave trade came through casual captures of prizes carrying slaves.' Yet, since in his greed and his callousness John Hawkins was the mental pre-

---

* The Hawkins myth has now been finally dispelled by Mr Rayner Unwin in his brilliant *The Defeat of Sir John Hawkins* (Allen & Unwin 1960). Hawkins' previous biographer, Dr J. A. Williamson (Oxford Press 1929) quaintly writes of 'the unspoiled negro of Tudor days' as 'wallowing in every horror known to savage man. It is no wonder' (asserts this author) 'that the Elizabethans saw in slaving nothing but a hunting of wild beasts.' In fact Hawkins and his men saw in slaving nothing but a quick way of making illicit gain.

† Miss Elizabeth Donnan, whose four monumental volumes *Documents Illustrative of the History of the Slave Trade to America* (Carnegie Institution of Washington, 1930; reprinted by Octagon Books Inc., New York, 1965) are both a model of scholarship and indispensable to any student of the Atlantic slave trade.

cursor of the English slave-traders of the succeeding centuries, he deserves some slight notice here.

The precise date at which the English adventurers began to accept slaving as a natural part of the Guinea trade is no longer known. Richard Jobson, author of *The Golden Trade*, an account of the Gambia published in London in 1623, was certainly against it. Jobson had been sent to Guinea by the patentees of James I's new *Company of Adventurers of London Trading into Parts of Africa*. He was a meticulous investigator, and was one of the first Europeans to find out about 'the silent trade', whereby the coast natives of Gambia would carry salt inland and there exchange it for gold-dust with a tribe they never saw; the salt was laid in heaps on the ground, the river traders withdrew, and returning later would find the salt removed and gold quietly substituted in its place.* Jobson, who was of course after the gold obtained in exchange for the salt, found the Mundingoes at the mouth of the Gambia River nervous, 'they having been many times by several nations surprised, taken and carried away'. Further upriver, the African trader with whom he was doing business, his friend Buckor Sano, showed him a group of young Negresses standing together, and told him they were slaves for him to buy. 'I made answer,' writes Jobson 'we were a people who did not deal in any such commodities, neither did we buy or sell one another, or any that had our own shapes; he seemed to marvel much at it, and told me it was the only merchandise they carried down into the country, where they fetch all their salt, and that they were sold there to white men who earnestly desired them.' Jobson and his colleagues replied that those were different kind of white men to themselves. Yet certain obscure references in English official documents of about this time seem to indicate that at least some Englishmen were fitting ships to 'take niggers, and carry them to foreign parts'. So long as the Spanish-Portuguese control of the New World continued – the crowns of Portugal and Spain had been united in 1580 – and so long as England had not acquired

---

* This form of 'silent trading' persists in Africa today. It enables wayside stall-holders to run more than one establishment at the same time. Coins are substituted for kola-nuts, etc., by the purchaser, the whole transaction taking place under the aegis of a little fetish hanging from the branch of a tree. The fetish prevents cheating.

Caribbean colonies, there was, anyway, no particular reason for the English to scamper into the slave trade.

John Hawkins' slaving exploits were inspired by what he learned in the Canary Islands, as well as by what his father, William Hawkins, had told him about Guinea and the West Indies. William Hawkins, who died when his son was about twenty-two, was a respected old sea-captain, twice Mayor of Plymouth and a member of Parliament for that town. He was renowned for his seamanship throughout the West Country and could also boast the unnerving privilege of being 'esteemed and beloved' by King Henry VIII. Following the example of contemporary French merchants, he had made a number of voyages to Brazil, first touching at the Guinea Coast. This early form of the Triangular Trade had nothing to do with slaving however, although William Hawkins did, in 1539, borrow a native Brazilian chief to display in England, the chief unfortunately dying on the voyage home to Brazil. It must have been under this old man's auspices that his son John became familiar with the Canary Islands, where he diligently enquired about trading possibilities in the Spanish transatlantic possessions. 'Amongst other particulars' Hakluyt tells us that young Hawkins was 'assured that negroes were very good merchandise in Hispaniola, and that store of negroes might easily be had upon the Guinea Coast.' This is the first crude reference in English – certainly in printed English – to the denizens of West Africa as 'merchandise'.*

Now, I think that we can agree that this casual use of the words 'merchandise' and 'store' already implies a distinctive and contemptuous attitude towards the African Negro as such. The dictionary definition of 'merchandise' reads 'the objects of commerce; wares; goods'. That of 'store' reads 'the source from which supplies may be drawn'. Lest I seem to state the obvious, I should explain that to my mind the implication of Hakluyt's use of these words flatly contradicts the new theory that, in these early days, racialism played little or no part in the launch-

---

* Professor Eldred Jones, in his *Othello's Countrymen, The African in English Renaissance Drama* (Oxford University Press, 1965) points out that Hawkins' own account of his 'third and troublesome' slaving voyage, published in 1569, is the first English publication to make consistent use of the term 'Negro' for the Africans living south of Cape Blanco. Hawkins refers to 'the Negro (in which nation is seldom or never found truth)'.

ing of the Atlantic slave trade – that 'race' (to quote a recent book on the subject) 'was not as yet a central question'.* This theory is slenderly erected on isolated instances of Elizabethan Englishmen enslaved by Portuguese slave-traders. There is little Andrew Battel, who imprudently landed from the *May Morning* one day in 1599 to pick fruit upon the Brazilian shore, was abandoned by his Captain, Cocke, was captured by the Indians, sold by them to the Portuguese, shipped to the Guinea Coast, and ended up the slave of what he alleged to be a cannibal tribe with the reassuring name of Ga-ga. Another Elizabethan heretic, young Anthony Knivet, was also sold by the Indians to the Portuguese. But these and similar cases would not seem to prove that European slavers or planters did not yet differentiate between white and black. A secondary argument (which we shall meet in depth when we leave the Coast of Guinea to inspect the sweaty turmoil of selected transatlantic plantations) stems from the grim treatment, on seventeeth-century sugar islands like Barbados, of the white indentured labourers, the white transported felons, the white religious deportees, and the kidnapped white persons lured, sent or sold across the sea. Often treated as badly as the Negro slaves, it is estimated that during the colonial period some quarter of a million British subjects were victims of this traffic. Yet these people proved stubborn and quarrelsome, independent and intractable. Undoubtedly they suffered torments, but they never came to be looked on, as were Negro slaves and their descendants, as chattel property – as, that is to say, an automatically inferior form of humanity, a kind of two-legged domestic animal.

To return to John Hawkins, that bold and famously secretive man, whom we left on a fact-finding mission in the Spanish-held Canary Islands, where (says Hakluyt) he had 'by his good and upright dealing . . . grown in love and favour with the people'. When he had learned all there was to know about his prospective merchandise, its stores and its West Indian markets, he returned to England to seek financial backers for his master-plan – or for that part of it which he was willing to reveal. Money for his purpose was not difficult to find: the success of

* See *Black Cargoes: A History of the Atlantic Slave Trade* by Daniel P. Mannix and Malcolm Cowley (London, 1963).

his first slaving voyage surpassed even his own expectations.

When Queen Elizabeth heard what he had been doing in Africa she branded it 'detestable' and declared that it 'would call down vengeance from Heaven upon the undertakers'. Apprised of the golden profits the shareholders had made from this first slaving voyage, the Queen herself invested capital in Hawkins' second expedition to the Guinea Coast.

## V

As the result of John Hawkins' three expeditions we have the first thoroughly documented account of English slave-traders. Hawkins gave his own version of his activities to the geographer Richard Hakluyt for publication and, concerning his third and disastrous voyage, swore evidence before the High Court of Admiralty. There are further records written, dictated or sworn by men who went with him. The Spanish ambassador in London, Guzman de Silva, wrote lengthy, agitated letters on the subject to his King, Philip II. De Silva thought that once the English had broken in upon the slave trade to the west there would be no holding them: 'It is important to stop this from the beginning' he urged, and, again: 'The 'greed of these people is such that they might arrange always to undertake similar voyages.' The royal archives of Portugal have also yielded contemporary Portuguese accusations against Hawkins. All this material has been scrutinized and annotated by modern scholars. A good deal of secrecy surrounded the preparations for the voyages, and the extent to which his London backers were aware that Hawkins was actually slave-trading remains uncertain. The eminence and wealth of those who invested in his expeditions – the Treasurer of the Royal Navy, the Master of Ordnance to the Navy, two future Lord Mayors of London, certain Privy Councillors and finally the Queen herself – make it unlikely that they were not fully informed of Hawkins' plans, especially as his outgoing cargo included peas and beans, shirts and (oddly) shoes for the Negroes he intended to capture.

Although one of Hawkins' biographers assures us that his hero's letters 'bear witness to an educated mind . . . and are better spelt and put together than those of many a nobleman of the time', Hawkins' own descriptions of his exploits are both illiterate and disingenuous. He shared the preconceptions of his contemporaries about Negroes and, as we have seen, judged them to be usually untruthful – an interesting charge coming from one who was not himself distinguished for his veracity. Some of his colleagues took a more liberal view. John Sparke, an officer on the *Jesus of Lubeck* expressed a partiality for the Negroes of Cape Verde, whom he thought the finest-looking and most 'civil' of any group he came across, and 'of nature very gentle and loving'. But even Sparke attributed their civility to 'daily traffic with the Frenchmen', thus early supporting the general European assumption that nothing negroid could be good in itself, and that it was only contact with Europeans which could render Africans urbane. Neither Hakluyt's publications, nor the verbal depositions of eye-witnesses, do more than conjure up in a general way the perils and the novelty of these voyages.

On the other hand, with Hawkins personally we find a break in the ranks of what, at this distance of time, are for us faceless men : the slave-traders. The members of this profession were not people liable to have their portraits painted, sketched or engraved. Some of them, like Nicholas Owen making his shell-pictures on the Sherbro River, whiled away the time with diaries in which they described how they dressed, where they slept and what they ate; but none of them, so far as I know, depicted his own features. Portraits of John Hawkins, however, do exist. An elegant and courteous man, he had 'a long curved nose, widely-opened eyes, carefully trained moustache and close-cropped pointed beard'. On board ship he dressed sumptuously in silks or velvets, with buttons of pearl and gold. He was in fact the precise antithesis of Charles Kingsley's popular picture of Hawkins as 'a grizzled elder in sea-stained garments', whom he makes 'waddle up' to Drake at Armada-time on Plymouth Hoe, yelping out in 'a broad Devon twang' an invitation to come and quaff a cup of wine with him. Hawkins was, on the contrary, a civilized man of persuasive charm, an astute dissembler, received at court, and even perhaps liked, by the Queen. He was indeed one of the few gentlemen-slave-traders his country produced, for, as Mrs Aphra Behn pointed out a hundred years later in her novel, *Oroonoko*, slave-trading captains were not well-considered. 'This commander' (she writes of the wicked captain of the slave ship which bore the princely Oroonoko away to Surinam) 'was a man of a finer sort of address and conversation, better bred, and more engaging, than most of that sort of men are; so that he seem'd rather never to have been bred out of a court, than almost all his life at sea'.

Hawkins' African depredations were confined to the more westerly regions of the Gulf of Guinea – that is to say to Cape Verde and Sierra Leone. He was limited by his ignorance of the severe navigational hazards of the Coast, although it seems that on his first voyage he took with him a Spanish pilot, who taught him the rudiments of sailing near in shore. On his first voyage his three small ships, with their complement of only one hundred men, lay off Cape Verde, with its smooth green hills, long strip of shining sand and its dangerous, concealed Almadia reef. So far as Cape Verde, his ships would have bobbed along under the heady influence of the North-East Trade Winds, he and his men buoyed up by that sense of exhilaration celebrated by Rudyard Kipling:

> There are many ways to take
> Of the eagle and the snake,
> And the way of a man with a maid;
> But the sweetest way for me
> Is a ship upon the sea
> On the track of the North-East trade.

Africa, however, soon takes over. At Cape Verde you get the first exhalation of what one Victorian traveller described as 'the hot breath of the Bights . . . the breath of Death himself'. For though, as has been suggested, the phrase 'the Gulf of Guinea' conjures up to the romantic arm-chair traveller a gale of exotic scents, to the initiate it is otherwise. There is the thick curtain of muffling heat, and the density of seething vegetation, and often added to these the stench of dead crabs lying on the mud at river-mouths, and decaying coco-nuts half-buried in the sand by natives anxious to rot the fibre free. To counterbalance this you have in Sierra Leone (whither Hawkins proceeded from Cape Verde) the vision of the mountains darkly rising in an arc behind the bay of what is now Freetown, one of the most splendid sights West Africa affords. At evening come the theatrical effects of fork-lightning quivering high over the sea, while the captive thunder rumbles through the mountain peaks with a noise which the first Portuguese mariners likened to the roar of a lion – hence their name for the country, Sierra Leone. This was the land at which Hawkins, with his three little ships and his arquebusiers in armour, arrived in the winter of 1562.

Hakluyt's record of this first of the voyages is curt and deliberately vague. 'Partly by the sword and partly by other means' Hawkins alleged that he had captured three hundred Negroes, whom he afterwards sold in the Spanish colonies across the Atlantic. But Portuguese complaints to the English Government stated that he had taken three times that number, many of them seized from Portuguese slaving ships by force of arms. On his next expedition, that of 1564, they first stopped at the islands of Alcatraz off Cape Verde. Eighty men in armour lumbered ashore and, failing to capture any Negroes, amused themselves by taking pot shots at some on the further side of a river. These Africans did not understand fire-arms, and were startled by their arrowless wounds. They 'used a marvellous crying in their flight with leaping and turning their tails, that it was most strange to see and gave us great pleasure to behold them'. This sport over, Hawkins went south along the coast until he reached what is now called Sherbro Island, one of the most peaceful and idyllic regions on the hauntingly beautiful coast-line of Sierra Leone. Here they lingered 'going every day on shore to take the inhabitants, with burning and spoiling their towns'.

On Sherbro Island, moreover, Hawkins came across some co-operative Portuguese who told him of an inland village where, they said, some one hundred women and children lived protected by only forty males. The Englishmen set off after this easy and tempting prey but, ignoring Hawkins' orders and inflamed by the conviction that the Africans kept gold in their huts, the soldiers split up, fanning out singly or two together and ransacking the village. While preoccupied with this they were surprised by a band of Africans who attacked them, wounded several, and pursued them back to their boats shooting at them with arrows and hacking to pieces those who were floundering full-armoured in the mud. Two hundred Negroes had by now gathered on the bank; seven of Hawkins' best men, including the captain of the *Salomon*, were killed; and thirty wounded. Learning of serious preparations to attack them currently being mounted by 'the king of Sierra Leone', whose army had lit a great fire as a rallying-point, Hawkins prudently withdrew. He had got his complement of slaves, and his men were dying or sickly 'which came by the contagiousness of the place'; he therefore set sail for the West Indies. On the way they struck tornadoes, and were eighteen days becalmed with insufficient drinking water, but, as one of his slavers tells us, 'the Almighty God, who never suffereth his elect to perish' sent them a north-west wind, and they made landfall on the wild and feathery Carib island of Dominica, where they collected rain-water before going on to sell their slaves in the Spanish colonies.

Despite Hawkins' financial success we may feel that in this second English brush with Africa that continent gave almost as good as it got. The coastal Negroes might not yet have fire-arms, but they had, as a first line of defence, their dreaded climate, and, as a second, courage and poisoned arrows.

It was on his third and last voyage (which ended in the loss of four of his ships captured by the Spaniards, and of many of his men and almost all his treasure) that Hawkins first encountered poisoned arrows. These were used by the Jalofs, up on the Senegal River. Two hundred men of Hawkins' now much more ambitious expedition landed before dawn at a village on the river bank, which they found deserted, the women and children in hiding and the men apparently fled. Suddenly, to the accompaniment of horrifying war-cries, six hundred Africans surrounded them, but proving in the end unable to stand up to the fire of cross-bows and arquebuses they partially withdrew. Hawkins decided to go back to his barges. This was accomplished without the loss of a single life, but with the booty of nine slaves only. The attack had been a signal failure, but at least no Englishmen had been killed.

Just two days later a curious illness broke out on board the ships. Men who had received superficial arrow-wounds which had seemed hardly worth talking about were seized with violent convulsions, and an arching of the back as in lock-jaw. Wedges of wood were jammed into their mouths until the fits subsided; but they always recurred and eight men died in agony within the week. 'On the lower deck' (writes Mr Rayner Unwin) 'it was rumoured that one of the captive negroes, with whom Hawkins had been closeted in an attempt at interrogation, had taught their captain to draw the poison from his wound with a clove of garlic. If it was so Hawkins did not choose to extend the application of the remedy.' Since his men were now terrified, and might well turn mutinous, and since native drums could be heard nightly throbbing the alarm throughout the forests, Hawkins decided to push on down the coast. Later, with a full stock of his living merchandise, he set out once more across the Atlantic, to meet shame and disaster on the Spanish Main.

So ended the pioneer English efforts at slave-trading. In 1588 Queen Elizabeth granted a monopoly to certain London and Exeter merchants for ten years of exclusive trading on the Senegal and Gambian coasts. But this company was concerned with the more anodyne aspects of the African Trade – bartering English goods for West African products. This was, incidentally, a profitable exchange : Towerson, for example, had found in the fifteen-fifties that for one copper basin he could get thirty pounds' worth of gold. The Queen herself invested one thousand pounds in a trading voyage of 1561, and gained a profit of sixty per cent. It was not until well into the following century that Englishmen resumed trading in slaves, and then it was chiefly by purchase and negotiation, and seldom by the seizure of free Negroes in their huts.

Having watched Hawkins at work, what are the images left in our minds by these brutal encounters of Englishmen with the 'civil . . . very gentle and loving' peoples of West Africa? The courtly captain, in jewelled doublet and hose, incisive on the poop; native villages in flames; screaming white men helpless in their heavy breastplates, struggling vainly as they sink ever deeper into the ooze; a discarded arquebus, perhaps, lying rusting on the yellow sand as the little sea-crabs prance in and out of their holes to the swish of the incoming tide?

Let us leave, for the moment, Cape Verde, Sierra Leone and the Rivers of the South and take a look at the trading forts and castles, strung out for four hundred miles eastwards along the Gold Coast from Beyin, Ankobra and Axim to Christiansborg, Prampram and Keta. Since a conducted tour of all of these forts is scarcely feasible, we may begin by the greatest of them all, Elmina. On the marshy salt-flats behind the town herons and egrets step light and leisurely through the shallow water. The long, carved boats of the fishermen lie drawn up on the fore-shore, a screen of nets on poles drying near them. The surf hurls itself along the beaches. It crashes against the high black rocks crowned by the bastions, colonnades and battlements of the fortress of Elmina – the Castle of the Mine.

Impregnable from the sea, Elmina is best approached, as I have myself approached it, from the land-side. Since this was also the direction from which most of the newly procured slaves, yoked in the stumbling slave-coffles described by Mungo Park, first came to the slave-mart and the dungeons of Elmina, we may as well follow it ourselves – pausing momentarily in the Ashanti rain-forests for a few unwelcome reflections on our way.

# Chapter 5

# The Castle of the Mine

## I

STAYING for some days in the hilltop fort of St Iago – built by the Dutch in the sixteen-sixties to protect the main Castle of St George at the Mine from landward assault – I found I never tired of gazing down at the stark yet complex beauty of the castle itself, or of wandering through its vast courtyards or along the tops of the curtain walls looking out to sea. Although powerful, the Castle of the Mine is also a sprawling building which, with its whitewashed walls and brick vaults and archways, seems to have grown out of the rocks on which it stands. By day the white walls shimmer in the sun and the heat, and the shadows cast by buttresses and towers are of an incredibly sharp purple-black. At night these walls are almost as brightly lit by the African moon. Sometimes I would leave my bedroom in the middle of the night to walk on what I liked to think of as my private rampart at St Iago, fascinated by the view of the silent castle and, behind it, the ceaseless tide of the Bight. Unlike many of the more modest trading forts along the old Gold Coast, Elmina is no tumbledown relic of trading days, but an unflinching architectural statement of the former European presence in the Gulf of Guinea.

Although I was quartered in the Dutch fort, I was at the same time the guest of a characteristically hospitable Ghanaian friend, the Vice-Chancellor of Kumasi University and by matrilineal descent the hereditary Chief of Elmina. His stone house, with a first-floor verandah, stands in the very centre of the town, overlooking the noisy, sunlit piazza on which the market-mammies would wave and shout up friendly greetings from below. He was in the process of constructing a new stool-house, to contain that symbol of his chieftainship, and, although a

55

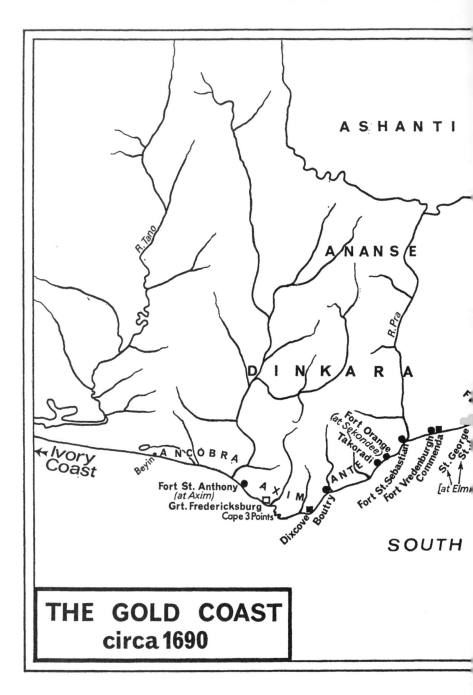

ASHANTI

ANANSE

R. Tano

R. Pra

DINKARA

←Ivory
Coast

ANCOBRA

Beyin

Fort Orange
(at Sekondee)
Takoradi

AXIM

Fort St. Anthony
(at Axim)
Grt. Fredericksburg
Cape 3 Points

ANTE

Dixcove
Boutry

Fort St. Sebastian

Fort Vredenburgh
Commenda

St. George
St.

[at Elm

SOUTH

**THE GOLD COAST**
**circa 1690**

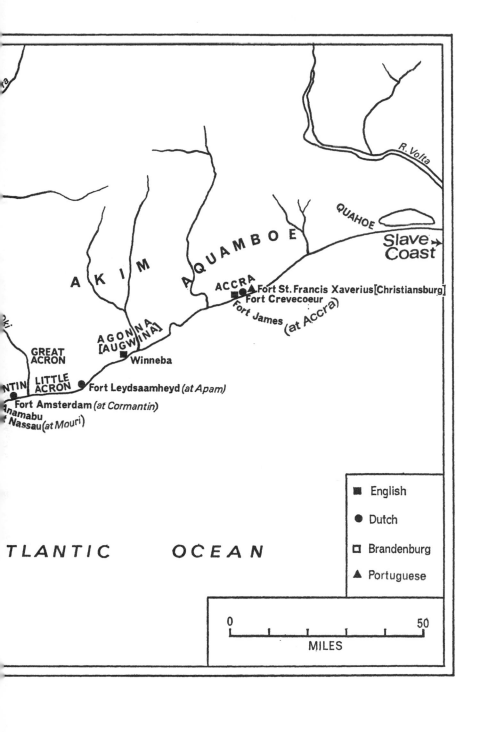

R. Volta

QUAHOE

Slave→
Coast

A K I M

A Q U A M B O E

ACCRA ▲Fort St. Francis Xaverius [Christiansburg]
■■ Fort Crevecoeur
Fort James (at Accra)

AGONNA
[AUGWINA]

GREAT
ACRON
■ Winneba

NTIN LITTLE
ACRON ● Fort Leydsaamheyd (at Apam)
● Fort Amsterdam (at Cormantin)
Anamabu
◆ Nassau (at Mouri)

A T L A N T I C   O C E A N

| | |
|---|---|
| ■ | English |
| ● | Dutch |
| □ | Brandenburg |
| ▲ | Portuguese |

0          50
MILES

devout Roman Catholic, he poured a libation of beer on the verandah to inform his ancestors that his guest was grandson of the Administrator who had negotiated the transfer of the Dutch stronghold to the British in 1872. Their reply was apparently cordiality itself.

We had driven down from Kumasi through the rain-forest, past lofty, lavish clusters of swaying bamboo, as high as the nave of a Gothic cathedral, and past the clumps of floppy wild banana trees which live in a rather promiscuous, haphazard way beside the forest streams. Like the mangrove swamps of the Niger delta, these cool forests, as you look into them, give you a sense of endless depth. Every so often you pass a bush path leading to some hidden village, and we drove through many villages on the motor-road itself. Towards evening, in these villages, the lithe and tall Ashanti youths form merry, idle groups to laugh and talk. Children are trotting back from school in neat school uniforms and bare feet, their slates and books balanced on their heads. The women pound fu-fu with precision, or are cooking in their houses. The young men's ample togas, worn over one shoulder with a careless elegance, lend the colours of the tropical birds to the dark, deep scene – magenta, peacock blue, bright yellow, emerald green or violet. As we drove on I reflected that these graceful and muscular youths with noble faces and beguiling smiles, and these little schoolboys, are but modern replicas of the race of Ashanti Negroes, prized and feared above all others by the owners of the colonial plantations to whom they were sold in chains.

Miscalled, in the West Indies, 'Coromantees' (from the coastal factory at Cormantine whence many of them were shipped), these young warriors were famous on the plantations for their efficiency and strength, but also for the haughty spirit which made them leaders and instigators of the dreaded slave revolts. Of these Ashanti slaves one West Indian planter, Dr Collins (author of a useful manual, *Practical Rules for the Management of Negro Slaves in the Sugar Colonies*, published in London in 1803) writes that 'being habituated from infancy to war, the necessary movements of which give flexibility to the muscles, and energy to the mind', the Coromantees were 'by far the most hardy and robust; yet bringing with them into slavery lofty ideas of independence, they are dangerous inmates on a

West Indian plantation'. A hundred years earlier, in 1701, Christopher Codrington, Governor of the Leeward Islands, wrote to the British Board of Trade: 'The Coromantees . . . are not only the best and more faithful of our slaves, but are really all born heroes . . . There never was a rascal or coward of that nation, intrepid to the last degree . . . My father, who had studied the genius and temper of all kinds of negroes forty-five years with a very nice observation, would say: "No man deserved a Coromantee that would not treat him like a friend rather than a slave." ' Bryan Edwards, the West Indian historian whom we have already met, endorses this view, but gives a warning against the Coromantees' gift for organizing slave revolts. He tells of the experience of a friend of his in Jamaica who had bought 'a parcel' of young Ibo and Coromantee boys. At the branding on the breast which automatically followed such purchases, the first youth, an Ibo 'screamed dreadfully, while his companions of the same nation manifested strong emotions of sympathetic terror. The gentleman stopped his hand; but the Koromantyn boys, laughing aloud and immediately coming forward of their own accord, offered their bosoms undauntedly to the brand, and receiving its impression without flinching in the least, snapped their fingers in exultation over the poor Eboes'. The fortitude of the Coromantees has been attributed by one writer 'to the prevalence of unusually cruel customs among the tribes of the Gold Coast' – presumably a reference to the tribal and status-symbol cuts incised facially in childhood. For the really cruel practices such as the former ritual human sacrifices at the Ashanti capital of Kumasi can scarcely have induced courage. There seems nothing morally fortifying about being murdered, or watching others being killed.

Further theories or as the American scholar Mr Philip Curtin calls them in his *The Image of Africa** 'the old libels of popular belief' had for generations asserted that the African and European nervous systems were different: 'that African women could give birth without pain, that the Negro nervous system was generally less sensitive in matters of touch and taste, though not in eyesight. The Negro brain, bile and blood had also been

---

* Philip D. Curtin, *The Image of Africa, British Ideas and Action 1780–1850* (Macmillan & Co., Ltd., 1965).

held to be of a different colour from those of other races . . . All these points' (concludes Mr Curtin) 'were corrected easily enough on the basis of a few years of medical practice among Negroes.' Yet these offensive assumptions had persisted a very long time, and formed yet further strands in the web of misunderstanding which, as we have already noticed, obscured the real nature of Africans to European minds.

The earliest Portuguese traders were not more immune to these misapprehensions than their successors. For they ran straight into fetish complications so soon as they started building, in late January, 1481, the Castle of St George at the Mine.

## II

King John of Portugal had ordered a careful survey of the Gold Coast on which the decision to build the Castle of the Mine was ultimately based. The name 'El Mina' was then still applied in a general way to the whole Gold Coast, for the Portuguese remained convinced that they would soon find the mines from which came the gold the Africans traded with them. In fact the difficulties of inland communication, and above all the Africans' determination to fend the white men off from the natural sources of supply, prevented either the Portuguese or any other European nation from reaching 'the land of gold' for four centuries; it was not until Sir Garnet Wolseley's punitive expedition to Kumasi in 1876 that Europeans came within reach of the gold mines. Not only did the Portuguese expect to acquire and work the mines themselves, they also exaggerated the supply of gold readily available, since the great quantities of gold ornaments which the Africans at first exchanged for brass or copper must have been the accumulations of centuries. But by the time it was realized that the coastal strip did not contain gold mines, the name Elmina, now limited to the Castle and the township, had come to stay. The Castle of St George, so christened by its founder and first governor, Diogo d'Azambuja, thus became known as what it was precisely not – 'the Castle of the Mine'. Gold, ivory and slaves flowed freely through it, but there was no working goldmine in the vicinity.

Before the building of the castle, its site, consisting of two African villages separated by a tidal river-mouth, was known as the Village of Two Parts. Chosen by the Portuguese for defensive and for navigational reasons, the site offered, as well, a massive rock formation from and upon which a stone fortress could be built. Setting a precedent always thereafter followed on the coast, the Portuguese first applied to the local king for permission to build. This dignitary, Kwame Ansa, showed marked foresight. He begged the Portuguese not to build a permanent settlement in his territory. In courteous and diplomatic terms he emphasized that he was sensible of the honour done to him and his people, but that he was dismayed by the evident grandeur and style of the Portuguese deputies sent out to negotiate with him. All the Portuguese with whom he had traded previously, he said, had been poorly dressed men, who were merely out to trade and were 'never happy until they had completed their lading' and set sail again for home. He was convinced that the grandees he now saw before him could never get used to the Gold Coast climate, and he suggested that there was no need for his nation and that of the King of Portugal to make any innovation in their trading habits. He politely suggested that the Portuguese should continue to come and to go as before.

It seems likely from this first recorded speech of a Gold Coast king that Kwame Ansa shrewdly foresaw dangers and troubles if a European nation got a permanent foothold on his coast. In the end, however, he allowed himself to be persuaded to lease them a part of the foreshore of Elmina. It is noteworthy that not until the European seizure of West Africa for colonial subjection was any European settlement regarded as being the property of the nation which made it. Elmina, Cape Coast and all the other forts were held on sufferance from the local African chiefs, were often subject to sudden assault if the settlers displeased their hosts, and equally often used as refuges by the natives in times of local war. Their existence gave the local people an employment and a protection, and these strongholds of foreign occupation inevitably created spheres of influence as time went by. But extra-territorial rights they could not claim. Where Europeans were concerned, the African kings and their counsellors always retained a sense of the strength of their own position. There are many recorded complaints of slave-traders who were obliged to stand bareheaded in the presence of some local king and treat him with an obsequiousness they would only have accorded to a monarch or a nobleman at home. The nascent theory of the superiority of white men to Negroes was never accepted by these last. It was riling for the Europeans to have to kow-tow as they did but, in their precarious position, there was absolutely nothing they could do about it. Suppliants for slaves, gold and ivory, they could not afford to alienate African potentates, who became more and more greedy for a mass of gifts which fell little short of tribute. One of the only European weapons in the field of bargaining was the lavish dispensation of brandy and rum. The deliberate policy of creating alcoholism on the Coast was one more corrupting by-product of the slave trade.

The Portuguese decision to build a great fortress and trading depot at Elmina was a logical one. They were anxious to be able to control the coastal trade, and to try to keep predatory foreigners away. They wanted a base in which to maintain military and naval forces, and a speedier turn-round for their trading ships. Instead of lying for weeks or months off the coast, waiting for small African traders from upcountry to bring down a few tusks, a little gold and some slaves, ships at Elmina would be able first to discharge their trade goods in warehouses, and then to stock up quickly from the Elmina stores (before the emphasis switched from the gold to the slave trade, Elmina slaves were simply kept in store-houses similar to those used for the tusks of ivory and other products of Africa). There was thus every reason to come to an agreement with King Kwame Ansa of the Village of Two Parts.

The expedition which now set out from Portugal in January 1482 seems to have been a model of efficiency. There were some six hundred men – soldiers, masons and carpenters. The ships were loaded with finished material for the details of the building – stone cut to form windows, doorways and gateways, tiles, bricks, lime, timber, nails and tools. The rest of the stone was to be quarried from the towering rocks between the mouth of the river and the sea. On landing, work was at once begun upon a central keep, and quarrying began. At this point the natives of the Village of Two Parts rose up in fury and attacked the Portuguese workmen. King Kwame Ansa had omitted to explain to his tenants that the rocks they were destroying had been since time immemorial the residence of an important sea-spirit, and so the object of reverence mixed with awe. The Portuguese assuaged the Africans with expensive presents, but hurried on with their building so that they might take shelter in it did the row – as well it might have done – blow up again. In less than a month, the chronicler tells us, the walls were 'built up to their full height and so was the tower and many houses within it were finished'. Diogo d'Azambuja now gave the castle its formal name. He sent most of his surviving men back to Portugal – although Elmina has never been malarial several had died – settling down himself as Governor with a complement of sixty men and three women. This sexual imbalance was presumably redressed by the village girls, for, hot-blooded believers in miscegenation, the Portuguese soon created a scattered half-breed population down the coast.

The inauspicious scuffle over the desecration of the fetish-rocks at Elmina* may have been dismissed by the Portuguese settlers as a tiresome incident of small significance, a mere expression of ignorant belief in a misguided religion which would soon give way before the truths of Christianity. For all their rapacity, the Portuguese did for many frustrating decades honestly try to convert the coast Africans, whose belief in miracles, visions and the survival or reincarnation of the soul in some form or other gave to two or three generations of Portuguese priests and friars a certain optimism about the possibilities of conversion. African amulets and charms were misinterpreted as being the equivalent of the venerated relics of Christian saints and martyrs. When the Portuguese first came across the grotesque figurines to which the Negroes paid such obvious deference, they assumed them to be much the same as their own *fetiços* or images of the Virgin Mary and the saints. The name *fetish* is thus no more of African origin than the other European term for this form of religion – 'ju-ju', which is thought to date from early French visitors to the Coast, who, seeing the same

---

* The rhomboid shape of the great courtyard at the English headquarters, Cape Coast Castle, built in 1682, is partially due to the sensible wish to avoid injuring another fetish rock, which was excluded from the fortifications in deference to local feeling. We may find a modern analogy in the trouble caused some years ago among workmen at Shannon Airport, when instructed to extend a runway across a well-known faëry ring.

63

little figures, called them 'joux-joux', or toys.* But in fact these figures were neither toys nor representations of African saints. They were objects into which some benevolent or at any rate potent spirit could be coaxed to reside, and there cosseted in the hope that he would stay and not be lured away by superior magic or by the prospect of better, handsomer treatment elsewhere. In the same way the fetish rocks, trees, pools, river bends and so on were the residence – sometimes permanent, sometimes occasional – of capricious spirits which could do good or harm to human beings at will. The charms which Africans wore from birth, and which were increased in number as the years went by, were also the tiny homes of a spirit personal to the owner. Each individual had his or her own attendant spirit, rather like a guardian angel but far more unreliable. There were charms to cover every conceivable contingency – charms to prevent your being witched, to avoid canoe accidents, to make you invisible to elephants, love-charms, hate-charms, a whole nervous, intricate, dark world of charms – a watchful, wary world as well.

The wide and specialist subject of African fetish may seem irrelevant to this study of the slave trade, but I do not think that this is necessarily so. It is, in fact, clearly germane to any judgement on the effects of the forced migration of millions of Africans into the New World. In buying, shipping and selling Negro slaves, John Hawkins and his merry men, for example, were not as they thought merely dealing in labour potential – we might more precisely say trading in muscle-power. Those mournful and tormented human cargoes took with them over the ocean not only their own tastes and habits, but their own traditional beliefs. In the fertile soil of the tropical Americas these transplanted well. The voodoo of Haiti is of direct African origin. In Cuba, Efik and Ibebo slaves re-created the secret society of the Niger, Egbo. In Bahia in Brazil, priestesses of the Yoruba god, Shango, still practise rites which Nigerian Yorubas can recognize today. As everyone who has lived in the West Indies knows, strange secret ceremonies take place after nightfall in the seclusion of the forested hills. By Caribbean waysides one often comes across inexplicable little objects made of cloth

* Although it has also been thought to come from the Mundingo word, gru-gru, but it is more likely that this last is another corruption of the French.

or bird feathers or animal skulls and bones. Indeed, in the cruel and alien setting of the plantations, the aid of fetish-spirits was needed as never before.

Many of the fetish charms of Africa were against being poisoned by an envious friend or a secret enemy. This particular anxiety carried with it the corollary of a considerable knowledge of poisonous herbs. The fear of being poisoned by a domestic slave, like the fear of being slaughtered in a slave revolt, made the lives of transatlantic planters and their families uneasy, and accounted for a good deal of the severity of the slave-laws. You might buy a parcel of youths and girls in the market of Bridgetown, Barbados, or Charleston, Carolina, but you could never really be sure what exact quantity of hatred, hostility and magic you were carting back to the slave-barracks of your comfortable Palladian home.

## III

For so long as their enfeebled grip upon the Gold Coast lasted – and it may be roughly said to have ended in 1637 with the fall of Elmina to the Dutch during the Eighty Years War* – the Portuguese maintained their Christian emphasis. Slaves were baptized wholesale immediately after purchase; their spiritual welfare was cared for throughout the plantations of Brazil. Inside the courtyard of Elmina was a chapel; a church dedicated to St George, for the use of those Portuguese and their slaves who lived in the actual town, and of the few free local African converts, stood outside the walls near the sea-shore, until pulled down as a security risk in 1596. A new church was built inside the castle courtyard two years later and, much altered by the Dutch who used it as a trade-store and market, still exists today, its white façade decorated with stripes of old Portuguese bricks. At Axim, to the far west of Elmina, and always an important centre for getting gold from the western rivers and gold-fields, they erected a fort dedicated to St Anthony; in 1563 some English seamen reported seeing a

---

* The Portuguese had become disastrously involved in the Eighty Years War (1568–1648) between Spain and the revolted Netherlands because of the union of the crowns of Spain and Portugal in 1580 – called in Portuguese history 'the long embrace'. The embrace lasted until 1640.

gigantic cross of wood standing beside a watch-house on a rock near the fort. Built on a promontory jutting out into the sea, Axim, which, again, was altered when the Dutch seized it in 1642, has perhaps the most romantic of all the settings of the Gold Coast forts, particularly when seen in the brief reddish twilight of a fine day on the Gulf. At Shama, near the mouth of the great Pra River, and now one of the most architecturally seductive of the smaller castles, the Portuguese put up what was evidently a rather primitive fortified station dedicated to St Sebastian. Shama was totally rebuilt by the Dutch. It has about it a miniature perfectionism, with little battlements and a steep semi-circular flight of yellow brick steps fanning down from the main gateway to the beach and the jumbled township below. European architecture in a tropical setting always has a fascination of its own. It is not hard, when clambering about these West African forts and castles, to distinguish stylistically the nationalities of their founders.

Not long before the construction of the Castle of the Mine, other Portuguese mariners had penetrated as far east as the powerful and sinister city of Benin, upriver from the Slave Coast. These were still the days before the Portuguese had become disheartened by the meagre harvest of their christian-izing zeal; as well as trading with the Bini, they hoped to convert them to the Faith. They were received in his spacious palace by the Oba of Benin, a theocratic ruler descended from a god and so heavily sheathed in polished gold that when he rose to his feet he had to be propped up by two slaves, who likewise operated his arms for him when he wished to gesticulate. This dread and interesting monarch subsequently sent a distinguished Bini 'of good speech and natural wisdom' as his ambassador to the court of Portugal. The ambassador and his wife returned to Benin loaded with gifts and accompanied by 'holy and most Catholic advisers' instructed to rebuke the Oba's subjects for their 'great idolatries and fetishes'. The king of Benin's approach to Christianity was courteous but lukewarm – which is not sur-prising since he himself was treated as a deity and cannot have wished for competition in his own field. He made some vague promises about encouraging his subjects to become Christians, but procrastinated over carrying these out. When chivied by the Portuguese friars, he finally detailed off one of his many sons and a handful of his greatest nobles to become converts. The selected Bini were baptized 'straightway', and taught to read and to speak Portuguese. According to Mr Michael Crowder's *History of Nigeria* 'to this day a section of the Benin royal palace speaks a language, quite unintelligible to the ordinary Bini, which is allegedly derived from Portuguese'.

At Whydah on the Slave Coast, where the Portuguese presence lasted until six years ago,\* an Augustine monk from São Tomé once invited the King to attend mass. When asked what his reactions were, the King replied that it was 'very fine' but that he preferred to stick to his own fetish. Gradually the Portuguese, and also the French who were the only other European nation to aim at all seriously at native conversions, became discouraged. Polygamy was one of a host of insuperable obstacles, West African humour and gaiety another. It was found that, attracted by the novelty of it all, Africans would diligently listen to religious instruction and seem to understand it, but as soon as the missionaries' backs were turned they forgot all about it – or, worse still, mocked it in what were termed 'their frolics', aided by friends who, as servants in European establishments, had learned to answer the catechism most satisfactorily and to speak 'pertinently of the creation, the fall of Adam, Noah's flood, of Moses and of Jesus Christ'. One experienced French trader on the coast concluded finally that the Negroes 'can conceive of nothing that is spiritual, but only sensual and palpable objects'. In fact, the real complication of African religious beliefs was that their conception of the spiritual was so potent, so immediate and so incredibly wide-ranging.

Of the daily life led by the Portuguese inside the Castle of the Mine no real records exist, any more than there are reliable estimates of the extent of their slave-trading. During the sixteenth and early seventeenth centuries improvements to strengthen the castle and bring its defences up to date were often carried out. The two big ditches to landward, spanned by wooden drawbridges, were deepened, and the medieval castle

---

\* There were French, English, Dutch and Portuguese stations at Whydah. For reasons of sentiment the Portuguese retained their fort, standing within an acre of vegetable garden and making a tiny enclave in French territory, until 1961, when the Republic of Dahomey annexed it. The Portuguese representative at Whydah burned his motor-car in front of the fort as a protest, whereupon Dahomey issued a celebration postage stamp showing the charred wreckage of the Citroën.

walls thickened to resist the ever-increasing fire-power of the guns of ships attacking from the sea. Even so the Dutch nearly captured Elmina in 1596. They succeeded in doing so in 1637, using the simple expedient of hauling cannon up the hill of St Iago, which was defended by nothing more formidable than a pretty little Renaissance chapel dedicated to St James. From this commanding hilltop, where the Dutch-built fort now stands, the invaders lobbed their cannon-balls over the river and into the great castle courtyard. Although no very grave damage seems to have been done, the Portuguese surrendered the Castle of the Mine into heretic hands, thus virtually abdicating their power on the Gold Coast.

Holland – or rather the United Provinces, of which Holland with its capital at Amsterdam was only one – first became interested in the Guinea Coast in rather the same way that Hawkins himself had done a generation earlier. A Dutch skipper caught on his way to Brazil by Portuguese from São Tomé island in the Gulf of Guinea, learned from his loquacious captors tempting details of their Gold Coast trade. Returning to the Netherlands 'he made a successful pioneer voyage thither, returning in 1594 with a valuable cargo of gold and ivory. Such were the vigour and persistence with which the Dutch exploited these new markets, that by 1621 they had secured between half and two-thirds of the carrying-trade between Brazil and Europe while virtually the whole of the United Province's gold coinage was minted with gold brought from Guinea'.* The Dutch West India Company, founded in 1621 by charter, as an implement in the Eighty Years War, soon became an almost exclusively slave-trading concern. It shipped Negroes wholesale from West Africa to the island of Curaçao in the West Indies, whence they could be smuggled into the Iberian colonies in the New World.

It was one of the new Company's more ambitious and unsuccessful ventures which sealed the fate of Elmina. In 1624 the Dutch had started a settlement of their own in northern Brazil. In 1636, John Maurice of Nassau (builder of the Mauritshuis in The Hague) was appointed its Governor, an office which he resigned in 1644. The Dutch colony had a short life, since the Portuguese took it ten years later. But, under John Maurice of

* From C. R. Boxer, *The Dutch Seaborne Empire, 1600–1800* (Hutchinson, 1965).

Nassau, there arose a massive demand for Negro slaves to work in the sugar-mills at Pernambuco and on other Dutch projects in Brazil. 'It is not possible to effect anything in Brazil without slaves . . .' the new Governor wrote: '. . . and they cannot be dispensed with upon any occasion whatsoever; if anyone feels that this is wrong, it is a futile scruple.' The 'futile scruple' had apparently been entertained by some of the first Dutch voyagers, whose Calvinist consciences had been affronted by seeing the Portuguese treatment of Negroes. Very soon they themselves were doing worse, proving to be slave-traders as callous and frequently as sadistic as, for example, their English rivals. A seventeenth-century French trader and authority on the Guinea Coast describes how, when his ship was lying at anchor off the Castle of the Mine, thirty or forty canoes a day came to him from Elmina and Commenda, 'all the blacks coming to complain of the hardships the Dutch put upon their countrymen; keeping some of them for a long time in the bilboes within the castle, exposed stark naked to the scorching heat of the sun in the day and to the cold dews in the night'. The Dutch general commanding Elmina personally showed this Frenchman three Negroes chained in such conditions on the land-batteries. He told him they had been fettered there for more than nine months, as a punishment for their part in an abortive native conspiracy to surprise the Castle of the Mine and destroy it by fire. A great number of the townsmen had been secretly mustered for this attack, and when it was forestalled they fled to other places on the coast, burning their houses before they left. If it was a bad day for the Gold Coast when the Portuguese first settled there, it was a worse one when they left and when the Dutch – avaricious and brutal, complacent and infected by one of the more inhumane versions of Christianity, that of Calvin – took their place.

For the people of the Gold Coast the Dutch flag fluttering in the sea-wind above the white battlements of Elmina, and at Axim, Shama, Dutch Commenda and other forts and trading stations down the Gulf, meant enslavement at a new and more high-powered pace. Outside Europe, the Dutch were neither a kindly nor an imaginative nation. The machinery of the slave trade to the west was now whirring smoothly, and its cruelties were paralleled across the Atlantic, on the plantations of

Surinam and the depot-island of Curaçao. Dutch planters and their wives – more particularly, it was noted by foreign observers, their wives – became a by-word for their revolting treatment of their slaves, whether the Negro slaves of the transatlantic colonies, or the Indian, Chinese or Javanese slaves in their oriental outposts at Batavia, or Malacca, or in the Banda Islands.

Any attempts to convert the Africans to Calvinism petered out towards the middle of the seventeenth century, when it became impossible to find *predikants* ready to face the West African climate. Some of these had at first ministered in Elmina and the forts, but religious practice was soon reduced to morning and evening prayers conducted by a lay-reader who also enlivened the garrison's week by periodic scripture-readings. In the mid-eighteenth century a cheerful-looking freed slave, the Reverend Jacobus Capitein, who had been ordained *predikant* in Amsterdam, was despatched by the West India Company to Elmina, where he found only a small European following, opened a school for Negro and half-caste children, and translated the Lord's Prayer and the Ten Commandments for their benefit. He ended badly, dying in debt in 1747. The bewigged Reverend Capitein, whose engraved portrait shows us his protuberant eyes, thick lips, and expression of benevolent optimism, was not replaced. So far as Dutch missionary activities in slave-trading times went, his appointment was the exception which proved the rule. The austere and discouraging tenets of Geneva were, in any case, unlikely to appeal to the warm hearts and happy minds of the West African Negro communities. Nor, as instruments of Christian proselytism, is there much to be said for the fetter and the lash.

## IV

The easy conquest of Elmina by the Dutch suggests that the defences had become dilapidated and Portuguese morale low. The general tone had perhaps become careless and sleazy. With the clattering arrival of the Dutch – those brisk, confident soldiers from the north, representatives of a young Republic, a triumphant commerce and a militant reformed Faith – all this was changed. Instead of the sibilant Portuguese tongue, to

which the free Africans and the domestic slaves at Elmina had
been for generations accustomed, the hideous language of the
Netherlands now rent the soft tropical air – the abrasive con-
sonants, the booming, oblong vowels of *Plattdeutsch*. The new
masters of Elmina set to work with a characteristic vigour. The
Portuguese had surrendered on 29 August 1637, after a siege
lasting only three days. The enemy commander, Colonel van
Koin, ordered an immediate survey of the Castle to be made by
one of his engineers named Commersteyn, and this, resulting in
the oldest known plan of Elmina, was completed in a week.
Quarters were allotted, store-rooms investigated, the Roman
Catholic Church turned into a mart, and its altar rails torn up.
The familiar figures of the saints vanished; instead, as years
went by, bleak quotations from the psalms were built into the
walls: 'Zion is the Lord's rest, it is His dwelling-place to
eternity' one can still read there, in Dutch, to this day. What
can have been more bewildering to the Africans than this rapid
switch of masters, the clang and din of conquest, the stamping
of the oiled leather thigh-boots, the glint of swords and muskets,
the cannon balls hissing over the huddled rooftops of the native
town? Then, too, there was the contrast in type between the
small, swarthy, jet-eyed Portuguese and the hulking red-faced
Netherlanders and German mercenaries, their fair hair hanging
to their shoulders beneath wide-brimmed hats with drooping
plumes. The comparative racial tolerance of Portuguese days
became at once a thing of the past, for the Dutch West India
Company forbade concubinage with African women. This was
a prohibition quite impossible to enforce; but the fact that such
unions were henceforward clandestine served to emphasize the
arrogant Dutch attitude to the Negro race.

For us, the advent of the Dutch at Elmina means improved
visibility, both there and further down the coast. Some of the
Governors kept diaries, and records of improvements. Two or
three accounts of the Dutch possessions were published in
Europe. It is possible to learn from such sources the use of
various buildings, the strength of the garrison, the daily routine,
what kind of food was eaten, how many anchors and how much
canvas was kept in the stores for sale to passing ships. On
Christmas Eve, 1639, two years after the Dutch had installed
themselves in the Castle, a young Nuremberg goldsmith,

Michael Hemmersam, who was twenty years old, arrived there as an enlisted soldier and stayed six years. His account of Elmina, published by his widow, gives vivid glimpses of life within the Castle, the gates of which were closed at nightfall and only opened with the dawn. Hemmersam describes the ringing of the castle bell to mark the hours, the geese and ducks (destined for the Governor's table) pottering about on a stretch of muddy water outside the walls, the reading and singing of psalms and hymns on Sundays in the great hall, which was hung with muskets and pikes. He even refers to the numbers of civet cats kept in the Cat Yard. These contributed to the manufacture of the scent that must only too clearly have been a priority essential to life in seventeenth-century African forts, where Europeans dressed as stuffily as they did in contemporary Europe, and reeked of sweat.

By 1645 the Dutch were maintaining Elmina with eighty-five Europeans and one hundred and eighty-four trained slaves. There was a Governor, a Treasurer, four European traders and nine men in charge of handicrafts, a lay-preacher (or 'sick-comforter') and a garrison of sixty-five officers and men. There was a devotional library containing seventy-two copies of the psalms. One of the lay-preachers, who came to Elmina in 1642, committed suicide when he fell ill there after four years. Although the sea-wind prevented the Castle (but not St Iago behind it) from being malarial, the soldiers' quarters were airless and unhealthy, and the untiled roofs leaked in rain. Contaminated water brought a variety of tropical diseases. Even for the officers fresh meat was hard to come by, and the lower orders ate smoked meat, flour, biscuits, cheese and butter. The slaves ate African food. Fruit and vegetable gardens were planted on the hillsides of St Iago, and, later, pleasure gardens with classical pavilions domed in thatch were scattered here and there behind the town. The officers seem to have indulged in long and heavy meals. Except for the seasonal celebration of some kermess or other, there was nothing to do with leisure but to drink – in the case of the Dutch neat brandy and rum – which everyone did to excess. The Dutch believed that the English at Cape Coast Castle drank far more than they did; the English believed the same about the Dutch. In fact, alcoholism was rampant in both camps.

There is no doubt that, under Dutch rule, the Castle of the Mine flourished. 'The castle is justly famous for beauty and strength, having no equal on all the coasts of Guinea' runs a French description of 1682:

> ... The general's lodgings are above in the castle, the ascent to which is up a large white and black stone staircase, defended at the top by two small brass guns, and four pattareroes, of the same metal, bearing upon the Place of Arms; and a *corps de garde* pretty large, next to which is a great hall of small arms of several sorts, as an arsenal; through which and by a by-passage you enter a fine long gallery, all wainscotted, at each end of which are large glass windows, and through it is the way to the general's lodgings, consisting of several good chambers and offices along the ramparts.

The Governor of Elmina lived in considerable grandeur, as a conversation-piece of Admiral de Ruyter in his tower bedroom, painted by de Witt in 1665, bears witness. This spacious room, one of two of identical size and shape, has five walls with windows facing outwards, and a long sixth wall on the Castle side. The Admiral, elaborately dressed and wearing a circular black hat with a moderately high crown and two white ostrich feathers, stands slightly to the left of the picture, while a plumed and turbaned figure symbolizing Africa kneels before him, holding a picture of one of the English forts de Ruyter had captured. The whole floor is raised as a dais with two steps leading up to it. This floor is of polished wood, the walls are hung with stamped Spanish leather. Beneath an open lattice window is a long table covered with a turkey carpet, and bearing a terrestrial globe and writing materials. At the back is a sumptuous canopied bed, with an embroidered coverlet and curtains of some thin material. There are two broad, armless leather chairs studded with brass nails. A door to the right is open, revealing a soberly dressed man leaning over a staircase rail. Except for the African figure, it might be the interior of any grand Dutch house of the period of de Hooch or Terborch. The Dutch imported their own bricks from Holland for vaulting, archways, stairs and sundials; they also brought out to the Gulf of Guinea things equally necessary to them – their own atmosphere and their own style.

The Government of Ghana now uses the Castle of the Mine

as a police barracks, which brings a certain lazy animation to the sunlit courts. But the huge *corps de garde*, the panelled corridors and galleries seem echoing and empty. You can stand in the room in which Admiral de Ruyter was painted, and look out over the same seascape that he saw. But the walls are now bare, and the spirit of Dutch power and Dutch certainty has gone with the salt wind from the sea. Down in the town and across the lagoon is an old Dutch graveyard, but of a far later period. In its centre a high obelisk rises. Shaded by giant trees and with worn gravestones and sarcophagi tilted amidst a rich tangle of foliage, it is a charming, melancholy place in which to linger and reflect upon death, and upon the vanished glory of de Ruyter's world. For, as the centuries floated by, the Dutch, too, lost their interest in their Gold Coast possessions. In 1872 the Castle of the Mine and the remaining Dutch strongholds were sold to the British. In a formal ceremony within the Castle courtyard it was handed over to Queen Victoria's representative, who happened to be my Irish grandfather John Pope Hennessy, then Administrator of the West African Settlements. In surviving letters he recorded how he, also, looked out at the sea and down at the town of Elmina from the same hexagonal room, in which he was temporarily lodged.

## V

With the capture of Elmina, Axim and Shama, the Dutch became the dominant European power upon the Gold Coast. None of these was, however, their earliest station on the coast. As early as 1612, a small Dutch fort, made of earth and brushwood, and protected by deep ditches, had been built at Mouri, only three and a half hours by foot from Elmina. They had the support of the people of Mouri, who for some reason believed that the Dutch would be more sympathetic, and easier to trade with, than the Portuguese. In 1624 this fort was taken over by the new Dutch West India Company, rebuilt, and named Fort Nassau in honour of the House of Orange. By this time, for newcomers, the Dutch were already slaving on a fairly extensive scale. In the five years 1619–23 they had shipped some fifteen and a half thousand Africans to the shores of Brazil. In 1625 the first shipment of Negroes was landed on Manhattan Island, called by the Dutch New Amsterdam. Thirty years later, slave ships were actually being sent out to Africa from New Amsterdam. When one of these, the *King Solomon*, reached Curaçao with three hundred and thirty-one slaves, the Company's vice-director on that island wrote to their New Amsterdam office that 'he wished there had been a thousand of them, so great was the demand'.

When the Dutch experiment at Pernambuco collapsed in 1651, the Portuguese regained control of the slave trade to Brazil, for they had always kept factories in Africa, though no longer on the Gold Coast. But the main importance of the Portuguese in the history of the trade lies in the fact that they were pioneers in the traffic. 'The Portuguese served for setting dogs to spring the game' – this was an expression used by a famous Dutch trader to describe the way in which the Portuguese had inadvertently shown other European nations how easy and desirable buying and selling West Africans could be. This Dutch trader was Willem Bosman, chief factor for the Dutch West India Company at the Castle of the Mine, and a real authority on West Africa, where he had spent fourteen years towards the close of the seventeenth century. If one can apply the incongruous adjective 'likeable' to any of the slave-traders, we might do so to this inquisitive, diligent and open-minded Netherlander, whose *New and Accurate Description of the Coast of Guinea*, written in the form of twenty letters, was published in Dutch in 1704, and in French and English versions in 1705. Bosman's activities were not confined to Elmina, and under his guidance we can visit the Court of Benin, as well as that of the King of Whydah, who supplied him with a thousand slaves a month. Far less intolerant of African religious beliefs than most of his European colleagues or rivals, Willem Bosman even learned to respect the worship, at Whydah, of snakes.

# Chapter 6

# A Snake in the Roof-tree

## I

WILLEM BOSMAN is likeable because he is observant, a good story-teller, alert, and pleasantly verbose. He strives, too, after accuracy, whilst unable to resist at times the traveller's tale – as, for instance, when he asks us to credit that the King of Whydah had between four and five thousand wives. Resident on the Guinea Coast at the end of that seventeenth century dubbed by Dutch scholars 'The Golden Age' of Dutch history, Bosman is really a forerunner of those 'old coasters' of Victorian days whom Mary Kingsley has so vividly portrayed – veterans of the West African coast whose hair-raising accounts of life on the Bights would intrigue and dismay greenhorns shipping out for the first time from Liverpool to take up trade posts on the Gulf. Had Bosman in fact been an old coaster, and had one come across him on board ship, he would have proved diverting company. As often happens with boat friendships, one might, whilst appreciating his company and his knowledge, have recoiled before some of his views. He shared, of course, with his colleagues the conviction that the slave trade was essential, and therefore beyond criticism. 'I doubt not but this trade seems very barbarous to you,' he writes in one of his twenty letters, branding being his momentary theme, 'but since it is followed by mere necessity, it must go on; but yet we take all possible care that they are not burned too hard, especially the women, who are more tender than the men.'

Bosman was an enthusiastic patriot, finding Dutch ship-masters superior to those of any other nation at skilfully packing six or seven hundred slaves in one ship, yet keeping the conditions healthy: 'For as the French, Portuguese and English slave ships are always foul and stinking, on the contrary ours are for the most part neat and clean . . . The slaves are fed three times a day with indifferent good victuals, and much better than they eat in their own country.' Here once more we encounter the professional slave-traders' assertions that the slaves were 'comfortable', and the total obliviousness to the mental torment inflicted by the sharp, bewildering loss of liberty, country, family and friends. Someone has declared that the greatest cruelties in world history have been perpetrated less by naturally cruel persons than by that very extensive and intractable breed – persons without any semblance of feelings at all. Fourteen years in the slave trade might have blunted the most sensitive perceptions, yet Bosman shows a genuine appreciation of African ways of life and displays, on the whole, a kindly disposition. At the same time he was a cynic and to some degree a prig. He criticized the heavy drinking of the wretched European factors and soldiers on the coast, an alcoholic dependency which, combined with the bad climate and the constant recourse to venery, cut short, in Bosman's view, their lives. 'But it is indeed convenient it should be so,' he writes of these youngsters' premature deaths 'another wants his place: if men lived here as long as in Europe, 'twould be less worth while to come hither, and a man would be obliged to wait too long before he got a good post; without which nobody will easily return rich from Guinea . . . the money we get here is indeed hardly enough acquired: if you consider we stake our best pledge, that is our lives, in order to it.' But despite his apparent cynicism, his sarcasm and his chauvinistic tendencies, there is much to be learned from Willem Bosman. His style is chatty and personal: 'You would really wonder to see how these slaves live on board.' He earnestly wishes to inform and to correct: 'not a few in our country fondly imagine that parents here sell their children, men their wives, and one brother another: but . . . this never happens on any other account but that of necessity or some great crime; but most of the slaves that are offered to us are prisoners of war, which are sold by the victors as their booty.'

In one of his letters, Bosman went into the methods of slaving in great and valuable detail. He singled out for this purpose his dealings with the people of Whydah on the Slave Coast, who were 'so diligent in the slave trade' that they could deliver one thousand Negroes each month. We learn that on reaching Whydah, the first business of a factor was to pay the King and his advisers a species of tax or tribute – 'about a hundred pounds in Guinea value'. In return for this the factor was given a licence to trade; this agreement was then publicized throughout Whydah by the town crier. Even so, before the European could actually trade with other people in Whydah, he must first of all buy the King's whole stock of slaves at a fixed price 'which is commonly one-third or one-fourth higher than ordinary'. If, by mischance or mismanagement, there were not enough slaves to fill a ship waiting in Whydah, the Europeans had no option but to trust the local traders with trade-goods to the value of one or two hundred slaves. These goods were then carried up sometimes as far as two hundred miles into the interior, and there exchanged for slaves at the markets – 'for you ought to be informed that markets of men are here kept in the same manner as those of beasts with us'.

Once brought down to Whydah, these up-country slaves were then clapped into prison. Later, during the serious negotiations with the European traders, they were taken out on to a plain, undressed and carefully examined 'even to the smallest member, and that naked too, both men and women, without the least distinction or modesty'. Those given a clean bill of health were put to one side, the rejects to the other. Slaves were 'thrown out' for being more than thirty-five years of age, for being maimed in arms, legs, hands or feet, for having lost teeth, for having grey hair or cataract. Venereal disease was also a reason for rejection. The next stage was branding with an iron already sizzling in the fire. These 'burning irons' had the arms or the name of the various companies embossed on them, and were deemed indispensable to avoid confusion between the slaves of the Dutch, English, Danish, French or Portuguese. Branding also prevented the African traders' sleight of hand, whereby they would craftily substitute bad slaves for good.*

The bargaining over, the newly-branded Negroes were returned to their prison, where they were kept on bread and water –

* This was, of course, the preliminary or traders' branding. On arrival in the transatlantic plantations, the slaves were branded a second time with their new owners' initials. The Society for the Propagation of the Gospel in Foreign Parts, which had inherited two plantations from Christopher Codrington in 1710, would brand their slaves, for instance, with the initials S.P.G.

'like our criminals' – for twopence each a day. The Company grudged even this modest expenditure, and the slaves were generally hurried on to the ship as soon as feasible, having previously been stripped of every shred of clothing that they owned. Unless the master of the ship was 'so charitable' as to give them a piece of cloth – which was frequently done – they remained stark naked for the duration of the Atlantic voyage. Bosman explains the segregation of the sexes on board and how the slaves lay 'as close together as is possible for them to be crowded'. He refers to the cannibal myth as being a genuine danger to the ships' crews : for the slaves from up-country 'very innocently persuade one another that we buy them only to fatten them and afterwards eat them as a delicacy'. These rustic slaves had to be watched with particular care, as they were liable to plot rebellion, kill the Europeans, and try to put the ship ashore or swim from it. Bosman himself had such trouble twice only. The first time he suppressed it by the simple expedient of shooting the ringleader through the head. On the second occasion his ship's master had fished up a discarded English anchor, and foolishly stowed it in the hold occupied by the male slaves. These Negroes had somehow obtained, and concealed, a hammer, with which they struck off their fetters, using the anchor as an anvil. Bosman is certain that they would have overpowered his own men, had not the crews of an English and a French ship lying nearby heard the Dutchmen's distress gun and swarmed over in open shallops to their assistance. The slaves were driven back into the hold, but some twenty of them, killed in the affray, represented a tedious financial loss for Bosman.

Willem Bosman's account makes it clear – were any further clarification needed – that by his time the slave trade was functioning with smooth efficiency, inside a recognized framework of tradition, convention and a kind of hideous respectability. Kidnapping was now an exceptional means of getting slaves to sell. As a method it was generally looked down on as a sign of poverty. The pirates of Usa, who haunted the swamps of the Benin River, were, according to Bosman, so poor that they stole anything – men, animals, goods – that came their way and sold them for food. Again, the trade of the people of Coto (also on the Slave Coast) was so meagre that they resorted to up-country slave-raiding parties, 'stealing men which they sell to the Europeans that come here with their ships. This is the best part of their subsistence, and indeed' (Bosman contemptuously adds) 'all I have to say of them.'

## II

In the course of his fourteen years' stint along the coast of Guinea, Willem Bosman became acquainted with many of the local potentates. With some of them he became positively intimate. His contacts ranged from that figure of legendary power and splendour, the Oba of Benin, to the poverty-stricken King of Gabon who earned his living as a smith and leased out his wives to Europeans on a piece-work basis. All these personages, their courtiers and their subjects were greedily involved in the slave trade.

The Oba of Benin accorded Bosman interviews in his audience chamber, deep in the labyrinthine palace of Benin, and ornamented with those marvellous bronzes of sacred snakes, leopards, Portuguese warriors and African deities which are now collectors' items of the greatest rarity and value.* The Oba, surrounded by his chief councillors, would be seated on an ivory couch beneath a canopy of Indian silk. The court of Benin had a certain similarity to that of Versailles, in that it was thronged with great nobles whose whole careers were spent within the palace precincts. They did not deign to trade directly, but left this, and all forms of agriculture, to their wives and slaves. The dress of the Bini noblemen struck Bosman as magnificent; when they left their houses they would fling richly fringed scarves over their robes of the finest white cotton, which were ample and pleated. Their wives wore long, full skirts of brilliant-coloured check, with bodices of delicate stuffs. Round their necks were strings of coral, on their arms iron or copper armlets (some of them wore leg ornaments as well) and their fingers were heavy with rings. Even the plebs of Bini were well-dressed, according to their means. They were a kind and civil race, and would give away anything for which they were asked,

---

* When the city and palace of Benin were pillaged and burned down by a British 'punitive expedition' of 1897, nearly two thousand five hundred of these bronzes were shipped back to Great Britain as loot.

even if they would have preferred to keep it themselves. They were also prompt business men, 'interested in cloths of all descriptions, brass armlets, looking-glasses, iron bars, fine coral, cowries from East India, beads and perfumes. In exchange they exported slaves, local cloths, pepper, jasper stones, leopard skins and ivory.'* In the palmy days of the slave trade the Binis supplied some four thousand slaves a year.

The feudal grandeur of Benin made a sharp contrast to some of Bosman's other slave depôts. The subjects of the needy King of Gabon were decked out 'in a particular dismal manner' with old European hats and perukes, old coats, shirts and breeches which they would get from the sailors in exchange for wax, honey, parrots, monkeys and fruit. In this soiled and pathetic finery they would strut about with pride. They also drank even more brandy than any other Negro group that Bosman had ever seen. The spinster Queen of Agonna, in whose territory the English fort of Winneba was built, seemed, to Bosman, an especially intriguing figure. She was the only female sovereign he had met along the coast, and when she needed a lover she bought 'a brisk jolly slave, with whom she diverts herself, prohibiting him on forfeiture of his head to intrigue with any other woman; and when the youth hath lost his charms or her passion palls, he is exchanged for another'.† One of Bosman's favourite kings was the seventy-year-old King of Little Acron – 'an extraordinary goodnatured man, with whom I have often been merry'. But the merriest of all this array of minor royalties was clearly the King of Whydah, to whom Bosman was constantly being summoned to play games and to feast. The King of Whydah wore gowns of violet silk, or silver or gold damask, and lived in a spacious, higgledy-piggledy group of clay huts, with four iron guns mounted at the gate, and soldiers on guard. Bosman and other European guests always laid aside their swords before entering the royal presence, and talked to him bareheaded. His nobles lay prostrate on the ground for so long as they were in the room with him, and, after meals, were given what scraps the Europeans had left 'which they very greedily

---

* Michael Crowder: *The Story of Nigeria* (Faber & Faber, 1962).

† Thus showing a distinct advance on the famous fifteenth century Hausa Queen of Zaria, Amina, who is 'said to have taken lovers in every city and executed them when she had done with them'. (Crowder, *op. cit.*)

eat, whether they like it or no, and though they have ten times better at home'. Bosman and the King of Whydah gambled for an ox, a hog, a sheep or some other animal, but never for goods or money. If Bosman won, the King immediately sent him his winnings; if he lost the King refused to accept anything. This King of Whydah had once made the error of marrying two of his own daughters, both of whom soon died, a loss which he had regarded as the judgement of heaven. In Bosman's time, to avoid further temptation, the King married his only surviving daughter to the English factor. When Bosman jestingly suggested that the King owed him a fine, as he had had first promise of this daughter, the King paid up merrily, and said that if Bosman really wanted her, she could easily be called back. But the rôle of commoner-consort did not appeal to Willem Bosman: 'Marrying a King's daughter in this country is not very advantageous' he comments ruefully. 'Otherwise I had not failed long since to have been happy that way.'

The country round Whydah, which was immensely fertile and planted with trees seemed to Bosman 'the most charming that imagination can represent; nor can I believe that any country in the world can show the like'. The people were courteous, good traders and thievish to boot. Sometimes they were altogether too industrious in so far that they would re-sow the soil as soon as they had harvested their grain with the result that the land went sour and periodic famines swept the country. During such famines slaves could be bought for a song, and had even been known to be given away to European traders.

The Dutch, French and English factors who lived or stayed at Whydah were all accommodated in huts within the palace compound. Bosman (we are not surprised to find) had got the best of these. The King had built for him a 'very large' lodging, with three warehouses and seven rooms, standing round an airy courtyard with a covered gallery on every side. 'The lodgings of the rest of the Europeans' Bosman noted, no doubt with satisfaction, 'are very mean and inconvenient.' It was in the dining-room of this house that Bosman had to give reluctant hospitality to a snake. One day he found this snake comfortably settled into the roof-tree just above the table at which he ate. Although it was within reach of human hands, no one could be persuaded to remove the revered reptile, and it stayed there for a fortnight. Some of the notables of Whydah came to supper, and the conversation* turning on snakes, Bosman pointed out his own specimen aloft, saying it must surely be starving as it had not eaten for fourteen days. His guests replied that this could not be so, and that the snake knew exactly how and when to get the food it wanted. The next time Bosman saw the King of Whydah he told him that 'one of his gods had made bold, though uninvited,' to eat at his table for fourteen days, and that he felt that the King should pay the snake's board as otherwise it would be necessary to have the snake expelled from the house. The King was delighted. He said that if the snake were left alone he would provide for it, and for Bosman as well. Soon afterwards a fat ox was sent over. 'At the same rate,' Bosman reflects 'I would willingly have boarded all the gods of the land, and I believe I should not have lost much by the bargain.'

Bosman called the King of Whydah, who, at fifty years old, was as spritely as a man of thirty-five, 'the most civil and generous negro that I have met . . . never better pleased than when we desire a favour from him'. But he was encircled by sycophants, who gradually persuaded him to become more obstinate in his dealings with Europeans. Not long after Bosman had left the coast for good, a new and uncouth element entered into Dutch trading methods. For reasons, presumably, of economy, the Dutch West India Company cut down the numbers of resident factors and entrusted the slave trade to what Bosman calls 'boorish ships' captains who were utterly ignorant of the manners of the people', and did not 'know how to treat them with that decency which they require'. In consequence the King of Whydah completely changed his attitude to the Dutch, reduced his hospitality to them and upped the price for slaves.

We have spent so much time with Willem Bosman because I think that he exemplifies a fact which I suggested at the beginning of this book: that not all of the Europeans engaged in the trade were villains or sadists. The civilized relations he established with so many of the local kings were based, it is true, on reciprocal commercial interests, but Bosman did at least try to

---

* Probably conducted in French, which many Whydah Negro traders spoke, or in the *lingua franca* of that part of the coast, a bastard Portuguese.

understand, and certainly appreciated, West African ways of life. Amiable though they might be to traders, these kings ruled their subjects by fear. Some of them never ate in public so that their subjects might believe that, being of divine origin, they never ate at all. The chiefs I myself have drunk brandy with in West Africa are geniality and hospitality personified; but I have never forgotten a procession I met about ten o'clock one hot morning upon the main road leading into Old Calabar. I saw it coming down the road in the distance, and could not at first understand what it was. It turned out to be a gaggle of some forty men and youths, preceded by a boy beating a gong, and by standard bearers carrying tall insignia of rank. They moved slowly down the dust-road, intermittently chanting, or more correctly yelling, some refrain. In the centre of the crowd was a yellow, wheeled go-cart in which, under a state parasol, was seated a richly robed chief, wearing on his head a cap of red velvet, cloth of gold and fur. His expression was one of grim but detached ferocity. He neither turned his head to right nor to left, but glared straight ahead as though only he existed in the world. To an old African hand this sight would have been banal. To me it seemed a sudden, brutal glimpse into that alien world of African powers with which Bosman and his kind had to deal. Nobody seemed to know who this particular chief might be. Their only information was negative – that he was certainly not the Chief or King of Calabar. I watched the procession as it shuffled and shambled noisily, fervently onwards, the great bright yellow umbrella bobbing, the gong beating, the little carriage jolting and swaying at a snail's pace. They wheeled right at a junction, and disappeared from view behind the Shell petrol station.

Once again, as so often in Africa, I was perplexed. Was the grim, furious look, with the unfocused orange eyeballs glinting, the stern, imperious mouth, part of a conscious act – an indigenous version of royal behaviour, the converse, so to speak, of Queen Elizabeth the Queen Mother smiling and waving a gloved hand from her limousine? Or was it just personal to this potentially alarming individual? And of what was the retinue composed – courtiers, servants or slaves? This last query brings us to an important subject which, from its ambiguity and complexity, I would give anything to shirk. That subject, made much of by the supporters of the Atlantic slave trade, and still brought up by its modern apologists, is the intricate subject of African domestic slavery. What were the obligations of African slaves inside Africa? Why were they enslaved in the first place? How were they treated by their owners? And were they, or were they not, as badly off in Africa as their countrymen shipped to live and die on the plantations of the New World?

## III

Eighteenth- and nineteenth-century apologists for transatlantic slavery, who fought Wilberforce and the abolitionists with notorious tenacity, resorted to a number of specious arguments. Some of these were frankly economic and cynical – slavery provided the life-blood of the colonies, and without it the colonial empire would wilt and so wither away. Others appealed to the authority of the Bible, emphasizing that slavery is accepted in the Old Testament and is nowhere condemned in the New.* Aristotle, whose *Ethics* define a slave as 'a living working-tool and possession', was also cited, as were Homer and Plato, the slave civilization of Periclean Athens, the slave caravans of Carthage and the Anglo-Saxon enslavement of the Celts. They argued, in fact, that slavery was inevitable. 'Slavery' wrote Voltaire 'is as ancient as war, and war as human nature.'

But when defending the slave trade itself, the apologists went even further. They persuaded themselves, and attempted to persuade others, that transatlantic slavery came as a boon and a blessing to Africans. By misinterpreting the mild, complex and frequently patriarchal system of African domestic slavery, they concluded that it was a state of bitter and savage servitude. Ignoring the fact that without the European demand there

---

* See C. W. W. Greenidge, *Slavery* (George Allen & Unwin, 1958), who quotes the following passage from *The Spirit of Islam* by the late Syed Ameer Ali, a distinguished Pakistani scholar, and a member of the Privy Council: 'Christianity as a system and a creed raised no protest against slavery, enforced no rule, inculcated no principle for the mitigation of the evil. Except for a few remarks on the disobedience of slaves (1 Tim. vi, 1–2) . . . the teaching of Jesus, as portrayed in the Christian traditions, contained nothing expressive of disapproval of bondage.'

would have been no export trade in slaves, they justified themselves by pointing out that it was the Africans who sold each other. Encouraged by lurid accounts of the sacrifice of slaves at the funerals of distinguished personages they produced the view – shared, as we have seen, by a man as intelligent as James Boswell – that to transport Negroes to the colonies amounted to an act of charity, almost, indeed, a pious duty. Willem Bosman, Jean Barbot and their successors in African travel-writing, objective though they set out to be, could not resist a very natural temptation to titillate the imagination of their readers – the sort of audience to which the *Newgate Calendar* appealed, an audience intrigued by reports of wild, exotic goings-on and of brutish behaviour. For the benefit of these smug, safe readers, the travellers deliberately dwelt upon the horrors of human sacrifice in Africa, and upon the allegedly callous way in which any African would sell any other. Thus their serious and instructive accounts of the peoples of the Gulf of Guinea glinted with shafts of pure audience appeal. European persons who were not even allowed two wives could read, fascinated, that the King of Whydah had five thousand, with each of whom he slept only three times. Descriptions of African slaves being dismembered alive, and of children of six, too small to wield a cutlass with any certainty, being deputed to chop off slaves' heads at funerals also aroused attention. Thus a whole mythology of the miseries of life in Africa grew up and flourished.

This mythology likewise influenced far more sober and enlightened writers. These could not resist the logical conclusion that Negroes in the West Indies were happy in their knowledge that they would be allowed to die from over-work in their hovels, instead of being flung headless into their African masters' graves. Since personalities are always more actual than generalizations, we may take the views of Bryan Edwards, the late eighteenth-century author of the *History of the British West Indies*, already quoted. Edwards was a humane slave-owner and strove his hardest to be fair. He took the trouble to cross-examine many of his slaves as to their former status in their own country, the method by which they had been sold to the Europeans, and what they thought about human sacrifice. One of these, Clara, 'a most faithful, well-disposed woman, who was brought from the Gold Coast to Jamaica the latter end of 1784' and had been born into domestic slavery at Anamabu, told Edwards that at her owner's death, she, her two brothers and several other slaves had been sold to pay his debts. Twenty other slaves had been killed at his funeral. Edwards then asked her which country she liked best – Jamaica or Guinea? 'She replied that Jamaica was the better country, "for that people were not killed there, as in Guinea, at the funeral of their masters" .' It is difficult to see what other answer, under the circumstances, Clara could have given ; in another passage of the same book Edwards complains of the West Indian Negroes' well-known and exasperating habit of invariably replying to any question in the sense which they judged most pleasing to the white interrogator. On the other hand Edwards seems to have been a model master (although, later, an absentee one), Clara was clearly in the privileged position of a house-slave, and her general recollections of an Anamabu childhood may well have grown so faint with the years that only the wholesale slaughter of twenty friends and relatives remained a vivid incident of her young life. Slave life in Guinea, even with the remote occupational hazard of being ultimately chosen as a funeral victim, can in no conceivable way have been as bad as life on the majority of the West Indian plantations. Many of the owners and overseers of these – as for instance in early nineteenth-century Antigua – had the convenient habit of turning out old or diseased slaves to die of hunger in the streets. Other planters were for long involved in controversy as to whether it was more economical to work your slaves to death in seven or eight years, and buy a fresh batch from the traders, or whether it was more prudent to work them less hard so that they survived longer.

Just as it was in the interests of slave-traders and planters to minimize the cruelties of the Middle Passage, so it was to their advantage to exaggerate and travesty domestic slave conditions in Africa itself. In his *The Image of Africa*, Philip Curtin has explained that :

with the growth of the anti-slavery movement in Britain, more attention was paid to the place of slaves in African society, and especially to the question of how an individual might be made a slave in the first instance. Social structure as a whole, however, was ignored, and there was little notice that the institution of slavery was part of a wider net of family and group relations. The European concept of slavery, derived ultimately from Roman law, stood in the way of understanding what slavery meant in Africa.*

'In the African system,' (writes another modern historian) 'slaves, though of inferior status, had certain rights, whilst their owners had definite and often onerous duties towards them.'† Slaves were used to till the earth for their owners, and were, in return, fed and clothed. Many of the tribes, notably the Mundingoes, treated their slaves very well: 'They are remarkably kind to, and careful of their slaves,' (we read in a late eighteenth-century account of the Mundingoes) 'whom they treat with respect, and whom they will not suffer to be ill-used. This is a forcible lesson from the wild and savage Africans, to the more polished and enlightened Europeans who . . . treat them [i.e. their slaves] as if they were a lower order of creatures, and abuse them in the most shocking manner!'

The status of domestic slaves in Africa differed, of course, from area to area and from tribe to tribe. The most usual method of enslavement was as payment for a bad debt – when a man would pledge himself and his family indefinitely in a form of serfdom to his creditor. Further reasons for enslavement were adultery, theft and certain other crimes. West African slavery was a vital part of a general social and political structure. In many tribes it was unobjectionable for a king's son or daughter to marry a slave. A child by a slave woman was regarded as the property of the father's family, but the father could, if he wished, make the child a freeman or freewoman before his own death. Moreover, gifted slaves could rise to positions of great power within the state, for, having no wide-flung family obligations, they were liable to be more trustworthy and less open to influence than many of the nobles themselves. The different African kingdoms had their own rules for the protection of their slaves. In Benin, for instance, no male Bini could be sold for export. Here, as almost universally elsewhere along the coast, the European slave-market was supplied by prisoners taken in war, by enslaved criminals or by Africans captured or kidnapped from other tribes.

A relevant account of the methods of purchase of such war-

* Curtin, *op. cit.*, p. 23.
† Crowder, *op. cit.*

prisoners is given by Captain William Snelgrave, an English slave-trader of the generation junior to Bosman's, and who, like Bosman, usually traded at Whydah. But Whydah was no longer Bosman's pastoral country of courteous Negroes ruled over by an hospitable and friendly king. In March 1726 the armies of the warlike inland kingdom of Dahomey had swept down upon the coast. Whydah resisted. It was conquered and laid waste. The European traders now found they had to cope with, and placate, a powerful warrior monarch who, save perhaps in sense of humour, was the antithesis of Bosman's snake-worshipping boon companion and host.

## IV

When, in command of the slave ship *Katherine* (which belonged to a private owner named Morice and not to the Royal African Company),* Captain William Snelgrave arrived at Whydah in March 1727, he learned from the factor at the English fort there of the devastation of the country by its conqueror, the King of Dahomey. The pretext for the invasion had been the King of Whydah's refusal to permit free passage of slaves from Dahomey to the coast. Forty European traders had been held prisoner and had only just been released. The destruction of Whydah had been so complete that it was no longer practical to trade there, so Snelgrave set off for the port of Jaquin in Ardra, a neighbouring kingdom which, not having even attempted to resist the armies of Dahomey had, though conquered, been spared pillage.

As faceless for us as is Bosman, William Snelgrave also was a remarkable and literate trader, who published a long book on his experiences on the Gulf of Guinea. The son of a slave-trader, he made his first voyages with his father, and must have had an iron constitution since he was on the Slave Coast and worked the Middle Passage for twenty-six years, from 1704 to 1730. On the subject of African slavery he gives us sensible information; enslavement came from capture in battle, from debt, and from

---

* The vicissitudes of the Royal African Company, which by Snelgrave's time could not afford to keep its coastal forts in good order, and could no longer compete with 'interlopers' or private traders, will be examined in a later chapter.

crime. To the usual arguments in favour of the Atlantic slave trade he adds two novel ones – that it helped to rid Africa of criminals, and that the planters had to treat their slaves well because they did not want to lose what they had bought. Snelgrave's attitude to his slaves during the Atlantic crossing combined humanity with self-interest. Writing of his own hair-raising experiences of shipboard slave-mutinies, he remarks that: 'These mutinies are generally occasioned by the sailors' ill-usage of these poor people . . . Wherever therefore I have commanded it has been my principal care to have the negroes on board my ship kindly used; and I have always strictly charged my white people to treat them with humanity and tenderness; in which I have usually found my account, both in keeping them from mutinying and preserving them in health.' Having survived several dangerous mutinies himself, and known other less wary captains who had been battered to death by their slaves, Snelgrave went to particular pains to allay his purchased Negroes' fears. He received 'the grown people' on board his ship with a reassuring speech, made through the linguist. He told them that they were now his property, that they were not going to be eaten, and that they had been bought 'to till the ground in our country, with several other matters'. This welcome-aboard piece was followed by instructions on how his new chattels were to treat the white men on the ship, and that should any sailor abuse any of the slaves, complaint was to be made to himself through the linguist and he would see justice done. The speech ended with a threat: any disobedience, and above all the crime of striking a white man, would be 'severely punished'.

According to Snelgrave – and although he is a bit self-righteous, there is no reason to disbelieve him – he had the male Negroes taken out of their irons soon after the ship sailed; the women and children he never fettered. The slaves had two good meals a day, and in fine weather could come up on deck from seven in the morning and remain there until sundown if they wished. Monday was nicotine-day: pipes and tobacco ('which they are very fond of') were issued all round in the morning. The holds in which the Negroes slept were cleaned by themselves, under white supervision, daily. This model slave-captain had always found trading at Whydah peculiarly enjoyable: 'As this was the principal part of the Guinea Coast for the slave trade, the frequent intercourse that nation had for many years carried on with white people had rendered them so civilized that it was a pleasure to deal with them.' But now in 1727 he had to deal with a very different sort of person – the victorious and somewhat barbaric King of Dahomey, to whom the nice conventions and affable negotiations of the Whydah slave trade were a closed book.

The King of Dahomey, who was referred to in the *Boston News Letter* and the *Gentleman's Magazine* as 'Trudo Adato, King of Dahomey and Emperor of Popo', was an awe-inspiring martial monarch who had known little or nothing of Europeans. What he did know he had gleaned from an English factor, Captain Bullfinch Lambe, who had been captured at Jaquin and taken to the King's court where he became a royal favourite. So curious was the King about England that he finally released Captain Bullfinch Lambe and sent him home with a Negro linguist from Jaquin named Tomo, three hundred and twenty ounces of gold, and eighty slaves. It was later rumoured in London that the King of Dahomey had sent a message to King George I by Lambe urging His Britannic Majesty to cease the export of Negroes to the colonies, but to buy them and keep them on the Guinea Coast to work at European-supervised plantations instead. It was also said that the motive for the invasions of Whydah and Ardra had been the King of Dahomey's determination to stop the Atlantic slave trade. This absorbing theory can now be neither proved nor disproved; but the King of Dahomey's readiness to trade with Snelgrave and other captains make its truth improbable.

Before leaving the court of Dahomey, Lambe had been required by the King to take a most solemn oath to return, but he had never done so. Equally, he had not even sent Tomo back to Dahomey, although the real motive of the expedition had been for Tomo to investigate London, and report verbally to the King on whether all that Lambe had told him about English life could possibly be true. This breach of oath by Captain Bullfinch Lambe (who, instead of hastening back to the Gulf of Guinea, had taken Tomo to Barbados and then sold him to 'a gentleman in Maryland') rankled with the King of Dahomey.

It did not incline him to think well of European honour, for to the African mind a solemn oath could never and should never be broken.

Leaving the ravaged port of Whydah, Captain Snelgrave sailed along the coast to Jaquin, where he anchored in the first week of April. Almost as soon as he arrived there he was sent for by the King of Dahomey, who was encamped in triumph forty miles inland. The very evening that Snelgrave and his companions entered the royal camp, a part of the Dahomeian army appeared dragging or driving more than eighteen hundred prisoners of war, probably from an area near the Pra River, which runs into the Gulf near the old Dutch brick fort of Shama on the Gold Coast. The Englishmen were allowed to watch the King personally pick out 'a great number' of these captives to be sacrificed on the spot to the royal fetish, or, as Snelgrave not inaptly called it, the King's 'guardian angel'. The remainder were put by for use as domestic slaves, or to be stock-piled for sale to European traders. Snelgrave was struck by the efficiency with which the prisoners were received from the soldiers' hands by specially appointed officials, who paid the value of twenty shillings sterling for every man and ten shillings sterling for each woman, boy or girl. This payment was made in the popular currency of cowrie-shells from the Maldive Islands.

The following afternoon a messenger from 'the Great Captain' – a dignitary delegated to negotiate with the Englishmen and to arrange the delivery of purchased slaves – announced that the King wished to see the Englishmen at once. Here again we come upon the imperious manners of the African kings, certain in the knowledge that as they had the human merchandise the Europeans desperately wanted they could call the tune. Snelgrave had brought the usual presents for the King of Dahomey. He was told to wait in a forecourt while these were being examined by His Majesty. The traders were then conducted to a smaller court where they found the King, splendidly apparelled, seated cross-legged on a silken carpet on the ground. He had very few attendants. Enquiring 'in a very kind manner' after the health of his guests, the King ordered that carpets should be spread for them near him. They learned that they, too, were expected to sit cross-legged, which Snelgrave says 'was not very easy for us', and which must incidentally have given the King a slight but tangible tactical advantage, for sitting cross-legged when you are not accustomed to it leads to cramp and the fidgets as well as back-ache and muscle-strain and is not, we may suppose, an ideal position for hard-headed bargaining. What, the King asked through the interpreter, might Captain Snelgrave want of him? Snelgrave, in his role of client, answered that he had come to trade and that he hoped His Majesty would quickly fill his ship with Negroes, so that he could soon get home to his country to tell his countrymen what 'a great and powerful king' he had seen. The King promised that the Captain's hope should be fulfilled, but first was there not the matter of customs? For the settlement of these taxes or tributes payable before buying could begin the King referred Snelgrave to one Zunglar, a person whom Snelgrave had known before as the Dahomeian agent in independent Whydah, and whom he strongly disliked. This 'cunning fellow' declared that, although a conqueror, the King of Dahomey would not exact more custom than had the vanquished King of Whydah in the old days. Snelgrave suggested in reply that 'as His Majesty was a far greater Prince, so I hoped he might not take so much'. The King, who had been assiduously following this conversation through the linguist, here intervened to say that it was precisely because he was a greater Prince that he should be paid more, not less, custom. But he made a concession in terms which startled Snelgrave: 'as I was the first English captain he had seen, he would treat me as a young wife or bride, who must be denied nothing at first'. This arresting simile made Snelgrave sharply accuse the linguist of mistranslation, but the King repeated his words and asserted that he wished the slave trade to flourish. Snelgrave answered that in that case the King must impose easy customs and protect slave-traders from the thievish natives of Whydah. The King then declared that he had been chosen by God to punish the King of Whydah and his subjects 'for the many villainies they had been guilty of both towards whites and blacks'. After a further palaver the King agreed to take, on this occasion only, one half of what the King of Whydah had taken. All was going well until the King, perhaps to create a sense of insecurity, suddenly went off at an unwelcome tangent on the subject of the broken oath of Captain Bullfinch Lambe. Why, he demanded point blank, had Lambe not returned? Where was he, anyway? And where was Tomo?

Snelgrave immediately denied all knowledge of Lambe, whom in fact he had never met, but said that he had heard that he had gone to Barbados, a sugar-growing island very far away from Great Britain. He hoped that Lambe would prove an honest man. The King declared that even if Lambe should prove faithless, this would not prejudice him against other white men. The slaves and gold that he had given Lambe were of no consequence – he said he valued them at 'not a rush' – and that if Lambe did come back and brought a large ship it would be instantly crammed with slaves.

The palaver with the King of Dahomey ended – or seemed to have ended – well: the customs reduced, as we have seen, to one half of those which the King of Whydah used to demand; Snelgrave to take slaves in the ratio of three men to one woman; the slaves to be sent down to the port of Jaquin, where he would choose only those that he liked. But, as usual in all such negotiations on the Coast, Snelgrave's troubles had only begun. A personage whom he calls 'the Lord of Jaquin' demanded higher customs than those agreed on, and Snelgrave could not report this back to the camp of the King of Dahomey as any messenger would have certainly been murdered by Jaquin men on the way. There were high seas which delayed his bringing his trade goods ashore and the African middle-men pestered him ten times a day for payment and refused to accept his promissory notes 'because the writing might vanish from it or else the notes might be lost and then they should lose their payment'. To the irritation of this typically West African pertinacity was added a porters' strike for higher wages. Snelgrave was even afraid for his life: 'Nay, I began at last not to think myself safe, one of the traders being so insolent as to present his fusil at me for refusing to take his bad slaves. For, though they came to trade, yet they were always armed with sword and dagger, and a boy carried their gun for them. These people were far different from the traders we used to deal with at Whydah.' The contrast Snelgrave found between the fierce and arrogant warriors of Dahomey and the more couth behaviour of the coastal traders he had known in days of yore is, possibly, analogous to that between the eighteenth-century Scots Highlanders, and the people of the Lowlands. Long accustomed to the sleek manners of the coast Africans, Snelgrave was not merely disconcerted, he was positively hurt by the aggressive tone of the subjects of the King of Dahomey.

After more than two months of wrangling, the King of Dahomey did himself at last intervene, sending 'the Great Captain' to Jaquin as his emissary to quell the recalcitrant traders. Snelgrave entertained the Great Captain at a dinner-party during which he was urged to buy an old female slave, but refused to take her on the grounds of her age. The King then ordered her to be thrown into the Gulf, from which the sailors of the *Katherine* rescued her. To Snelgrave's surprise, this old lady proved worth her weight in gold, for, once at sea, she undertook the task of keeping quiet the female slaves 'who used always to be the most troublesome to us, on account of the noise and clamour they made'. On this voyage they were 'kept in such order and decorum by this woman, that I had never seen the like in any voyage before'. At her journey's end this invaluable duenna was sold to the surveyor general of customs of Barbados and the Leeward Islands.

Snelgrave had reached Whydah in March 1727, and he did not leave the roadstead of Jaquin, with a cargo of six hundred Negro slaves, until July. The tedious passage took seventeen weeks. They made landfall at Antigua, 'where the cargo of negroes (who had stood very well) came to a good market'. Loading at Antigua with sugar, he set sail at the end of February 1728 and entered the mouth of the Thames in April 'having been sixteen months on this remarkable voyage'. In England he fell ill, and could not return to the Guinea Coast for a whole year. When he got back to Whydah and Jaquin he found local wars still raging, with the King of Dahomey, however, as dominant as before. His friend Mr Testesole, the governor of the English fort at Whydah, had been murdered by the Dahomeians, and chaos prevailed. Although European traders looked forward to, and encouraged, tribal wars, the King of Dahomey proved almost too martial. A professional soldier, he could hardly take time off to organize a competent slave trade on the old lines, and business, in consequence, declined.

And now, having spent some time upon the Gulf of Guinea, we may as well leave it before we, too, develop low fever, pains in the head, the bloody flux, sleeplessness, melancholia, alcoholism or any of the other ills to which factors and slave-traders were liable. Let us set off for the Spanish Main. It will be neither a healthful nor a stylish voyage, however, since the Atlantic breezes will be sickly with the stench from between decks. Many deaths may occur *en route*. Sharks, greedy for Negro corpses, will shadow the ship all the way to Barbados; nor will that island nor Jamaica nor Antigua nor any of the other West Indies seem quite so halcyon as we should hope to find them. Moreover, like Captain Snelgrave and his fellows, we shall be back on the Coast of Guinea all too soon.

# Chapter 7

# Westward Ho!

## I

WE SPENT in our passage from St Thomas to Barbados two months
eleven days . . . in which time there happened much sickness and
mortality among my poor men and negroes, that of the first we
buried 14, and of the last 320 . . . whereby the loss in all amounted to
near 6560 pounds sterling. The distemper which my men as well as
the blacks mostly die of, was the white flux, which was so violent and
inveterate, that no medicine would in the least check it; so that
when any of our men were seized with it, we esteemed him a dead
man, as he generally proved.

Captain Thomas Phillips, from whose journal of the voyage
of his slave ship *Hannibal* in 1693 and 1694 this passage comes,
had also one hundred cases of smallpox amongst his slaves, only
twelve of whom, however, actually died of it. A further twelve
had drowned themselves off Whydah before the voyage had
begun, 'they having a more dreadful apprehension of Barbados
than we can have of hell, tho' in reality they live much better
there than in their own country; but home is home etc.'

In taking a ship for the Atlantic crossing we can do much
worse than choose the *Hannibal*, a Guinea vessel of four hundred
and fifty tons and thirty-six guns, which had been bought for
Phillips by his 'patron and benefactor', Sir Jeffrey Jeffreys, and
had set sail from the Downs in October 1693, in the reign of
William and Mary. We could of course select any of a vast
number of ships of different periods and different nationalities,
since in our hindsighted case History itself is our travel agency.
But Captain Phillips, a careful and not altogether unsym-
pathetic man, will serve to get us off to Barbados, and instruct
us on the way. His losses, both in slaves and seamen are, also,

fairly typical of these lengthy and hazardous voyages on over-crowded ships; and in this connection it is necessary to remember that the conditions in which the sailors lived on board were almost as bad as those of the Negroes themselves. The crews' only relief came from drinking 'raw unwholesome rum' mixed with 'unpurged black sugar' with which, in the case of the *Hannibal,* they had secretly stocked up at São Tomé. Although Captain Phillips, who thought this drink caused illness, flogged men whom he found swilling it, and threw the punch into the sea, a good deal would seem to have remained on board, for the white flux did not set in until after the ship had sailed from the Gulf. For some reason which he could not understand, the white men and boys of his crew never contracted the smallpox, even though they were tending the Negroes who had caught it. The slaves themselves seemed to recover merely by drinking water and anointing their pustules with palm-oil: 'But what the smallpox spared, the flux swept off, to our great regret, after all our pains and care to give them their messes in due order and season, keeping their lodgings as clean and sweet as possible, and enduring so much misery and stench among a parcel of creatures nastier than swine; and after all our expectations to be defeated by their mortality.' Captain Phillips, who had several times fainted dead away in the 'trunk' or slave prison of the King of Whydah, did not relish his trade. 'No gold-finders can endure so much noisome slavery as they do who carry negroes; for those have some respite and satisfaction, but we endure twice the misery; and yet by their mortality our voyages are ruined, and we pine and fret ourselves to death, to think that we should undergo so much misery, and take so much pains to so little purpose.' Out of seven hundred Negroes embarked on the Guinea Coast, Phillips could deliver only three hundred and seventy-two alive in Barbados, where they sold for nineteen pounds a head.

Phillips' *cri de coeur* came at the very end of the voyage, and was provoked by its disappointing results. In other ways he was a thoughtful and even kindly man, who ran his ship well, let the Negroes out of their fetters once he was at sea, and saw to it that the slaves' chief food, a kind of porridge made of ground Indian corn, was flavoured with salt, malaguetta pepper and palm oil. Three days a week they were given boiled horse beans, at which, he relates, they would beat their breasts and cry out aloud with delight. When his officers urged him to follow the example of many slaving captains and 'cut off the legs and arms of the most wilful' of the slaves 'to terrify the rest' he refused

to entertain the least thought of it, much less put in practice such barbarity and cruelty to poor creatures, who, excepting their want of Christianity and true religion (their misfortune more than fault) are as much the works of God's hands, and no doubt as dear to him as ourselves; nor can I imagine why they should be despised for their colour, being what they cannot help, and the effect of the climate it has pleased God to appoint them. I can't think [he concludes] there is any intrinsic value in one colour more than another, nor that white is better than black, only we think so because we are so, and are prone to judge favourably in our own case, as well as the blacks, who in odium of the colour, say, the devil is white and so paint him.

Phillips organized his cargo with great care, appointing thirty or forty Gold Coast Negroes as overseers of the Whydah ones, to keep the peace and spy out any plotting. Each of these 'guardians' was given a cat-o'-nine-tails as a badge of office 'which he is not a little proud of, and will exercise with great authority'. The slaves were fed twice a day, at ten in the morning and four in the afternoon; those sailors who were not distributing the victuals manned the great guns and stood to arms to prevent any attempt at revolt. Besides being filthy and long-drawn-out, the voyage of a loaded slave ship was tense and nerve-searing for the handful of white men on board.

There is one aspect of Captain Phillips' account, which, though he does not go into detail, is important and by its implications, unpleasant. The Negro men, he tells us, were fed upon the main deck and forecastle, so as to be 'under command of our arms from the quarterdeck'. The boys and girls were fed upon the poop. But the African women 'eat upon the quarter deck with us'. For the treatment of Negro women on slavers we must supplement the *Hannibal*'s log from other equally reliable sources. Disagreeable, indeed repellent, as this subject may seem, it is one of the greatest pertinence to the history of the coloured populations of the West Indies, the Southern States of America and the other transatlantic slave plantations. For the humiliations which African women were forced to endure on the

Middle Passage cannot fail to have conditioned their attitude, and consequently that of their descendants, to the white men who claimed to own them. We may begin with the evidence of a Negro slave.

## II

Ottobah Cugoano, the kidnapped Fantee who ended up as London servant to the miniaturist Cosway, and from whose book, published in 1787, we have already quoted, had been taken as a boy to Cape Coast Castle, there sold, and transported to Grenada. He does not describe the voyage in much depth, just calling it 'the brutish, base but fashionable way of traffic'. He does, on the other hand, refer to a plot amongst the women and the boy slaves 'to burn and blow up the ship, and to perish all together in the flames; but we were betrayed by one of our own country-women, who slept with some of the head men of the ship, for it was common for the dirty filthy sailors to take the African women and lie upon their bodies; but the men were chained and penned up in holes'. John Newton, the famous slave-trader turned clergyman and Abolitionist, writes that while not necessarily universal in slave ships, the forced use of Negro girls by the officers and men on board ship was 'too commonly, and, I am afraid, too generally prevalent'. Newton himself tried to prevent such incidents on board his own ship: 'In the afternoon' (his Journal for a January day in 1753, when he was lying off Mana, records) 'while we were off the deck, William Cooney seduced a woman slave down into the room and lay with her brutelike in view of the whole quarter deck, for which I put him in irons. I hope this has been the first affair of the kind on board and I am determined to keep them quiet if possible. If anything happens to the woman I shall impute it to him, for she was big with child. Her number is 83.' But many slave-captains were not so scrupulous; Newton likens the white men's behaviour to that of a Cossack horde sacking a town. 'When the women and girls' (he writes) 'are taken on board a ship, naked, trembling, terrified, perhaps almost exhausted from cold, fatigue and hunger, they are often exposed to the wanton rudeness of white savages . . . In imagination the prey is divided on the spot, and only reserved till opportunity offers.'

Although they could not speak English, these shivering creatures could not fail to understand the manners and the gestures of the seamen – the international language, the Esperanto, of lust.

'Perhaps' (Newton continues) 'some hard-hearted pleader may suggest that such treatment would indeed be cruel in Europe; but the African women are negroes, savages, who have no idea of the nicer sensations which obtain among civilized people. I dare contradict them in the strongest terms.' He explains that he 'had lived long and conversed much, amongst these supposed savages'; that he had been often alone in a town at night in a house filled with trade goods and with only a mat for a door, and had never suffered any harm. 'And with regard to the women, in Sherbro, where I was most acquainted, I have seen many instances of modesty, and even delicacy, which would not disgrace an English woman. Yet, such is the treatment which I have known permitted, if not encouraged, in many of our ships – they have been abandoned, without restraint, to the lawless will of the first-comer.' The sailors did not even trouble to ask a slave woman for her consent, and on most of the ships Newton had known 'the licence allowed, in this particular, was almost unlimited'. The surgeon, Alexander Falconbridge, who was a contemporary of John Newton, and published his *An Account of the Slave Trade* in 1788, writing of the slave-dances on deck in fine weather, when slaves 'who go about it reluctantly, or do not move with agility' were flogged with the cat-o'-nine-tails, and of the glass beads issued to the women to amuse them, likewise states that 'on board some ships, the common sailors are allowed to have intercourse' with the African women, although he believes it was only with those 'whose consent they can procure'. According to this witness some of these shot-gun romances ended in suicide, since African women had 'been known to take the inconstancy of their paramours so much to heart as to leap overboard and drown themselves. The officers are permitted to indulge their passions with them at pleasure, and sometimes are guilty of such brutal excesses as disgrace human nature'.

While both these authorities, and many others too, take care to be objective and to say that debauching the Negro women on board was not an undeniably universal practice, it would not be logical to suppose that there were many exceptions. To be a seaman on a slaver was, as we have seen, to live for months in conditions almost as dreadful as those of the slaves. The stench of death and disease was forever in your nostrils. In rough or wet weather the 'air-ports' on the slave decks were closed, and all fresh air shut out. Falconbridge, who had made many voyages as a slave ship surgeon, gives a solitary example of what, on such occasions, followed. 'Some wet and blowing weather' (he writes) :

having occasioned the port-holes to be shut, and the grating to be covered, fluxes and fevers among the negroes ensued. While they were in this situation, my profession requiring it, I frequently went down among them, till at length their apartments became so extremely hot as to be only sufferable for a very short time. But the excessive heat was not the only thing that rendered their situation intolerable. The deck, that is the floor of their rooms, was so covered with the blood and mucous which had proceeded from them in consequence of the flux, that it resembled a slaughter-house. It is not in the power of the human imagination to picture to itself a situation more dreadful or disgusting. Numbers of the slaves having fainted, they were carried up on deck, where several of them died and the rest were, with great difficulty, restored. It had nearly proved fatal to me also.

And Falconbridge was serving on the better class of English slaver.

To work on ships which often were merely floating coffins – the ships taking slaves to Rio de Janeiro were in fact called *tumbeiros* from the Portuguese for tomb – was at once brutalizing and nauseous. Amongst other signal disadvantages of life aboard we may count a particularly bold breed of rat which infested the ships, destroying any clothing they found, biting men below deck, and defecating on the faces of those who slept. Seventeenth- and eighteenth-century ship conditions were bad enough, and the seamen of those days a rough lot. But the men who were persuaded, or who volunteered, to enlist on a slave ship were, in the words of the famous Liverpool slave-captain, Hugh Crow, who published his autobiography in 1830, 'the very dregs of the community'. Some had escaped from jails, others were criminals in fear of the law. Many were gentlemen's sons 'of desperate character and abandoned habits', who wished to escape creditors or to flee the country for some other reason.

'These wretched beings' writes Crow 'used to flock to Liverpool when the ships were fitting out, and after acquiring a few sea-phrases from some crimp* or other, they were shipped as ordinary seamen, though they had never been at sea in their lives. If, when at sea, they became saucy and insubordinate, the officers were compelled to treat them with severity; and, having never been in a warm climate before, if they took ill, they seldom recovered.' Under all these circumstances it is hard to suppose that any but a saintly captain would deny his sullen crew what diversion they could find with the slave women on a long and tedious Atlantic crossing; nor is it easy to see how even the strictest and most well-intentioned master could control the sexual activities of his men by day or night. The callous and wanton demoralization of these African women, at home so gay, so carefree, so courteous and so merrily clad, each with an allotted part to play in the busy life of her village community, surely formed one of the most criminal and, in its long-term results, one of the most durable by-products of the slave trade.

Amid so much accumulated horror, the ample records of which might make one permanently lose one's wavering faith in human nature, a single redeeming fact emerges – but it redeems neither captain nor crew. Writing of slavery in Jamaica as 'a situation that necessarily suppresses many of the best affections of the human heart', the historian Bryan Edwards remarked that if slavery 'calls forth any latent virtues, they are those of sympathy and compassion towards persons in the same conditions of life; and accordingly we find that the negroes in general are strongly attached to their countrymen, but above all to such of their companions as came in the same ship with them from Africa. This is a striking circumstance: the term *shipmate* is understood among them as signifying a relationship of the most endearing nature'. What is more poignant, what more revealing of the true character of Africans than such life-long friendships forged in fetters and in blood? Yet, on arrival in the West Indian islands, or on the North American coast, even this solace was often denied the shipmates, for the processes of sale to the planters too frequently split up families, lovers or friends. Of all these processes perhaps the most barbarous was that known as 'sale by scramble'.

* A crimp was a man who impressed or decoyed sailors.

## III

When a ship laden with slaves dropped anchor off a West Indian port, excitement would prevail on board. The reaction of officers and men was very far removed from the fear and distaste with which they had made landfall in the Gambia or off the mangrove swamps of the Bight of Benin, just as the translucent green waters of the Caribbean Sea, the foam swirling gently over white coral reefs about which black-and-yellow-striped fish darted formed the antithesis to the dangerous thundering surf of the Gold Coast. The long and noisome voyage was over, the prospect of shore-time in European-run taverns and brothels was near, the second, and worst, lap of the Triangular Trade was completed once again. The lovely, melancholy islands of the Caribbean can never have been a more welcome or refreshing sight.

In their merciful ignorance, the slaves, too, rejoiced. Their irons were struck off, they were given fattening foods, and rubbed with oil until their black skins shone in the clear, cool dawn. Suddenly they felt a sense of freedom, curiosity and joy. But, as John Newton wrote:

This joy is short-lived indeed. The condition of the unhappy slaves is in a continual progress from bad to worse . . . perhaps they would wish to spend the remainder of their days on ship-board, could they know beforehand the nature of the servitude which awaits them on shore; and that the dreadful hardships and sufferings they have already endured would, to the most of them, only terminate in excessive toil, hunger and the excruciating tortures of the cart-whip, inflicted at the caprice of an unfeeling overseer, proud of the power allowed him of punishing whom, and when, and how he pleases.

Today, the islands of the West Indies have become, for the undiscerning tourist, purely places of pleasure. In those days they were places of pain.

On shore, the arrival of a well-stocked Guineaman gave a thrill of anticipatory satisfaction to two mainly unattractive groups – firstly to the ships' agents and the slave-auctioneers, secondly to the owners of plantations and their vulturine overseers. Although, on the whole, the climate of most of the Caribbean islands is healthier and more balmy than that of West Africa, mortality amongst the Negro field-hands and other labourers was high. I have earlier referred to a perennial controversy between certain planters as to whether it was best to give their slaves a moderate amount of work, feed them well and generally so treat them that they might live to an old age; or whether it were not more profitable to strain their strength to the utmost, use them harshly and feed them poorly, so as to wear them out 'before they became useless and unable to do service', purchasing new ones from the ships to replace those who had died. This controversy, the arguments on both sides of which had been calculated to a nicety, was, for instance, raging in the island of Antigua in the fifties of the eighteenth century. It had been concluded that to wear slaves out and buy a fresh stock was cheapest in the long run, and there were then a number of Antiguan estates on which slaves seldom survived more than nine years. Some planters, like the Codringtons who owned Betty's Hope plantation on Antigua, and the little islet of Barbuda as well, planned and operated 'slave nurseries' which were filled with little boys and girls bought off the boats.*

Even when the captain had successfully brought his ship to the West Indies his anxieties were not invariably over. Navigation down the islands was tricky; in 1791, for example, the deck and other portions of a small French Guineaman containing the bodies of some shaven slaves, was washed up on the beach at Antigua, and such was not a rare occurrence. At St Christopher, in April 1737, there was a sensational mass suicide attempt by the slaves on board the *Prince of Orange*, out of Bristol, and commanded by a Captain Japhet Bird. 'At our arrival here' (a letter from on board, published in the *Boston Weekly News Letter*, relates) :

I thought all our troubles of this voyage were over; but on the contrary I might say that dangers rest on the borders of security. On the 14th of March we found a great deal of discontent among the slaves, particularly the men, which continued till the 16th about five o'clock in the evening, when to our great amazement above an hundred men slaves jumped overboard . . . out of the whole we lost

---

* 'However, in my opinion, if I bought negroes, I would buy them at the age of 10 or 12 and send them to Barbuda; they would at that age come cheap, would live better and at little expense there, and I doubt not would do well' (letter to Sir William Codrington of Dodington Park, the absentee owner of Betty's Hope and of Barbuda, from his overseer who was also his nephew, June 1790; preserved among the Codrington Papers at Dodington).

33 of as good men slaves as we had on board, who would not endeavour to save themselves, but resolved to die and sunk directly down. Many more of them were taken up almost drowned, some of them died since, but not to the owner's loss, they being sold before any discovery was made of the injury the salt water had done them.

This particular panic was found to have been caused by a St Christopher slave with a perverted sense of humour, who had trotted on board to tell the new arrivals that they were first to have their eyes put out and then be eaten. 'This misfortune' (the letter ends) 'has disconcerted the Captain's design of proceeding to Virginia' – where he hoped to sell slaves left on his hands in St Christopher, then suffering from a shortage of sugar.

Once the slaves had been put ashore, selling began in earnest. The moribund or 'refuse' slaves were landed first, and sold off at a tavern *vendue* or public auction. At these they were usually purchased by Jews, as a speculation, or by surgeons. In Grenada you could buy a slave who seemed to be dying of the flux for as little as one dollar; most of these refuse slaves, who were carried on shore, always died. Some captains would march the healthy slaves through the streets of the little tropical town at which they were landed, streets animated by that rather languid flurry peculiar to West Indian life, streets in which the 'seasoned' Negroes from previous ships would roll their sea-shell eyes at the procession of straggling bewildered newcomers. The fresh slaves would then be lined up in a yard for a minute physical examination by prospective purchasers. But a more popular mode of sale was often the 'scramble', the date and hour of which would be advertised beforehand.

The surgeon Falconbridge, who had attended many a scramble in his time, describes one at which he saw two hundred and fifty Africans sold on a Caribbean island which he does not name. In a scramble, all the Negroes, by an agreement between the captains and the purchasers, bore the same price. 'On a day appointed' (he writes) 'the negroes were landed, and placed altogether in a large yard belonging to the merchants to whom the ship is consigned. As soon as the hour agreed on arrived, the doors of the yard were suddenly thrown open, and in rushed a considerable number of purchasers, with all the ferocity of brutes.' The theory of the scramble was that any Negro, Negress or infant you could lay your hands on was yours to buy. 'Some instantly seized such of the negroes as they could conveniently lay hold of with their hands. Others, being prepared with several handkerchiefs tied together, encircled with these as many as they were able. While others, by means of a rope, effected the same purpose. It is scarcely possible to describe the confusion of which this mode of selling is productive.' Violent quarrels amongst the purchasers broke out. The Negroes themselves were so appalled by this bestial onslaught that several clambered up the walls of the yard and 'ran wild about the town'. These refugees were soon recaptured. On another voyage from Africa, Falconbridge witnessed a scramble on board ship. The Negroes were herded together on the main and quarter decks, which had been darkened by an awning of sailcloth so that the purchasers could not 'pick or choose'. 'The signal being given, the buyers rushed in, as usual, to seize their prey; when the negroes appeared extremely terrified, and near thirty of them jumped into the sea. But they were all soon retaken, chiefly by boats from other ships.' At one scramble at Port Maria, on the rocky north coast of Jamaica, Falconbridge says that the African women were especially alarmed, shrieking and clinging to each other 'through excess of terror at the savage manner in which their brutal purchasers rushed upon, and seized them'.

Such was the shattering prelude to life on the old plantation.

## IV

As a general rule, the captain's duty towards the slaves he had brought across the Atlantic ceased with the voyage. The owners' agents then took over and arranged sale by auction, scramble or private negotiation. Often, however, owing to the time of year – sugar was not ordinarily available before June, although it could at times be obtained in April and May – or to temporary poverty on one island, or to the poor quality of some of the slaves, the agent could not sell a whole shipload of Africans in the same island, or in a single mainland port such as Charleston. The captain had then to proceed from place to place, peddling his slaves piecemeal, sometimes for weeks or even months. In principle, however, once the captain had handed his human cargo over to the agents, he set about loading up with sugar when possible; if there was no sugar to be had, he returned home in ballast. Since, from fear of Negro revolts, Guineamen carried a larger crew than ordinary merchant ships, a number of the seamen would be paid off at, say, Barbados, and hang around there waiting for employment on some other ship. This employment was often hard to find. Bad captains were, indeed, known to have deliberately maltreated their men in West Indian ports, with the intention of forcing them to jump ship; others would sail for home without warning superfluous seamen who were carousing on shore. 'It was no uncommon thing' (according to one witness who attested before Parliament at the time of the Abolitionist agitation) 'for the captains to send on shore, a few hours before they sail, their lame, emaciated, and sick seamen, leaving them to perish.' The authors of *Black Cargoes* relate that these dying men were called 'wharfingers' in Kingston, Jamaica, where they would languish on the wharves. At more modest ports they were termed 'beach-horners'; and in the inscrutable, malevolent-looking island of Dominica, with its precipitous green mountains and lack of harbour, they were popularly described as 'scowbankers' – 'scow' being the current word for large flat-bottomed boats or lighters.

Profits from the slave trade were large, but also chancy. In the autumn of 1774, for example, the snow *Africa*, a two-masted, square-rigged ship of one hundred tons burthen, which had been captured from the French during the Seven Years War, set sail from the port of Bristol for New Calabar.* The *Africa* had been bought and outfitted by a syndicate of eight Bristol merchants, and stocked up with the usual trade goods – brandy, rum, guns, laced hats and waistcoats, Indian and Manchester cottons, multi-coloured china beads, iron bars, copper rods and so on – to the total cost of £4,445 14s. 0d. A further £1,247 2s. 0d. had been spent on fitting the ship out, making a total of £5,692 16s. 0d. The syndicate appointed Captain George Merrick, who knew the Africa trade, to the command, and supplied him with the necessary certificates

---

* For details of the *Africa*'s voyage I am indebted to the interesting paper by my friend Professor Walter Minchinton, of Exeter University, published in *The Mariner's Mirror* for July, 1951.

authorizing him to trade on the African coast and also in the Atlantic colonies. His written instructions ordered him to go to New Calabar, and there barter his cargo

for good healthy young negroes and ivory, and . . . not to buy any old slaves or children but good healthy young men and women, and buy all the ivory you can and when you are half-slaved don't stay too long if there is a possibility of getting off for the risk of sickness and mortality then become great . . . let no candle be made use of in drawing spirits or to go near the powder . . . We recommend you to treat the negroes with as much lenity as safety will admit and suffer none of your officers or people to abuse them under any pretence whatever, be sure you see their victuals well dressed and given them in due season . . . We recommend you to make fires frequently in the negroes' rooms as we think it healthy and you have iron kettles on board for that purpose. We recommend mutton broth in fluxes, so that you'll endeavour to purchase as many sheep and goats to bring off the coast for that purpose as you conveniently can.

In March of the following year, 1775, the syndicate, which called itself 'John Chilcott & Co.', wrote two letters. One was to Messsrs Akers and Houston, their agents on the island of St Vincent, warning them that the *Africa* should be with them in the beginning of May, and asking them to take the cargo over from Captain Merrick and to sell the slaves for the usual promissory notes – 'the sight of the bills we expect will not exceed twelve months, and if they are sold at St Christophers we expect a part of somewhat shorter sight.' Their second letter was under cover to the first, and addressed to Captain Merrick, telling him to do whatever the agents required, to get rid of his Negroes quickly and to come back home 'unless a freight offers for Bristol worth staying a fortnight'. These merchants, some of those grave men we saw bending over a map at the opening of this book, ended this note: 'We recommend dispatch and frugality, Your friends and owners, John Chilcott.'

The crew of thirty-one – a ship of the *Africa*'s size engaged in normal trading would only have carried a complement of ten to fifteen men – were paid half their wages on arrival at St Vincent; the slaves disposed of, Captain Merrick sailed his empty ship back to Bristol with a crew of seventeen, twelve of whom had set out thence on the voyage to New Calabar. The Negroes had fetched a total of £5,128 12s. 6d. The total proceeds of the voyage on the vessel amounted to £5,650 8s. 0d., which by deducting miscellaneous operating charges left a net balance of £5,442 8s. 0d. This meant that, for the owners of the *Africa*, not only was there no profit but a very definite loss. The fact that the ship brought back no freight from the Colonies and had, so to speak, achieved only two laps of the Triangular Trade, would seem to have accounted for this dismal result.

The story of the snow *Africa* is interesting because it illuminates one of the hazards of investment in the slave trade. The syndicate's instructions on the treatment of Negroes were probably genuinely humane, although they could be categorized under what one French writer on the subject has neatly termed '*la sollicitude intéressée*'. The records of Captain Merrick's murky doings in the Niger Delta, of the quantity of slaves he shipped, and of how he fared on the Middle Passage seem, unfortunately, no longer to exist. The saga of the *Africa* cannot, I think, be taken as typical, for is it not otherwise unlikely that so many merchants of so many nations should have plunged into the trade. More representative – to take ships' names at random – is the case of the *Enterprize* from Liverpool, which left the Mersey for Bonny in 1803, slaved quickly, and got rid of the whole cargo (save for one Negro girl who was subject to fits) at Havana, returning to Liverpool in 1804 with a net profit of nearly twenty-five thousand pounds. About 1800 the *Louisa*, also from Liverpool, returned from Jamaica with a profit of nearly twenty thousand pounds. The owners of the *Fortune*, again a Liverpudlian vessel, which carried a cargo of Congolese slaves to the Bahamas in 1805, made a profit of over thirteen thousand pounds, which the owners judged insufficient. The *Fortune* scarcely lived up to its name, for the slaves sold slowly, and during the long delay, the trading mate and one sailor ran off, thirty-four of the seamen were impressed into, or volunteered for, the Royal Navy at Nassau, the third mate and six seamen died on the voyage, and two of the other sailors were drowned.

# V

'I hope the slaves in our islands are better treated now than they were at the time that I was in the trade' (wrote the

Reverend John Newton retrospectively of the years 1736 to 1755, when he had been, off and on, an eager young slaver). 'And even then, I know there were slaves who, under the care of humane masters, were comparatively happy. But I saw and heard enough to satisfy me that their condition, in general, was wretched in the extreme.' The only islands which Newton had been able to investigate personally had been Antigua and St Kitts, but by the time that he was writing his *Thoughts upon the African Slave Trade*, the legislatures of some British West Indian colonies had passed certain ameliorative laws. In Jamaica, for example, the Consolidated Slave Law of 1784 abolished cruel and severe punishments, made regulations for slaves' working hours, their clothing, their spare time and the length of their meals. Female slaves who had borne six children were exempted from all labour. Scrambles on board ship were forbidden, and so was the separation of African families. This last prohibition (involving an interpreter) was awkward to enforce, but to the historian Bryan Edwards goes the credit for getting through the Jamaican House of Assembly a law by which 'the Guineamen' were compelled, under solemn oath, to do their utmost to see that this clause was respected. None the less, Edwards strangely maintained that the West Indian planters were 'entirely innocent and ignorant of the manner in which the slave trade is conducted (having no other concern therein than becoming purchasers of what British acts of Parliament have made objects of sale)'; yet in fact the new slave regulations were primarily the planters' answer to rising criticism in Great Britain, and to the spread of the movement to abolish the slave trade, with all that movement's volcanic implications that the next step would be to abolish Negro slavery itself. A further strong influence in favour of improving slave conditions in the British West Indian possessions was the settlement there after the American Revolution of loyalists from the mainland states, who brought with them a type of slave altogether more advanced than those of the sugar islands. Young discharged officers settled there also, forming 'a better description' of planter, with a more civilized concept of duty towards their slaves.

Edwards, as we have seen, did strive to be historically impartial. He did not deny evidence of 'excessive whippings and barbarous mutilations' of slaves, and even glossed this with a condemnation: 'If they happened but seldom, they happened too often.' By and large, though, he took the Jamaican planter's traditional, roseate view of the state of West Indian Negro slaves. He describes those newly landed from the ships as 'presenting themselves, when the buyers are few, with cheerfulness and alacrity for selection, and appearing mortified and disappointed when refused'. He also comments on their 'loud and repeated bursts of laughter' at the discovery of a blemish on any of their fellows during the medical inspection which preceded sale. When the buyer had completed what Edwards calls 'his assortment' he clothed his new slaves in a coarse German cloth called oznaburgh, and gave them hats, handkerchiefs and knives. Since they could not know what work or conditions were in store for them, and since the squalors of the Middle Passage were now past, they may indeed have trudged off to their destinations in a genial, or at any rate an optimistic, mood.

On arrival at their future home, the new or 'unseasoned' Negroes were distributed amongst the huts and provision grounds of older, established and experienced slaves. On his own estates Edwards had at first forbidden this custom which he judged 'an insupportable hardship' for the slave hosts. These latter surprised him by begging that his decision be reversed – the young newcomers seemed to the old people to replace children who had died or had been left in Africa, and the girls (of whom there was always a shortage) were potential wives for their sons. An agreeable mutual relationship was quickly established, and the adoptive parents were venerated by the new arrivals as if they had in fact been their own progenitors. A further reason for this anxiety to adopt and guide was that the older Africans 'expected to revive and retrace in the conversation of their new visitors, the remembrance and ideas of past pleasures and scenes of their youth'. But the solace of adopting a young man or woman, boy or girl, fresh from Africa was frequently shortlived for, worn out by the Middle Passage, many of the 'new Negroes' died before their three-year seasoning period was over. On the Worthy Park plantation and its outlying properties in the parish of St John, Jamaica, for instance, in the year 1794 alone, thirty-one new Negroes died, chiefly from dysentery. There was also the heavy infant mortality usual amongst the slave population of the sugar colonies.

This infant mortality, together with the fact that the slave-women's birth-rate was often inexplicably low, increased the demand for 'new Negroes' off the ships. Professor Ulrich Phillips, who in 1914 published a study of the Worthy Park plantation, found that in the year 1792 there were three hundred and fifty-five slaves there. Of these one hundred and fifty constituted the main field gangs; thirty-four were artificers and jobbing foremen; forty were watchmen, gardeners and cattlemen; thirteen were in the hospital corps; twenty-four little boys and girls made up the 'grass gang'; thirty-nine were young children and thirty-three were invalids or superannuated. The domestic staff at Worthy Park was twenty-two slaves strong. That same spring the owner began buying Congoes and Coromantees from the slavers' agents – one hundred in 1792, and eighty-one more in the following year. It was amongst these new Negroes that the mortality rate was so high. Two of the thirty-one were thought to have committed suicide.

Robert Price, an absentee landlord of Penzance in Cornwall, was the owner of Worthy Park. He was presumably the sort of proprietor Edwards had in mind when, writing of 'the inheritance or accident' by which many of the white planters in the West Indies had acquired their land and their slaves, he points out that: 'Many persons there are, in Great Britain itself who ... find themselves possessed of estates they have never seen, and invested with powers over their fellow creatures there, which, however extensively odious, they have never abused.'

Edwards was neither an enemy to the slave trade, nor to the state of slavery as such, although he rather ruefully admitted the innate injustice of perpetual servitude. Composing his monumental work in London, he looked back with nostalgia to 'the time of crop in the sugar islands' as 'the season of gladness and festivity'. During this harvest period the health of the Negroes and their inextinguishable vitality quite visibly improved, since all hands were allowed to chew as much luscious sugar-cane as they could manage. All of them – save those condemned to the Hades of the boiling-houses – grew temporarily strong and fat. The sick Negroes improved, and 'even the pigs and poultry' fattened on the cane-refuse. To Edwards, and to many other planting gentlemen of his kind, the blissful scenes on a well-run plantation at crop-time seemed 'to soften, in a great measure, the hardship of slavery, and induce a spectator to hope, when the miseries of life are represented as insupportable, that they are sometimes exaggerated through the medium of fancy'. But it was not the miseries of Negro slavery that were exaggerated through the medium of fancy; it was the depth and the duration of those limited outbursts of happiness in which the African slave managed, triumphantly, to indulge.

We have noticed that, on the steaming Gulf of Guinea, the comforting myth of the savagery and low mentality of Africans gained welcome sway over the minds of European slavers, and was spread by word of mouth and published books through Europe. Born of a callous and insolent ignorance, this myth crossed the Atlantic in the shark-ridden wake of the slave ships. There it took root and flourished in the sunlit, brooding islands of the West Indies, where the pale-green sugar-canes, acre upon acre, billowed and rippled in the breeze from the blue-green sea. It echoed through the high stuccoed drawing-rooms of the Bay Street mansions of the merchants and plantation owners in Charleston, South Carolina. In the bayous of Louisiana, in the Golden Isles of Georgia, in the cotton-fields beside the Mississippi River, in the thriving slave-markets of ominous New Orleans, in the trim offices of the Jewish slaving magnates of Newport, Rhode Island, it became an article of faith. So, in vast areas of the United States it appallingly remains today. But once established over the Atlantic, the myth not so much suffered a sea-change as it gained a new dimension. This appendix to the myth of Negro inferiority might be called the *Myth of the Merry and Contented Slave* – or, alternately, *Thanks for the Middle Passage*. Its components can best be envisaged as a series of vignettes in the mode of the lovely coloured engravings of slave festivals based on the pictures of the eighteenth-century painter Agostino Brunyas. In this fictive slave existence turbaned Negroes and Negresses sang as they worked the cane or cotton-fields by day, spent the night drinking, dancing and making love, reared happy families of sportive piccaninnies, and liked and respected the white masters, their indolent whey-faced wives and their spoiled children. According to this theory, which swept back to Europe and was long believed there, the slaves had, like Bryan Edwards' faithful old body, Clara, one further and capital cause for gratitude – they had been saved from the funereal practices of the Guinea Coast.

In an illogical, interlocking way these two myths, that of Negro stupidity and that of slave happiness, supported one another mutually. Those planters who, like the author of *Practical Rules for the Management of Negro Slaves* (published in 1803), went so far as to admit that slavery 'is not so desirable as freedom . . . because a slave is subject to an authority that may be exercised in a manner cruel, capricious or oppressive, from which the sufferer has no means of relieving himself', asserted that even in the hands of a bad master, a slave's 'lot is infinitely less deplorable than might be imagined; for he does not sublime misery in the laboratory of the imagination. His powers . . . are not felt if not applied to the organs of sense; and, let tyranny cease but for a moment to act . . . the slave forgets his oppression, and discovers enjoyments more great than those of an epicure at a banquet . . . Indulge to satiety his animal appetites, and a negro makes no account of his degradation'.

This neat conviction that should a slave by some mischance fall from his naturally happy state, he still could not suffer as a white man would have suffered, was widespread. The shape of Negroes' skulls, their pigmentation, the way their hair grew, all were quoted to prove that they had a different and a much less delicate nervous system than Europeans. An exception was sometimes made for the black mistresses of white men – either slave girls or free Negresses. Here the superlative beauty of so many African women was openly admitted. It was also on occasion praised. In 1765 an elderly white Jamaican poetaster celebrated the imaginary arrival from Africa of a negroid Venus – a classical Black Madonna, so to speak. We may as well look at four of the verses of this curious eulogy, which was entitled *The Sable Venus*. The country of origin of the sable Venus is indicated as being Portuguese Angola:

Sweet is the beam of morning bright,
Yet sweet the sober shade of night;
　On rich Angola's shores,
While beauty clad in sable dye,
Enchanting fires the wond'ring eye,
Farewell, ye Paphian bowers.

When thou, this large domain to view,
Jamaica's isle, thy conquest new,
   First left thy native shore,
Bright was the morn, and soft the breeze,
With wanton joy the curling seas
   The beauteous burden bore.

Her skin excell'd the raven plume,
Her breath the fragrant orange bloom,
   Her eye the tropic beam:
Soft was her lip as silken down,
And mild her look as ev'ning sun
   That gilds the Cobre stream.*

Gay Goddess of the sable smile!
Propitious still, this grateful isle
   With thy protection bless!
Here fix, secure, thy constant throne;
Where all, adoring thee, do ONE,
   ONE deity confess.

Thus, in that period of calculated literary artifice, even the Middle Passage could be romanticized. Let us now dismiss myth and romanticism, and turn to scrutinize plantation realities.

* The Cobre, a river on the southern coast of Jamaica, on the western bank of which stands the old capital, Spanish Town.

# Chapter 8

# The Sugar Islands

## I

THE TERM 'the Sugar Islands' – as evocative in its own way as 'the Gulf of Guinea' or 'the Guinea Coast'? – became for generations the popular manner of referring to the English and French colonies in the Antilles. It was a very exact definition, once sugar had finally ousted the small-holding tobacco plantations with which these islands were at first littered, but it could of course have been applied with equal justice to the huge Spanish sugar-producing possessions – Cuba, Hispaniola and Porto Rico – as well. Slave conditions on all the West Indian islands were clearly not identical, but also they were not too various. Since our aim here is to get the sight and smell of plantation slavery, we had better for the moment consider how it worked out in practice on some of the British and the French islands, leaving aside the Spanish territories. It was to supply the Iberian colonies with Negro labour that England, France and Holland first embarked upon the slave trade; but soon these countries acquired West Indian colonies themselves and, after some fruitless experiments with white indentured labourers, transported criminals, and kidnapped persons, they too fell back on the expedient of shipping Negroes from Africa in bulk for the cultivation of their island plantations. Dr Eric Williams has stressed, in his *Capitalism and Slavery*, that the origin of trans-atlantic Negro servitude was thus 'economic, not racial; it had to do not with the colour of the labourer, but the cheapness of the labour'. Another authority, Professor Ulrich Phillips, calls the Africans in the colonies 'latecomers fitted into a system already developed' – that is to say a system which killed off the first, Amerindian slaves in the Indies, and which had subsequently almost broken down under the difficulties and the

NEW
MEXICO

TEXAS

Arkansas

Mississippi

NO
CARO

SOU
CARO

Charles
GEORGIA

LOUISIANA   WEST FLORIDA

Pensacola Bay

New
Orleans

EAST FLORIDA

NEW
BISCAY

GULF   OF

MEXICO

Havana

CU

OLD

Vera Cruz

MEXICO

YUCATAN

BAY OF
HONDURAS

PACIFIC

OCEAN

Po
B

0                     500

MILES

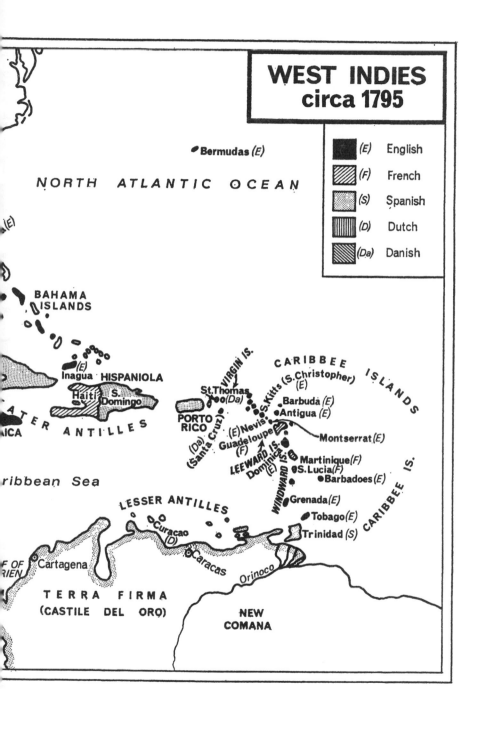

# WEST INDIES
## circa 1795

| | | |
|---|---|---|
| ■ | (E) | English |
| ▨ | (F) | French |
| ▦ | (S) | Spanish |
| ▥ | (D) | Dutch |
| ▧ | (Da) | Danish |

●Bermudas (E)

NORTH ATLANTIC OCEAN

▪(E)

BAHAMA ISLANDS

(E)
Inagua HISPANIOLA

CARIBBEE ISLANDS

VIRGIN IS.

St.Thomas
●●(Da)

S.Kitts (S.Christopher) (E)

Haiti S. Domingo

PORTO RICO

(Da) (Santa Cruz)

Barbuda (E)
●Antigua (E)

ATER ANTILLES

(E)Nevis
Guadeloupe (F)

Montserrat (E)

ICA

LEEWARD IS.
Dominica (E)

Martinique (F)
●S.Lucia (F)
●Barbadoes (E)

WINDWARD IS.

CARIBBEE IS.

ribbean Sea

LESSER ANTILLES

Grenada (E)

●Tobago (E)

Curacao (D)

Trinidad (S)

Caracas

F OF RIEN

Cartagena

Orinoco

TERRA FIRMA (CASTILE DEL ORO)

NEW COMANA

expense of employing European labourers. 'Both Indian slavery and white servitude' (he writes) 'were to go down before the black man's superior endurance, docility and labour capacity.' In his *A View of the Art of Colonization*, a pamphlet published in London in 1849, the distinguished colonial statesman, Edward Gibbon Wakefield, asseverated that the reasons for Negro slavery 'are not moral, but economical, circumstances; they relate not to vice or to virtue, but to production'. Much research has been done on the plantation as a political and economic institution, but the results of these valuable and scholarly studies can scarcely be called visual. They no more aid us in reconstructing the life that faced the African slave on the plantations than statistical tables of the numbers of Negroes shipped annually over the Atlantic help us to understand what weeks on a crowded slave ship were actually like.

The realities of daily living in the Sugar Islands during the long, long period of slave civilization are as hard to envisage clearly as those of African civilization on the Gulf of Guinea. A cloud of beguiling legends obscures the harsh truth, just as at evening the soft mists shroud the dense green mountain peaks of the islands, to be dissolved at sunrise and swirled by the sea-winds away. Thus, the legend of the contented slave is counter-balanced by the legend of an easy white prosperity, and of gracious living in pillared plantation mansions staffed by willing and affectionate darkie retainers. For those who find sea-battles romantic, there are the legends of fighting ships and deeds of derring-do in and out between the islands of the Caribbean – islands which were themselves the prizes as well as the theatres of European wars. There is the legend of a balmy, languorous climate, tropical yet temperate, with warm sparkling days and cool, refreshing nights. Still abetting and encouraging these legends today there is the undeniable beauty of the Caribbean scene, changing from island to island, seductive, beguiling. Yet this innate beauty is everywhere scarred by poverty and encrusted with filth. The shacks roofed with rusty tin on which the rain-rods clatter, the overcrowded shanties like old chicken-coops, the unpaved streets and pitted, puddly roadways are as much the relics of the slave days of the islands as are the slums of British cities those of the slave days of Britons during the Industrial Revolution.

It is thus that the memories of several sojourns in the West Indian islands over nearly thirty years are, for me personally, extremely mixed. The High Woods of Trinidad, where the Flame of the Forest rides far above one's head, the coral-sand beaches of Blanchisseuse, silent but for the rustling of the waves against the reefs, form but one wing of a diptych, the other wing of which is dark with the hovels and the greasy rum-huts of the larger part of Port of Spain. Similarly the mysterious smoking sulphur springs and plumy forests of Dominica seem offset by the horrible little town of Roseau, with its neglected museum, pretentious cathedral, disgraceful living conditions and its broken streets through which the lean and mangy mongrels roam. The same contrasts may be found in St Lucia, in Martinique, in Guadeloupe and elsewhere along the Antillean chain. But I think, on balance, that the beauty of the islands wins. Nor is this beauty solely natural: mysterious shadowy houses like Farleigh Hill in Barbados, the great grand free-standing architecture of the piazza in Spanish Town, Jamaica, are never to be forgotten, once seen. Moreover, an integral part of the strange enticement of the West Indies is surely to be traced to the generosity and friendliness of the largest section of their inhabitants – the descendants of the slaves. That this should be so has always seemed to me perfectly incredible, but so I have always found it to be. I think it of interest that the inborn generosity of the West African should have survived not the Middle Passage merely, but centuries of exploitation and abuse, followed by decades of a freedom which meant, in fact, white hostility and neglect. Our friend Willem Bosman wrote of the Benin Negroes of the late seventeenth century as 'generally goodnatured and very civil, from whom it is easy to obtain anything whatever we desire by soft means . . . and if we want anything, and ask it of them, they will seldom deny us, though they have occasion for it themselves'. 'The mind that is heroic cannot fail to be generous,' wrote a St Kitts lawyer named Clement Caines.* 'The negro is generous to excess. He bestows on others not only what he wants himself, but what he can hardly do without.' Mr Caines, who had in his time managed eight St Kitts estates with a total complement of one thousand

* *A History of the General Council and General Assembly of the Leeward Islands*, 2 vols, Basseterre, St Christophers, 1804.

Negroes, knew his subject well. 'The West Indian labourers moulder away' he wrote in another passage. Summing up the lot of the Africans in the Sugar Islands he resorted to a sonorous, Gibbonian prose: 'This devoted race became, therefore, the slaves of toil in the hands of the cultivator, the slaves of pomp in the hands of the vain, the slaves of lust in the hands of the concupiscent, and the slaves of caprice and whim in the hands of everybody.' Caines' evidence forms an interesting contrast to that of Bryan Edwards and certain other contemporary writers on Caribbean slave-conditions. It may, later, help us to form a fairly accurate picture of what, for Negro slaves, a lifetime of captivity on a West Indian sugar plantation meant.

As we hack our way, machete in hand, through the luxuriant thickets of legend and illusion that grew up protectively around the West Indian estates, we may never reach the precise truth, but we may at least get near it. We may find, I think, that Negro slavery was hardly a happy state; that prosperity, ever at the mercy of poor crops, of hurricanes, of slave epidemics and revolts, as well as of enemy raids and invasions, was distinctly intermittent; that many planters went bankrupt, and that their health was ruined by the climate or their own debauchery; and that the cultivation of the sugar-cane, the sweet source of such bitter misery, was as precarious as it was tough. The Swedish scientist Wadström,* who took part in an expedition to West Africa in 1787 to 1788, and published his *Observations on the Slave Trade* in London in 1789, and an essay on African colonization in 1794, declared that 'in no age or country was ever avarice more completely disappointed, or humanity more shockingly outraged than in the flattering but ill-judged introduction of the sugar cane into all or most of the British West Indies, especially the Ceded Islands† . . . its premature and forced cultivation has, within our own memory, swept masters and slaves, the oppressors and the oppressed, into one common grave'.

---

* Carl Bernhard Wadström was Chief Director of the Assay Office in Sweden. He gave anti-slave trade evidence before the Privy Council and the House of Commons during the two great enquiries into the slave trade, in 1789 and 1791.

† i.e. Montserrat, Dominica, Saint-Vincent and certain other French islands ceded by the Treaty of Paris, 1762.

There is a beauteous plant that grows
In Western India's sultry clime,
Which makes, alas! the Black man's woes,
And also makes the White man's crime.

The opening stanza of *The Black Man's Lament* or *How to Make Sugar* by the Quaker novelist Mrs Amelia Opie forms an adequate preface to a subject which may well seem perilously dull – that of sugar-production in the days of slavery. The ballad, composed to enlist the sympathy of ringleted, rosy-cheeked Georgian children in the Abolitionist cause, was illustrated with harrowing colour woodcuts of West Indian plantation life. It was published in London in 1824. In a series of pictures resembling a strip-cartoon we see the Negroes and Negresses herded together by white drivers wearing nankeen trousers, cut-away jackets and huge cartwheel panama hats as they flourish their long snake-like whips over the lines of hoeing slaves. Cane shoots are being planted in the plats; the harvest is being cut; the coppers of the boiling-houses heated; the barrels stowed aboard European-bound ships. Consciously naïf, the ballad, like its illustrations, was based on established facts.

Many people, particularly in this technological age, are fascinated by the processes of manufacture. They are thus happily immune to the only form of real boredom that travel can offer – the tour of a rubber factory, the dredging of tin from some rust-coloured, mud-congested Malayan lake, the liquefaction of sugar-cane. To those who do not share this general curiosity, I think that there are few more desperate predicaments than finding themselves expected to make intelligent comments when peering into vats and sorters and sifters, when climbing spiral steel staircases to look at things that spin and steam and click and whirr. Only natural enthusiasts or, we may suppose, the trained members of surviving royal families can take such experiences in their daily stride. The stiff, silvery rubber groves of Malaya are, in their sunless shadowy way as lovely as the trembling green sugar canes beneath an azure sky. The finished products of both now seem essential to living. But the stages in between leave one with a general confused impression that the process of turning a natural product into an artificial one seems primarily accompanied by a whole flock of quite abominable smells. Raw rubber, for example, stinks; nor am I likely to forget five days marooned on a French ship loading sugar at the back-of-beyond port of Pointe des Galets on the South Indian Ocean island of La Réunion-Bourbon, when the fecal stench of raw sugar invaded the cabin and hung like a nauseous gas about the few streets of that strange, but not altogether unexciting, little town. Prejudiced as I am, I propose, therefore, that we spend the minimum of time on the topic of West Indian sugar planting and, like Mrs Opie, limit that strictly to its effect upon the slaves. We shall then be entitled to question whether an African was really happier on Worthy Park plantation than in a rural village near Old Calabar.

First brought to the New World by Columbus, the sugar-cane was introduced to the French Antilles by Governor Aubert in 1640; it took so well that only twenty-five years later, Louis XIV's great minister, Jean-Baptiste Colbert, was congratulating one of Aubert's successors on the huge profits of the trade. As the Swede Wadström indicates, sugar was at no time an easy crop to rear. The conditions it demands are precise, and it is exacting and implacable. Low plains, with a rich soil, tropical heat, great humidity at the roots and violent sun as it grows – these are essentials. In the French islands the volcanic alluvial plains of Saint Domingue, the Basse-Terre of Guadeloupe, and the *mornes* of Martinique were found best suited to the sugar-cane. In the British islands the favourite soils for it were the ashy loam of St Kitts, and the chocolate-red earth of Trelawney parish in Jamaica. The next best thing was provided by a mixture of clay and sand called 'brick-mould' which was deep, warm, mellow and fairly easy to work. Barbados offered a black earth, as did Antigua and some of the Windward Islands. In whole areas of all of the islands, however, it was necessary to fight to the death with a tenacious mixture of clay, limestone, flint and 'soapy marle' which required a very brawny and very large labour force to conquer it. Replanting of the shoots was often done in semi-fluid marshland, infested by mosquitoes.

The labour-gang first cleared and weeded a selected piece of land. Resultant areas of fifteen to twenty acres, called plats, were divided from one another by cart-roads. These plats were next subdivided by rows of wooden pegs, which cut them up into smaller squares of three and a half feet each way. Hoe in hand, the Negroes were then lined up in a row, one Negro to a square, and set to digging holes some five or six inches deep. An able field-hand was expected to dig at least one hundred or one hundred and twenty of these holes in a ten-hour day – but working days were often far longer than this. To catch the autumn rains, planting took place between August and early November, although a January plant could turn out well. When growing, the canes were at the mercy of hurricanes, droughts, and of diseases called, in the English islands, the black and the yellow blast, as well as of the borer pest.

The essence of the monotonous and back-breaking work of holing was synchronization, usually achieved by the liberal use of the overseer's whip. The holes had to be dug in a straight line and when one line was completed the Negroes were supposed automatically to fall back with all the discipline of a line of guardsmen or a chorus of ballet-dancers, to begin the next. Listen to Mrs Opie's jingle-jangle:

> But woe to all, both old and young,
>   Women and men, or strong or weak,
> Worn out or fresh those gangs among,
>   That dare the toilsome line to break!
>
> As holes must all at once be made,
>   *Together* we must work or stop;
> Therefore the whip our strength must aid,
>   And lash us when we pause or drop.
>
> When we have dug sufficient space,
>   The bright-eyed top of many a cane,
> Lengthways, we in the trenches place,
>   And *then* we trenches dig again.

When the sugar-crop was being harvested – that time we may recall, of 'healthy merry-making' for the slaves – the crushing mills and the boiling houses worked twenty-four hours a day:

> But when the crops are ripen'd quite,
>   'Tis then begin our saddest pains;
> For then we toil both day and night,
>   Though fever burns within our veins.

That mill, our labour, every hour,
  Must with fresh loads of cane supply,
And if we faint, the cart-whip's power,
  Gives force which nature's powers deny.

The sugar-mills, run by water, by cattle or by man-power (and, in flat and breezy islands like Barbados, by the wind) twice crushed the bundles of cane between heavy rollers. The resultant trash was used as fuel for the boilers, while the precious juice ran off in a lead-lined wooden trough to the receiver, whence it continued on its way along another leaden gutter to the torrid boiling-house. Here it was clarified with an ad-mixture of white lime, was cooled, and passed through to the curing-house. Work in the boiling-house during crop-time was considered 'the most unhealthy to which a negro can be applied', and only strong and well-seasoned slaves were meant to be employed there, since the heat induced dropsy, first sig-nalled by a swelling of the face and legs. 'If you select a new negro, whose form of body and activity promises a subject well adapted to the coppers, and place him there without remission for a crop, it is fifty to one that he falls into those disorders' wrote Dr Collins in his *Practical Rules*: '. . . and if he is not hurried out of the world by the complaint, as many of them are, he will be very long in recovering his former state of health . . . Some negroes seem to have been adapted to it [i.e. the boiling-house] by nature, and will endure being kept at the coppers throughout the season without injury; but there are not many who are so happily organized. Those with sores on their legs should not be permitted to approach the coppers on any account.' Long night-shifts in the mills or the boiling-houses induced drowsiness, resulting in loss of fingers in the crusher, or of lives over the coppers. Here, as in the fields, overseers armed with whips formed an essential adjunct to the suffocating scene.

It was customary in the Sugar Islands to divide up the slaves – all, of course, save the skilled artisans and house servants – into graduated gangs, one of the several advantages of which was that they were easier to oversee. Many estates did this in a rule-of-thumb manner according to age rather than to physical capacity, a system (or lack of it) which real experts thought both wasteful and careless. The recommended plan was to select the heftiest Negroes, regardless of age or sex, and put them into what was called 'the strong gang'. To these were allotted 'the rudest labours of the plantation'. The next gang was composed of weaker or smaller Negroes. Then came a gang of youngsters employed in weeding, stumping, planting and manuring by hand – 'a service which, for their lightness and agility, they perform as well as the larger negroes and with more good will, if not oppressed with loads too heavy for their feeble shoulders.' Then came the grass gang:

composed of small negroes, just emerged from the nursery; and who, for want of other employment, would escape from their nurses, and employ themselves in mischief, such as in breaking canes, or pilfering from the absent negroes, or in setting fire to their houses, and in many such other amusements, by the practice of which they are initiated into early roguery and become adepts in the science in time . . . Let them be formed into a grass-gang, and put under the care of some discreet aged woman, whose duty it should be to collect them early in the morning and to lead them to some part of the estate, where they may pick grass or vines . . . In this manner they may bring five or six bundles daily . . . It is of great advantage to introduce your young people early into habits of labour, as so much of it will be required from them in their future progress through life.

Annual drafts were made from the grass gang. When the piccaninnies attained the age of nine or ten they were promoted to the grade above them, the weeding and manuring gang. In this they stayed until they were fourteen, when, if manly enough, they were transferred to the holing gang. In this way 'you obtain a perpetual succession of recruits, gradually trained and habituated to labour, and fitted for every purpose whatever of the plantation'. Dr Collins omits a point stressed by Mr Clement Caines – that grass-picking was one of the most heart-breaking jobs on a plantation, as the grass had to be plucked and gathered single blade by single blade.

This brief account of slave-tasks is compiled from a number of authorities writing towards the end of the eighteenth century, when, under humanitarian pressure from Europe, plantation conditions were considered to have radically improved. But as late as the seventeen-sixties atrocious cruelties were still being practised, and British planters would swap witty stories of how they had given some male or female slave 'a cool hundred' or how they had spent the morning 'peeling' some of their slaves.

Since a Negro's evidence against a white man was not admitted in law in the British or Dutch colonies the Africans had no redress against the excessive floggings, or the hacking off of their ears, noses or fingers which formed the sadistic pastimes of the more alcoholic or psychopathic planters. Alone amongst the European nations, the French had long before distinguished themselves by enacting a species of protective slave law, the so-called *Côde Noir*, drawn up by Colbert as one of his great series of ordinances – reformation of justice, 1667, of the criminal code, 1679, of the commercial code, 1678, of the marine code of 1681 – and promulgated as law in March 1685 two years after his death.

The first object of the *Côde Noir* was to protect Catholicism in the Antillean islands, by banning heretics from running plantations and by expelling the Jews; the second was to see that the slaves were properly looked after, so as to prevent pillage and revolt by Negroes whose owners starved them and so drove them to crime. The *Côde* also aimed to protect Negro slaves against sadistic or murderous masters who 'exercise a tyranny which would horrify the most barbarous of nations'. In this Edict slaves were still recognized as chattels, subject to seizure and sale in the same way as a defaulter's more inanimate possessions, but owners were directed to give their slaves enough to eat, forbidden to sell separately a mother and her children under the age of puberty, or to condemn Negroes to death, prison or mutilation without the judgement of the normal tribunals of justice. Slaves were not to be worked for a longer period than that between the rising and the setting of the sun. On the other hand the French master had the right to lash, or put chains on, his own slaves, and to decide, when escaped Negroes were recaptured, whether they should merely be branded or have a limb cut off. The death penalty was imposed for any attack on white persons, and for theft. A slave was, however, allowed to summon before a tribunal a master who did not fulfil his duties under the *Côde*. This last idealistic clause seldom worked out in practice. Although the basic purpose of the *Côde Noir* was to make plantations in the French West Indies safer and more productive, it is noteworthy that, unique amongst the European colonial powers of that date, France drew up and issued laws, which did to some mild degree limit the autocratic powers of the planters over their slaves. There was no equivalent in the British islands for close on one hundred years.

## III

Now that we have gained some idea of the training, the curriculum and the graduated phases of the life of a West Indian slave from the day he was sold in the Guinea-yard – head shaven, teeth polished, body well-oiled– until the day when he died of premature old age, it may be of interest to glance at the time-table by which he worked. This specimen time-table is compiled from the regulations on model, late eighteenth-century plantations. Conditions on the great majority of others, which were not run on 'humanitarian' lines, may be adduced, I think, from these.

The working day began just before sunrise, when the slaves, huddled in sleep beneath the ragged blankets of their cabins, were wakened by the tolling of a bell, or by the peremptory summons of blasts upon a conch-shell. It frequently happened that this summons turned out, too late, to be a false alarm, for the watchmen would confuse the blue-white radiance of the tropical moon with the orange dawn of the rising sun. Clad in their coarse woollen garments, and laden with hoes, bills and breakfast provisions, the slaves would be marched off to the cane-fields. Each gang was attended by an overseer – a white employee of mentality too low even to have become a planter – and a Negro 'driver'. Both carried long whips. In the French islands a breed of mastiff was also used in a policing capacity. On the work-site, roll was called in the raw morning air, and the names of absentees noted. So soon as these lay-a-beds showed up they were punished with 'a few stripes' of the cart-whip. When the early morning was chill and foggy – as so often in those islands it can be – the slaves found especial difficulty in hauling themselves off their plank or earthen pallets, for in the cold 'the sensations of the negro' were 'distressful beyond the imagination of an inhabitant of frozen regions'. The clinging dank mists before the dawn made them not brisk but sluggish, not active but inert; and neither whipping nor verbal encouragement could get them working properly until the tropical sun was riding high. Work continued until nine o'clock, when they had a three-quarters of an hour breakfast period in the shade, eating food prepared by some of the women slaves. A mid-day bell called them for a second rest of up to two hours, during which they ate a mushy meal to which salted or pickled fish had been added; and a nap was permitted. Those who preferred a large evening meal, and were not tired enough to sleep, would spend this lunch-break collecting food for their own pigs and poultry. Resumed at two o'clock, work continued until sundown or after, when another bell signalled the end of the day. If the slaves had worked much harder than usual, or if the rain had clattered down all day, drenching their woollen cloth-ing and their conical brimless felt hats, a tot of rum was on occasion issued in the evening. They would then retire to their cabins – described by one planter as far excelling in comfort 'the cabins of the Scotch and Irish peasantry' – and sleep until the strident conch-shell proclaimed the rising of another sun.

Once the West Indian planters were placed on the defensive, and found themselves and their alleged humanity attacked, they became vocal on the subject of the simple comforts of their slaves. The stinking cabins with earth-floors, fifteen feet long and divided into two compartments were, it was admitted, too low to let most of the Negroes stand upright inside them. They were made of wattle and plaster, and supported by wooden posts. But the earth flooring was described as 'commonly dry enough', and the palm-thatch formed 'an admirable covering'. A fire was kept burning all night in the middle of one of the rooms, the smoke escaping slowly through the thatch, or out of the door-hole. On good estates the bedstead was of boards, with a mat and blanket; a rough table, two or three stools, some earthen jars, a pail, an iron pot and a pile of calabashes for use as plates and cups completed the equipment of these hovels. Artisans and domestics had larger houses and, if of a thrifty turn, could buy linen sheets and mosquito nets, and acquire a plate or two of Staffordshire ware which they proudly displayed upon a crude shelf. The Negro cabins were assembled in a random fashion near the sugar-factories and being 'always intermingled with fruit-trees, the banana, the avocado pear (the negroes' own planting and property)' they supported, from a distance, the romantic view of slavery by their 'pleasing and picturesque appearance'.

On most estates Negroes were expected to spend part of each Sunday cultivating their fruit and vegetable gardens; in many cases they were ordered to do this, since the produce of their plots served to supplement the low-calorie rations – grain or dried horse-beans and other animal fodder – which were shipped out from European ports for the slaves' sustenance. On very many estates the Negroes' diet was at starvation level; here malnutrition and debility prevailed.* The slaves also kept their own pigs, goats and chickens, and made bark-ropes, baskets and earthen pans. Sunday mornings were market mornings, when Negroes would flock to the towns to sell their vegetables and fruit, their livestock and their artifacts.

When, in the first half of the eighteenth century, Methodist missionaries penetrated to the British West Indian islands, they were shocked to find Negroes working their grounds, and buying and selling at market, on Sundays; and that, in the slave hamlets, the day 'closed in noisy riot and debauchery'. 'Britain and Protestantism may well blush at this,' wrote one missionary some decades later† 'when it is known that in the colonies of Catholic states the Saturday and not the Sunday is given to the slaves to work their grounds and to supply their wants; that Sunday is *there* a day of *rest*, and of *worship* also; and that in

---

* In one of his great abolitionist speeches in the House of Commons, that of 18 April 1791, Wilberforce, who had just made the point that four or five thousand slaves, and sometimes nine or ten thousand, were under 'the care' of a solitary medical practitioner, continued: 'It was also in evidence that they were in general underfed. They were supported partly by the produce of their own provision-ground, and partly by an allowance of flour and grain from their masters. In one of the islands, where provision-grounds did not answer one year in three, the allowance to a working negro was but from five to nine pints of grain per week: in Dominica, where it never failed, from six to seven quarts: in Nevis and St Christophers, where there was no provision-ground, it was but eleven pints. Add to this that it might be less, as the circumstances of their masters might become embarrassed; and in this case both an abridgement of their food and an increase of their labour, would follow.' – Clarkson's *History of the Abolition of the African Slave-Trade* (Longmans, London, 1808), vol. ii, p. 230.

† Richard Watson: *A Defence of the Wesleyan Methodist Missions in the West Indies* (London, 1817). Secretary to the Committee for the Management of the Wesleyan Methodist Missions, Watson based his survey of the state of Christianity in the British West Indies on eye-witness accounts and on old reports in the Committee's archives.

addition to this, the numerous saints' days in the Romish calendar, affording many holidays to the slave in the course of the year, give a further amelioration to his labours, and additional opportunities of acquainting himself with religion.' These early Methodists were stubbornly resented by the planters, who feared that their doctrine that all men were equal before God would disturb the uneducated mass of Negro slaves. The Methodists had found the standard of morals and of Christian religious feeling very low amongst the white population of the islands, and non-existent amongst the blacks. The Anglican clergy in these colonies did not consider the Negroes 'any part of their charge'. They baptized neither newly imported African slaves, nor ones born in the colonies, 'except if a planter desired to have a favourite negro baptized, and then the rite was administered. The price of the fee was from one to two dollars.' No clergymen catechized or instructed slaves, nor did they perform any marriage ceremony for Negroes. According to another missionary, Joseph Taylor, 'Attendance of the slaves at church was neither enforced, desired, nor given'. The clergy were not wholly to blame; they were few in number, and the planters opposed any idea of their trying to minister to Negroes. If a slave managed to creep to church he was not allowed further than 'the aisle or some obscure corner, and even there seats are not always provided for them'. 'I do not believe' claimed another reverend witness 'that one hundredth part of the slaves ever attended church.' In St Vincent, with a slave population of thirty thousand, there was no church whatever, and the legislature had 'lately been moved to prepare a law restricting the labours of missionaries of every kind'. The educated ex-slave, Ottobah Cugoano, wrote in 1787: 'Even in the little time I was in Grenada, I saw a slave receive twenty-four lashes of a whip for being seen in a church on a Sunday instead of going to work.' For the Negro slave the Sabbath thus became a day composed of work, of market-chatter and of a well-earned and, let us only hope, a thoroughly drunken evening revelry.

In theory it could have been asserted that, the week's labour over, a Negro family might count Sundays and holidays as times of comparative serenity. But in the lives of even the most resigned of slaves there was no margin of safety, and no vista of hope. A hard-working and trusted Negro, living with his wife and family in a well-constructed hut surrounded by an ample vegetable garden, had nothing whatever to look forward to. His master's death or indebtedness, or wish to please a neighbour or a friend, might mean this Negro's sale, and his despatch, without his family, to lonely servitude on some distant plantation, some other island or, likely enough, to the sunless silver-mines of Mexico. West Indian slavery offered the Negro monotony without security. The only freedom that he knew was the freedom to suffer and to fear.

Superficially, the lot of the domestic slaves was far better. Contemporaries who did not admire the coarse quality of much plantation hospitality, would pass scathing comments on the 'superfluity of servants' that encumbered a vainglorious West Indian household, and the great kitchens, 'culinary deserts', where food was cooked without the aid of bellows, jack or grate. The primitive, rickety basis of gracious living in the West Indian islands required a cohort of house-slaves, some of them employed as messengers and running footmen, and as 'pack horses and carriage wagons'. Expert cooks, valets, lady's maids and hairdressers might be cosseted; the planters of Martinique and Guadeloupe would send favourite or promising Negroes to Paris to be instructed in the domestic arts. But one and all of these 'servants' were at the mercy of the whims of the master or the mistress – and, as in Dutch Surinam or any other European colony, the white women were notoriously more cruel to their slaves than were the men. Sometimes, for stock-breeding purposes, a handsome or intelligent male domestic would be told off to sleep with his master's Negress or mulatto mistress, a precarious assignment provocative of searing jealousies. Should a petted domestic slave topple from grace, he or she would be either sold away, or consigned to one of the estate's field-gangs, where pretty rough treatment would be meted out by those who had watched and envied them in their days of prosperity and ease.

Negro girls and young women employed about the house were looked on as fair game by their masters, who made them available to inexperienced adolescent sons and to male house-guests. Negro valets and footmen acted as agile and experienced pimps. Like most human crimes, this debauching of young

Negresses caught up – slowly, stealthily, deviously – with its perpetrators. For the girl who had been raped or clumsily seduced by a son of the house was perfectly liable to be the possession and lady's-maid of one of his sheltered young sisters, whose insidious adviser and confidante she would become. 'It is of the nature of slavery to contaminate whatever touches or approaches it' Caines, the lawyer of Basseterre, declared. 'The very system of slavery has a deteriorating effect upon the character of the whites', another witness added. The steady undermining of European morals by crafty domestic slaves, was, like the pollution of pure English by 'nigger-talk' in the Southern States of America, but a single by-product of the slave trade. It may be counted as one weapon in the African's considerable armoury of retaliation. Others included the subtler forms of child-murder; obeah practices; poisoning; and, most terrible of all, powerful and organized slave revolts.

## IV

The first line of defence for any vanquished or occupied nation, as for any camp of war-prisoners, is calculated cunning and deceit. It was thus that the Negro slaves in the European colonies made lying their second nature. An analogy can be found in the history of Ireland. More than seven centuries of brutal English oppression produced a race of the most persuasive, adept and incorrigible liars in the world. It is the perennial complaint of foreign tourists in Ireland that, when they ask the distance by road to some specific Irish town or lake, the answer will be flexibly adjusted to what their interlocutor assumes that they would like to hear. If you are looking exhausted, and the place you ask for is another forty-five miles distant, you will in all probability be assured that it is only eight. This placatory instinct lay at the origin of the famous Irish desire to please. Certain it is that for those of genuine Irish blood – as against those of Anglo-Irish stock – the truth is not always easy to enunciate. One hears oneself saying something pleasing, but it simultaneously strikes one that the statement may not be wholly true. The lie was, similarly, the first refuge, or the outer bastion, of those downtrodden Irish of the colonies – the African slaves.

Generation after generation of planters and their families would complain of this inbred and incurable mendacity – Negroes were claimed to be 'the greatest liars upon the face of the earth . . . so expert too that no Persian ever managed his horse or drew his bow with greater dexterity than a negro lies; nor indeed was he ever more carefully trained or practised to do it . . . The face, too, with which even babies lie is wonderful. Without altering a feature, averting or winking their eyes, or betraying the least symptom of knowledge which they wish to conceal, they listen unmoved to interrogations repeated over and over again, in the loudest voice and with the severest menaces'. These piccaninnies were patiently taught to lie by their mothers and fathers with all the earnest diligence white parents would employ to ensure that their own offspring were instructed in Latin or riding or arithmetic. The water-tight lie became a vital piece of the slave-baby's equipment at the outset of his sad career. Theft, although in the colonies it incurred punishment as automatic as that it met with in the towns and villages of Africa itself, was also included in the wise child's stock-in-trade. The conical sugar-loaf hats of Negro men became receptacles for stolen food – a handful of biscuits deftly swept off a table when the master was not looking, even 'a large junk of salt beef or pork'. These hats may still be seen in Jamaica today, where they now chiefly tend to contain legitimate possessions such as packages of cigarettes or matches.

It is obvious that in these circumstances there could be no thread of mutual confidence between black and white. Ill-treatment bred theft and deceit, theft and deceit engendered further ill-treatment. The houses of the planters might look elegant and be, in certain cases, luxurious; but they were built on a quicksand of suspicion and they rested on the hollow, rotting foundations of distrust. Out in the fields, the Negroes would employ yet another weapon – a species of go-slow which even the cart-whip could not invariably circumvent. 'A slave being a dependant agent,' writes Dr Collins 'must necessarily move by the will of another, which is incessantly exerted to control his own; hence the necessity of terror to coerce obedience . . . From their gratitude you are not to hope much, the relation subsisting between the master and the slave forbids it, nor is there any principle on which you have a right to form such an expectation.' Yet slavery could not totally pervert the nobility of the African character, nor always stifle their native loyalty. 'There have not been wanting instances' (writes the same author) 'of attachment from slaves to their masters which have astonished the world, and disposed it to think favourably of the principles of negroes.'

Theft, lying and malingering might be classed as the Negroes' main form of passive resistance to slavery and oppression. Their action-programme included skilful murders; the use of witch-craft; and of terrorism in the form of slave revolts. In between these two areas of behaviour there fell attempts to escape and join the 'maroons' or refugee Negroes who established successful communities in remote mountain valleys and lived the lives of highwaymen or outlaws; and the most final escape-form of all – suicide. Slave suicides in the islands were as frequent as aboard ship, or off the African coast, for the Negroes were convinced that on their deaths they would return across the sea to the happiness and freedom they had known at home.

So as to get the Negroes' more revengeful and terroristic activities into perspective, it is important to consider the devilish behaviour of many owners and overseers to their slaves. As we have seen, in the hands of the so-called 'good masters' the worst the slave had to fear was starvation, whipping and being sold away from his family and friends. In the hands of callous white men there was no limit to the cruelties with which the Negroes must contend. It was in recognition of these Euro-pean crimes, and in an effort to protect the slaves against them, that the French had enacted their *Côde Noir* of 1685. But the French *Côde* had in Wilberforce's words been 'utterly neglected in the French islands, though there was an officer appointed by the crown to see it enforced. The provisions of the *Directorio* has been but little more avail in the Portuguese settlements, or the institution of a Protector of the Indians in those of the Spaniards'. To show the pathetic futility of ameliorative regu-lations in the West Indian islands, Wilberforce quoted the case – for which there were two reliable eye-witnesses, a Captain Cook and a Major Finch – of a Negro girl in the British island of Barbados. Here there was a by-law forbidding any white man to administer more than thirty-nine lashes to an errant slave. The two gentlemen whose evidence Wilberforce quoted heard shrieks coming from a house at nightfall; they broke down the front door to find a young Negress chained to the floor and being flogged by her white owner until she was almost dead. Upon their protests, the man stopped the flogging but cried out in exultation: 'that he had only given her thirty-nine lashes (the number limited by law) at any one time; and that he had only inflicted this number three times since the beginning of the night' adding 'that he would prosecute them for breaking open his door; and that he would flog her to death for all any one said, if he pleased; and that he would give her the fourth thirty-nine before morning'.

This, and many similar incidents, occurring in the period of abolition agitation proves that the contention of Bryan Edwards and other pro-slavery planters was incorrect. These defenders of the *status quo* asserted that the abolitionists, in their 'malignant and unmerited aspersions' were confusing the behaviour of the West Indian planters of the Age of Reason with the brutishness of the buccaneers and first rough settlers of the previous century – gregarious folk who could not bear to eat alone and would enliven a drunken evening with whipping and torturing their slaves. Since sadism knows not the frontiers of chronology, and since the word of a slave was never taken before that of his master, it seems inherently improbable that overseers and planters were less cruel in the seventeen-eighties than in the sixteen-eighties: improbable and, in cool fact, untrue.

When Sir Hans Sloane, the eminent physician, botanist, and creator of the Herb Garden in Chelsea, published his *Voyage to the Islands of Madeira, Barbados, Nevis, St Christophers and Jamaica* in two huge volumes (1707 and 1725) he incidentally recorded slave punishments which he had seen. Sloane had gone out to the West Indies in 1686 as personal physician to the Duke of Albemarle, the new Governor of Jamaica, who died in the island in the following year. Sir Hans reported that for certain flagrant crimes Negroes were nailed to the ground, with crooked sticks strapped to each limb. They were then slowly burned alive, first the hands and feet, and then 'burning them gradually up to the head'. Lesser crimes were punished by castration or chopping off half of one foot with an axe. Efforts at escape were rewarded by putting very heavy iron rings round their ankles or their necks, and by a spur forced into the mouth. Slaves were whipped until their bodies were raw, when pepper and salt was rubbed into the wounds, or melted wax poured over them. Sloane admitted the 'great constancy' with which the Africans supported these tortures, and emphasized that these punishments were 'inferior to what punishments other European nations inflict on their slaves in the East Indies'.

To turn from the Dark Ages of the reign of James the Second to the enlightened days of the reign of George the Third, what do we find? Skimming at random through the monumental mass of evidence accumulated by Clarkson, Wilberforce and their supporters we come across an overseer who killed a Negro by tossing him into a copper of boiling cane-juice 'for a trifling offence'; this overseer lost his job and had to pay a fine to the value of the dead slave. In another case, fully reported in the *Jamaica Gazette*, a planter so unmercifully whipped a fourteen-year-old girl who was late for work that she fell motionless to the ground, and was dragged by her heels to the hospital, where she expired. This murderer was tried by jury, but acquitted on the grounds that 'it was impossible a master could destroy his own property'. Another master slit the mouth of a six-month-old Negro child from ear to ear; tried, again, by jury he was fined forty shillings; the verdict having been 'Guilty, subject to the opinion of the court, if immoderate correction of a slave by his master be a crime indictable'. In 1780 a certain General Tottenham (presumably of Irish extraction) was promenading through the streets of Bridgetown in Barbados when he passed a Negro youth 'about nineteen, entirely naked, with an iron collar about his neck, having five long projecting spikes. His body both before and behind was covered with wounds. His belly and thighs were almost cut to pieces, with running ulcers all over them; and a finger might have been laid in some of the weals. He could not sit down, because his hinder part was mortified; and it was impossible for him to lie down, on account of the prongs of his collar'. The boy implored the General's help, explaining that it was his master who had punished him and who, now that the youth could no longer work, had told him that as he could not earn his keep he would be given nothing to eat. In one Jamaican slave revolt, the inflamed Negroes killed an European child at its mother's breast. They were gibbeted alive, and bravely lasted nine days. A contemporaneous captain of a slave ship seized from its mother a ten-month-old Negro child who would not eat and flogged it with a cat-o'-nine-tails. When the child's legs swelled, the captain ordered its feet to be plunged in scalding water. The toe-nails and skin coming off, these were replaced by oil-cloth, and the child was tied to a heavy log. Two or three days later, since it still refused sustenance, the captain flogged it once again until, within a quarter of an hour, it was dead. The captain, who forced the mother to throw the corpse into the sea, went unpunished.

## V

In the sphere of active as against passive forms of Negro resistance to plantation slavery, the analogy with the peoples of an enemy-occupied country also obtains. We find plotting, potent but unidentifiable ringleaders, secret assassination and sabotage. The maroons, or fugitive Negroes skulking in mountain or valley hideaways, may be likened to the Yugoslav or Italian partisans of the Second World War. They lived by armed raids and robbery; they persuaded or forced other slaves to join their bands; they killed or kidnapped imprudent white or mulatto persons caught wandering alone through their forests. The haphazard methods of stocking up slave ships on the Guinea Coast or down in the Congo or in Angola meant that witch-doctors of both sexes were often transported in a parcel of fresh slaves. These obeah figures inspired the awe and evoked the terrified loyalty of the other plantation Negroes, and they brought over with them a dark knowledge of obscure, insidious things. Experts in vegetable poisons, they found in the florid vegetation of the Sugar Islands appropriate substitutes for the leaves and roots of Africa. Thus was the domestic hearth of the planter or the overseer constantly in peril. The victims of their own victims, white men and women had to depend on slave sentries to guard their houses at night, on slave cooks and other servants to sustain their lives by day. A cook could introduce a slow and subtle poison into the master's food; and although there were many poison trials, this branch of murder easily went undetected in a climate inimical to the health of European and Negro alike. In the French islands certain Negresses employed in European nurseries were specialists in the murder of white babies. Others abolished older children by the use of silent weapons which left hardly any trace. Prime amongst these was the thin, sharp and decorative scarf-pin of the slave woman's gaudy madras turban – thrust through a child's brain the pin would leave virtually no wound. Another form of retaliation was murder by fetish, or, as it came to be called in the West Indies, by obeah. Applied by one knowledgeable practitioner of obeah this method, which drew its efficacy from the Africans' polytheism and absolute belief in the power of fetish, could paralyze, or could at any rate seriously damage, a complete plantation estate. Although the obeah men and women were usually old and hoary-headed, and wore the forbidding, grim expression of the priestess of the sea whose dance I watched at Bonny in the Niger Delta, it was almost impossible to find out who was or was not one of them, for, in general and even to save their own lives, their fellow-slaves could not be influenced to denounce them.

In an account of West Indian obeah sent by the Agent of Jamaica to the Lords of the Committee of the Privy Council, and attached by them to their slave trade report of 1789, Mr Long, an expert on the subject, treated in detail its effect upon plantation life. He emphasized that:

the professors of Obeah are, and always were, natives of Africa and none other; and they have brought the science with them from thence to Jamaica, where it is so universally practised, that we believe there are few of the large estates possessing native Africans, which have not one or more of them . . . The negroes in general, whether Africans or Creoles, revere, consult and fear them . . . The trade which these impostors carry on is extremely lucrative; they manufacture and sell their Obies adapted to different cases and at different prices. A veil of mystery is studiously thrown over their incantations, to which the midnight hours are allotted, and every precaution is taken to conceal them from the knowledge and discovery of the white people.

Attributing 'a very considerable portion of the annual mortality among the negroes of Jamaica to this fascinating mischief', Mr Long describes the 'farrago of material' of which obies were composed – 'blood, feathers, parrots' beaks, dog's teeth, alligator's teeth, broken bottles, grave-dirt, rum and eggshells'.

Rule by fear and fetish was not, of course, confined to Jamaica; it was found in all the islands and on the plantations of the mainland as well.

As we noticed when considering fetish on the African coast, the belief in these charms worked both ways: they could be used offensively to cause the death of an enemy, and protectively to neutralize any such suspected attack. Fetishes would be hung up to keep thieves away from huts, hog-sties and provision grounds, as well as to induce a fatal decline in someone you did not like, and whose only available defence would then be to purchase a more powerful and more expensive fetish. For generations the white people of the islands laughed at the fetish objects, treating them as a harmless African form of scarecrow. The Jamaican insurrection of 1760, however, changed the views of Europeans on that island, since it was discovered that the revolt had been instigated by an old Coromantee oracle, who had administered the fetish oath to the conspirators, and handed them out 'a magical preparation which was to render them invulnerable'. The Jamaicans thereupon passed a law for the suppression of obeah, but neither the fear of being hanged nor the most scrupulous investigations could deter the slaves. It was therefore concluded that 'either this sect, like others in the world, has flourished under persecution; or that fresh supplies are annually introduced from the African seminaries'.

The earlier instinct of the British colonists to dismiss obeah as a foolish superstition, and fetish objects as scarecrows or toys, found its parallel – with even more violent results – in the French islands, and specifically in Saint-Domingue. This western half of the Spanish island of Santo-Domingo had been ceded to the French by the Treaty of Ryswick in 1697; by 1791 it was the richest colony of France. Here African polytheism, with the beliefs of the natives of Dahomey predominating, had been gradually interlaced with tattered threads of Roman Catholicism to form the widespread and indomitable religion of Vodun, which is still vigorous in Haiti today. Even so astute a student of Saint-Domingue as its late eighteenth-century historian, Moreau de Saint-Méry, treated Vodun (or, as sensationalist English Victorian travellers called it, 'Voodoo') as a corpus of mere superstition, a colourful caprice of the slaves which gave them welcome opportunities for dancing, singing and playing the drums, exhibitions sometimes watched by the Europeans as an entertaining pastime. It was not until the vast and successful slave-rising of 1791, which swept the white planters from the island, and crippled the power of their opponents, the freed people of colour, that it was belatedly realized that Vodun could be used to unite and inspire Negro slaves on plantations all over the islands. The drum-beats which white persons had regarded as dance-rhythms merely, resumed the rôle that they had played in Africa – that of sending messages across hundreds of miles of territory, and of summoning the Africans to war. The rebellion of 1791 to 1793, which took both whites and free coloureds so totally by surprise, had been planned under the aegis of certain *houngans* or Vodun priests and it is of pertinence to note that the first three Negro rulers of the kingdom of Haiti – Toussaint Louverture, Dessalines and Christophe – absolutely forbade Vodun assemblies. The wily Toussaint banned every form of African dance as well; Christophe and Dessalines contented themselves with the security measure of forbidding Vodun dances only.

The prevalence of obeah in most of the Sugar Islands, the dominance of its more codified and sophisticated form, Vodun, in others, incidentally defeated one of the planters' chief aims – to keep members of the same African tribe on any estate as separated from each other as possible, and to try to circumvent the development of a common language in which the slaves could plan and plot. But even the most tyrannical plantation owners did not attempt to forbid what seemed to be innocuous Sunday night 'hops', nor could they ferret out Negroes who crept to secret and nocturnal rendezvous presided over by fetish priests. The result of these clandestine conferences were minor or major slave revolts.

The Jamaican slave-revolt of 1760, which was a cause of the laws against obeah subsequently passed by the island Assembly, began on two plantations in St Mary's parish, Frontier and Trinity by name. On neither estate had the Negroes been noticeably badly treated, and indeed the overseer of the Trinity Estate, an Englishman named Abraham Fletcher, had been so humane to his slaves that he was allowed by the rebels to go unmolested. The leader of the revolt was a Coromantee who had been a chief in Guinea, and whose name was Tacky. Over

RIVER SHARBROW

Nicholas Owen's house
beside the Sherbro
River, drawn, *c* 1755,
by himself

Upper part of an
Afro-Portuguese ivory
casket, showing a
Portuguese caravel
(? sixteenth century)

A painting by de Witt. Admiral de Ruyter in the
Castle of Elmina, *c* 1665

A view of Cape Coast Castle in 1682 (after Greenhill)

The courtyard of the Castle of Elmina, 1956

In the Niger Delta, *c* 1830

(*Opposite above*) The Benin River, near Benin city

(*Opposite below*) The overgrown ruins of part of the thirteenth-century fortified walls of Benin city, which were twenty-eight miles round

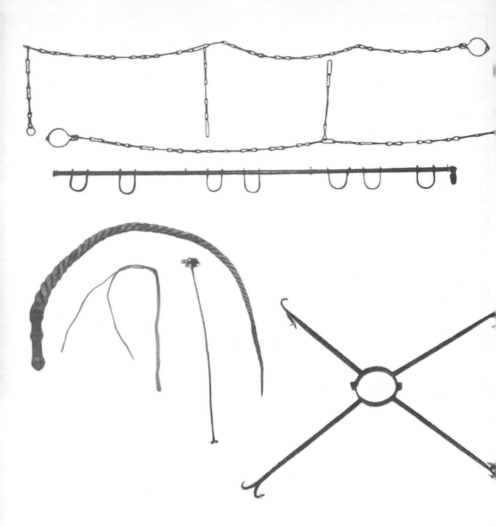

Branding irons, fetters, and whips used
by slave-traders

(*Opposite above*) The Myth of the Merry and Contented
Slave: a festival on St Vincent, 1794,
from an engraving after A. Brunyas

(*Opposite below left*) Thumb screws and
mouth openers

(*Opposite below right*) Fate of a rebel Negro in
Surinam, *c* 1772, from an engraving by
William Blake

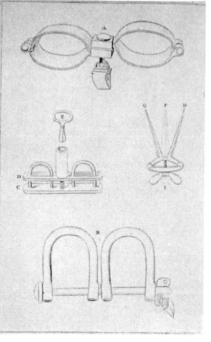

A West African slave market. In the centre a
French captain, to the right a French factor
(From the painting by A. F. Biard, Wilberforce Museum, Hull)

Forests of the Niger Delta

Efik trader's house, Calabar

Thomas Clarkson:
A portrait by C. F.
von Breda

AM I NOT A MAN AND A BROTHER.

Seal of the
Committee for the
Abolition of the
Slave Trade
formed in 1787

one hundred slaves fresh from the Gold Coast formed the core of the rebellion and were, as we have seen, given by an obeah man a magic preparation to render them invulnerable. Assembling at one o'clock in the morning, they broke into the fort at Port Maria, killed the sentry and seized arms and ammunition. Joined by slaves from neighbouring plantations they marched inland up the high road, attacking Ballard's Valley, Esher and other sugar estates, burning houses and canes and slaughtering white men, women and children as they went. They were further alleged to have drunk their victims' blood diluted with rum. Tacky, the chief, was killed in the forests; of the three other ringleaders two were hung up in irons and left to die, whilst another was forced to sit upon the ground, chained to an iron stake, and slowly burned alive, beginning with his legs. Up aloft, his two fellow conspirators survived on their gibbets for nine days, chattering to a crowd of friends who surrounded them and at times exchanging jokes with each other – 'I remember' wrote an English eye-witness, 'that both he and his fellow sufferer laughed immoderately at something that occurred – I know not what.'

The only method by which the bewildered planters could find out who, in such rebellions, were the obeah-men responsible, was, rather naturally, by bullying or bribing a captured rebel into giving names. In the Jamaican revolt of 1760, one of the prisoners denounced his obeah leaders on the promise that his own life would be spared. The chief of these priests was then executed, although he defiantly declared up to the moment of his death that 'it was not in the power of the white people to kill him.' 'And the negroes (spectators)' (runs the account of his execution) 'were greatly perplexed when they saw him expire. Upon other obeah-men, who were apprehended at that time, various experiments were made with electrical machines and magic lanterns, but with very little effect.' It would seem that, in this tentative, puerile pitting of European technology against African magic, African magic had won.

Gazing even so briefly upon these plantation scenes, lit by the fitful, lurid flames of cruelty and smoky with suspicion and distrust, we may well begin to wonder who, if anyone, did in fact benefit by the Atlantic slave trade? The answer is the thousands of persons indirectly but profitably involved: the absentee landowners living in their country-houses and their city mansions in Europe; the shipowners and merchants of Bristol, or Lisbon, or Nantes; the manufacturers, exporters and importers; and the governments and monarchies of Europe which levied taxes on commercial prosperity. These governments and monarchies had striven for decades to monopolize the slave trade through their own agencies. The government agencies – Royal African Company, *Compagnie des Indes* or Dutch West India Company, amongst others – were gradually defeated by the hawk-like slaving privateers, called 'interlopers'; but these agencies' efforts and their shaky organizations require some mention here.

## Chapter 9

# 'The Attractive African Meteor'

## I

IF, OF all the forms of sea-borne commerce in the eighteenth century, 'the African trade' was the most risky, it was also, when successful, one of the most profitable. Implicit in it was a breathless element of gambling, for nobody could predict the results of any single slaving voyage: 'The African commerce holds forward one constant train of uncertainty' wrote a knowledgeable citizen of Liverpool in 1797:* 'the time of slaving is precarious, the length of the middle passage uncertain, a vessel may be in part, or wholly, cut off, mortalities may be great and various other incidents may arise impossible to be foreseen'. The planters, moreover, might ultimately prove unable to honour their long-term bills.

On the other hand, since the price of slaves on the coast varied little and was seldom exorbitant, their food on the Middle Passage reckoned at ten shillings per head, and their freight at £3. 5s., the gain on each slave sold in the colonies was well over thirty per cent. Thus, in the years 1783 to 1793, the net profit to the town of Liverpool on an aggregate of 303,737 slaves sold was almost three million pounds, or about three hundred thousand pounds per annum. This was the golden harvest which accounts for all – for the fetid, feverish weeks upon the African coast, for the vile and dangerous Atlantic

---

* 'Circumstantial Account of the True Causes of the African Slave Trade, by an Eye Witness, Liverpool, 1797', printed in *Liverpool and Slavery* (Liverpool 1884) and partially reproduced in Donnan, vol. II. Although the eye witness balanced his figures with all the cupidity and care of some Swiss hotel-keeper, his results underestimate the profit per slave and were corrected by Gomer Williams in his *History of Liverpool Privateers*.

145

crossing, for the sordid scramble in the Guinea-yard, for the callous division of Negro families condemned to a servitude which offered no future and held out no hope.

'This great annual return of wealth may be said to pervade the whole town,' the same Liverpudlian authority continues: 'increasing the fortunes of the principal adventurers, and contributing to the support of the majority of the inhabitants; almost every man in Liverpool is a merchant, and he who cannot send a bale will send a bandbox, it will therefore create little astonishment that the attractive African meteor has from time to time so dazzled their ideas that almost every order of people is interested in a Guinea cargo; it is to this influenza that so many small ships are seen in the annexed list.' At this time in Liverpool there were ten merchant houses of major importance engaged in the slave trade, together with three hundred and forty-nine lesser concerns. Small vessels taking up to one hundred slaves were outfitted by minor syndicates, organized by men of all professions. Attorneys, drapers, ropemakers, grocers, tallow chandlers, barbers or tailors might take shares in a slaving venture – some of them investing one eighth of the money, some a sixteenth, some a thirty-second. These investors of modest means were known as 'retailers of blackamoors' teeth'. Shipbuilding in Liverpool was gloriously stimulated by the slave trade, and so was every other ancillary industry connected with ships. Loaded shop-windows displayed shining chains and manacles, devices for forcing open Negroes' mouths when they refused to eat, neck-rings enhanced by long projecting prongs like those seen by General Tottenham in the streets of Bridgetown, Barbados, thumb-screws and all the other implements of torment and oppression. People used to say that 'several of the principal streets of Liverpool had been marked out by the chains, and the walls of the houses cemented by the blood, of the African slaves'. The Customs House sported carvings of Negroes' heads. 'It was the capital made in the African slave trade that built some of our docks' wrote a late Victorian Liverpool essayist. 'It was the price of human flesh and blood that gave us a start.'

With so much at stake – in 1790 it was estimated that abolition of the slave trade would cost the city over seven and a half million pounds – Liverpool merchants naturally formed the most vocal and the most highly organized of all the interested pressure groups opposing Wilberforce's movement. 'What vain pretence of liberty can infatuate people into so much licentiousness as to assert a trade is unlawful which custom immemorial, and various Acts of Parliament, have ratified and given sanction to?' ran one rhetorical question current in the city at that time. So far as slave-trading was concerned, Liverpool may be said to have gone down with flags flying; for in the last sixteen months before Abolition became law, her merchants managed to ship forty-nine thousand, two hundred and thirteen slaves from Africa to the Sugar Islands in one hundred and eighty-five vessels. Very suitably the last slaver to sail from a British port – the date for the official end of the slave trade was set at the first of May 1807 – was a Liverpool ship under command of our friend the famous local slave captain, Hugh Crow. This cosy individual, who towards the end of his life became one of the sights of Liverpool, was a Manx boy by birth and had spent seventeen years in the slave trade. He was respected as a shrewd, bluff, kindly and realistic man, who treated his Negro cargoes with such urbanity that former 'passengers' of his were alleged to run to welcome him when he made landfall at some West Indian island with a fresh load of slaves.

The degree of Liverpool, and indeed of Lancashire, involvement in the slave trade is well exemplified by an advertisement published in that city when Abolition was at length seen as imminent. 'Valuable Articles for the Slave Trade' were to be disposed of 'under Prime Cost in Consequence of the Expected Abolition'. The list included a vast quantity of 'negro guns', about ten thousand 'fine gold-laced hats', ten thousand gross 'negro knives, the whole cast iron', ten thousand gross pieces of 'fine negro linen', three tons of 'brilliant diamond necklaces' (at three shillings a pound, and made, of course, of glass), ten thousand dozen 'negro looking-glasses', and five thousand quarters of horse-beans. There was also three tons weight of 'hand and feet shackles and thumb screws' at a $1\frac{1}{2}d.$ a pound. Specimens were to be seen on exhibition at the Exchange – 'except the thumb screws, the sight of which it is thought would too deeply wound the feelings of those not inclined to purchase'.

To live and traffic in a recognized centre of the slave trade was not, for the people of a European sea-port, a matter of shame but a matter of pride. In France where *le trafic noir* generally constituted only one fifth or one eighth of the total commercial activity of any port, it was found none the less that this particular form of trade so affected all the others that any Atlantic port from Dunkirk to Bayonne might rightly be called *un port négrier*. But to Nantes itself was reserved the supreme slave-trading title: *la ville des négriers*. There grew up in Nantes great commercial dynasties rooted in the black traffic and bound together, in the French *bourgeois* fashion, by family marriages of reason: the Montaudoins, the O'Schiells, the Wailshes, the Bouteillers, the Grous, the de Guers. These Nantois merchant princes would pool their resources to fit out slaving expeditions. Such family patterns were, to a lesser degree, repeated in every French Atlantic port and, in the words of Professor Gaston-Martin,* *'justifient l'apparente boutade que toute la bourgeoisie maritime du XVIIIe siècle est, peu ou prou, négrière'.* Monsieur Gaston-Martin emphasizes the 'varied but tyrannical' tastes of the African slave-markets, the scarlet cloths, the mirrors and glass objects, the gleaming copper and brass – tastes formed and ruled by *'l'amour du clinquant et du bruit'.* As in England and in Holland, the slave trade stimulated French home production but though the Saintonges, the Nantes country, and the Basse-Normandie could supply brandies, Berry could supply serge and druggets, Choletais canvas, Mazamet bolts of linen, and Rouen the popular mock Indian and Guinea cottons which were dyed with indigo from the Sugar Islands, French slavers had to import mirrors, knives, arms and clay-pipes from Flanders, Holland and Germany. The officers were also allowed to ship French silks, fine glassware and porcelain for private sale to West Indian planters, a part of the cargo known as *'les pacotilles'.* The captain and officers on a French slaver lived in a comparative elegance and even luxury, with silver on their tables, fresh meat and poultry, and excellent wines. The crew drank *vin du pays* in quantity, and ate salted bacon, dried vegetables and preserved Irish beef. The slaves had to put up with their usual monotonous diet of beans, rice and gruel, sometimes, on French ships, improved by dried

* Of Bordeaux University, and author of *Histoire de L'Esclavage dans les Colonies Françaises* (Presses Universitaires de France, 1948) and of *Nantes au XVIIIe siècle: l'ère des Négriers* (Alcan, Paris, 1931).

turtle meat from Cape Verde, as well as by green vegetables when obtainable, and by cassava (otherwise known as manioc). These last were rough-and-ready precautions against the scurvy.

However rich and flourishing the French merchants investing in the slave trade might become, the impetus of slaving on French seaports and French industries was always less than the effect of its equivalent in England. In the earlier eighteenth century Bristol, Chester, Exeter, Liverpool, London, Lancaster and Plymouth all shouldered this lucrative burden; after the Act of Union of 1707, Glasgow – which as a Scottish port had been forbidden to take any part in trade to English colonies – also got on the strength. But the trade in slaves soon became concentrated on three ports – London, Bristol and Liverpool. In the first half of the century Bristol, as Professor Minchinton writes* 'wrested the leadership from London', and was, for a short mid-century period, the dominant British port in the trade. From fifty-two slaving ships equipped in Bristol in the peak year 1739, the city's interest in slaving declined noticeably, until in the decade 1795 to 1804 'only a total of twenty-nine vessels sailed for Africa'. This was a direct result of the swift and dazzling rise of the attractive African meteor on the over-cast shores of the Mersey. Upstart Liverpool had won the day. 'In 1792, when the trade was at its height,' wrote a Liverpool historian earlier in this present century,† 'it was estimated that Liverpool enjoyed five-eighths of the English trade in slaves, and three-sevenths of the whole slave trade of all the European nations.'

The defiant ascendancy of Liverpool (the city whose build-ings were said to be cemented with Negroes' blood) was attri-buted by contemporaries to its merchants' astute discovery of the potential value of a contraband slave trade with the Spanish Indies. Up to 1730 Liverpool's new prosperity had depended upon the sale to the West Indies of Manchester cottons. Soon these cottons were being smuggled into the Spanish possessions; and if cottons could be sold there illegally, why not slaves also? With the capital thus accumulated Liverpool entered the slave trade to the English colonies and could offer slaves to the

---

* *The Port of Bristol in the Eighteenth Century* by Walter Minchinton (Bristol Branch of the Historical Association, Bristol University, 1962).

† R. Muir: *History of Liverpool* (London, 1907).

planters of Jamaica and the other islands at four and five pounds less a head than the merchants of Bristol or of London. This question of the contraband slave trade with the possessions of the Spanish Crown brings us face to face with a once-famous monopoly, the *Asiento*, and with those other monopolistic but not successful prohibitionary efforts – the chartered slaving-companies of certain European powers.

## II

Some of the people we have so far seen have been Company men – Thomas Phillips, for instance, of the *Hannibal*, who slaved under the aegis of the Royal African Company; others, like John Newton, were controlled by private masters; others, again, were what were known as 'interlopers', determined persons working for themselves, poachers on the companies' alleged preserves. We shall indeed continue to watch such individuals – shortly, as it happens, we shall be joining the dissolute garrison of Cape Coast Castle, and visiting the care-worn factor of English Commenda as he struggles to protect his mud-and-oyster shell ramparts against the indefatigable on-slaught of the tropical rain. Both Sir Dalby Thomas, the general commanding at Cape Coast in the reign of Queen Anne, and Mr William Baillie, the Commenda factor some years later, were employees of the Royal African Company which owned and maintained the insalubrious castle and the dilapidated Commenda fort. To understand these men and their colleagues better, we must now envisage them within their frame. This frame, or proscenium, is formed by the rigid rules of the char-tered company. The backdrop to the stage is the lurid one of international war.

Like the private life of most individuals, the public and political life of nations is geared to survival and success. But it may also be described as one tireless effort at organization, at giving chaos form and unity, restraining anarchy and com-bating crime and greed. To render the fluid solid, the fleeting permanent, the unattainable captive, this would seem to be and to have always been the primary aspiration of human life. Just as the artist strives to enhance reality by interpreting it, so the merchant, law-protected, struggles to transmute it into gold. It was to give shape, speed and increased prosperity to the export trade in Africans that the European chartered slaving companies were born. Fool-proof in theory, looking neat and purposeful on paper, these particular chartered companies seldom lived up to expectations for long. Their finances were too top heavy. The risks involved were too great. Their monopolies were almost impossible to enforce.

The European device of the chartered company was, from its outset, an association for foreign trade. With the conquest of overseas territories these associations automatically became colonizing ones. The charters, granted by the state, set forth prescribed rules. Merchant members of a company might, if they could, employ exclusively their own capital in some single company venture, or they could pool their money with that of others in a joint-stock investment. Companies in colonial or foreign-trading areas were granted special and exclusive rights, and could exercise, in the name of their governments, treaty-making and law-enforcing powers. The history of such trading companies is, on the whole, ancient and honourable. The English Merchant Adventurers, for example, were incorporated as early as 1359, in the reign of Edward III. The British Eastland, aiming at the Russian trade, came into being in the reign of the first Tudor sovereign, Henry VII; the Hudson's Bay Company in that of the Stuart King, Charles II. To recall a few more: there was the English Virginia Company; there were the various or successive *Compagnies Africaines* of France (such as those of Cape Verde, of Senegal, of Guinea, of the West Indies and so on); there was the Dutch West India Company, incorporated in 1621; the Danish Company; the Swedish West India Company; the Brandenburg Company; and that famous and expensive English combine, the Royal African Company. Some of these were either incidentally or wholly slave-trading companies. Others, obviously, were not.

We are here concerned with chartered companies which conducted, and tried to protect from interlopers, the vast human traffic in Negroes to the western colonies. Since the capital outlay – building and equipping ships, paying crews more numerous than those of ordinary merchant-men, maintaining forts along the Guinea Coast – was very considerable, the resort to joint-stock companies was necessary from the beginning. As these companies glided into debt, and were forced to borrow at a high interest, the State was faced with demands for subsidies. These demands relentlessly increased. In its heyday the Royal African Company alone was receiving a grant of £10,000 a year, and the upkeep of its African establishments ran at £20,000 *per annum*. The Danish Company on the coast received 93,000 kroner. All monopolies arouse hostility: in the case of these African chartered companies the monopoly was resented by adventurers who were officially excluded from trading, by home manufacturers who found their export trade artificially restricted, and by the transatlantic planters who complained that the companies never shipped sufficient slaves and charged more for them than privateers. Further, the international proliferation of these companies inspired jealousies and gave rise to wars – wars often private and undeclared, but, on occasion, wars on an international scale as well. In the longest, bloodiest and most widespread of the European conflicts of the first half of the eighteenth century, the War of the Spanish Succession which lasted from 1702 until 1714, the chief objective of the English, Dutch and German allies was to ensure that the descendants of Louis XIV were kept off the thrones of Spain, the Spanish Netherlands and the Spanish Indies – but, for the English, the secondary war-aim was to get legal rights to the *Asiento*, granted by the Spanish crown to the French Guinea Company in 1702. By this time the Spanish word *asiento* – literally a contract or agreement – had taken on the specialized meaning of the monopoly for shipping African slaves to the colonies of Spain. 'Inevitably' (writes a leading historian of the Spanish Empire) 'it was used as an instrument of Spanish foreign policy. Charles II and William III of England both failed to secure the *Asiento* for their subjects. Political circumstances . . . favoured the French.' So did religious circumstances, since the Spaniards were averse to granting the monopoly to an heretic nation. The fact that this *Asiento*, at length secured by the English at the Treaty of Utrecht in 1713, turned out, in the words of another historian, to be 'a glittering illusion' merely confirms the hackneyed fact that the fruits of martial victory are scarcely ever as covetable as they seem. The single word *Asiento* flits through every history book dealing with the transatlantic colonies or with the slave trade in a manner which, were it not for the dull prose that tethers it, we might liken to the will-o'-the-wisp that this monopoly actually proved to be.

The origin of the *Asiento* lay in Spain's lack of forts on the coast of Africa, and her consequent dependence on the Portuguese, the Genoese and, from 1702 till 1713, the French to supply slaves to the Spanish colonies. Although the legendary wealth and power of the Spanish crown was also largely an illusion, it became an obsessive one amongst the other nations of Europe. Also, despite the lack of effective centralization, the weakness of a succession of feeble Hapsburg occupants of the Spanish throne, the venality of Spain's viceroys in the colonies, and the inadequacy of her naval and military power, the sheer extent of the Spanish possessions in the west made them for many generations far and away the most rewarding market for the traders in slaves. Moreover, we are here less concerned with the sorry economic and political truths sheltering behind the grandiose façade of the Spanish Empire than with the effect which English or Dutch credulity about it had upon the fate of individual African villagers paddling their canoes across the Calabar River, or stumbling down in slave-coffles from up-country Gold Coast towns. Quite as much as the European soldiers and horsemen who fought on smoking battlefields at Blenheim or at Oudenarde, at Ramillies or Malplaquet, the peasantry of West Africa had a personal and anonymous stake in this war of prevention and aggrandizement. While a Yorkshire or a Norman youth pressed into his country's service might lose an arm or a leg in battle so, in far-off Africa, might his Negro contemporary – an Ashanti boy, or an Ebo – be enduring the equally novel experience of being manacled and fettered, branded, lashed and thrown into a slave ship's hold. For the battle-maimed of Europe there were such refuges as the Royal Chelsea Hospital or the Hôtel des Invalides. The Africans made captive were headed for the silver mine or the plantation. In the holocausts on Flanders fields thousands of European men were doomed to die that their governments might keep, or seize, the coveted *Asiento*. In Africa their counterparts and fellow-sufferers, the captive Negroes, were doomed to live.

As I have suggested, the Spanish noun, *Asiento*, with its attendant, varying and usually unreliable statistics of slaves shipped under its licence, haunts history books with repetitive monotony. It was not until, seated one winter's morning at a polished table in the Kress Room of the Harvard Business School, I was brought a bound and printed copy of this contract, published in London after the English had won the monopoly in 1713, that the noun *Asiento* took on for me a species of reality. This thin, square volume, with a triumphantly heraldic title-page, contained the legal clauses of the *Asiento*. Lurking in these precise and well-spaced paragraphs lay the fate of how many long-dead Africans, the mute and unknown victims of the cruellest form the business of making money has yet found. Even so, in those tranquil surroundings, snowflakes drifting densely outside the windows, silence and comfort within, it was hard to connect the anodyne and elegant appearance of this English version of the *Asiento* with its callous commercial implications and its criminal results.

# III

By the Asiento Treaty of 1713 a monopoly to transport to the Spanish colonies a total of almost five thousand slaves a year for a period of thirty years was granted to the British South Sea Company. This particular chartered company had been founded in 1711 for the purpose of general trading with the overseas territories of Spain, including the Pacific islands. It throve so swiftly and so well that in 1718 King George I himself became its Governor; two years later the bulk of its enthusiastic shareholders found themselves ruined in the financial collapse known to history as 'the South Sea Bubble'.

Despite this spacious scandal, the South Sea Company continued feebly to function. Together with the slaving monopoly, the Spaniards had, with reluctance, granted permission for the British to send one ship, laden with British manufactured goods, to the annual fairs at Porto Bello and at Vera Cruz. This concession led to much contraband traffic by British smugglers, which in turn provoked retaliation by the Spaniards. The Anglo-Spanish war of 1739 interrupted the *Asiento* trade; although the contract was renewed for another four years at the Peace of Aix-la-Chapelle in 1748 the British relinquished the

*Asiento* in 1750 on payment by the Spanish Government of £100,000. Under the *Asiento*, the British Company had been granted facilities at a number of Spanish transatlantic ports, where it sold many of its slaves and thousands of others landed for 'refreshment'. At Buenos Aires the Company owned a factory, and in 1717 purchased the estate of El Retiro near the city. This suburban area, still known today as *El Retiro de los Ingleses*, was used as a huge slave depôt. The South Sea Company's slaving activities largely consisted of shipping seasoned slaves from Jamaica and other West Indian islands, for it owned no forts on the coast of Africa. These all remained in the hands of the Royal African Company until the middle of the eighteenth century. After the Royal African Company's dissolution in the years 1750 to 1752 the coastal forts and castles were kept up by a committee of English merchants dependent on Government subsidies.

Chartered in 1672, the Royal African Company was heir to its predecessor, the Company of Royal Adventurers of England Trading to Africa. This by-product of the Restoration of Charles the Second had been created in the year 1663, under the patronage of the King's brother, James, Duke of York, later King James the Second. Hardly had the Company been formed, when the Dutch Admiral de Ruyter set sail for Africa, capturing every English factory and stronghold with the exception of Cape Coast Castle, which had excellent defences, and where the African townspeople showed an aggressive loyalty to its owners. The news of how the English had been, in Samuel Pepys' words, 'beaten to dirt at Guinea' provoked the Royal Company to appeal to Charles the Second for support. The result was the outbreak, in 1665, of the Second Anglo-Dutch War – a conflict popularly interpreted as a war for the West African trading stations. In fact, at the war's end in 1667, Cape Coast Castle alone remained in English hands. By the peace treaty signed at Breda in 1667 the Dutch kept the forts and factories they had conquered, and, for a short time, controlled the trade in slaves; but the English soon began to establish new forts along the coast, and they reconstructed Cape Coast Castle on a large and important scale. In 1672 the Royal African Company was chartered and, in return for a trade monopoly, undertook to keep up the Castle and the forts. The Company's objectives in

Africa were dual: the import into England of such local products as gold, ivory and dye-wood, and the export to the West Indian plantations of Negroes as slaves. In spite of royal patronage and rich shareholders, the finances of the organization were always strained; it has been estimated that to make a decent profit one hundred thousand pounds' worth of English goods would have had to be shipped to West Africa annually, but this total value was never fully reached. The upkeep of the African forts was a major item of expenditure, and helped to push the Royal African Company further and further into debt.

Expensive though they proved to the Company, these fortified trading stations on the rim of Africa were never manned on a lavish scale. Thus, in the year 1676, the establishment agreed upon for Cape Coast Castle consisted of sixty-one white men – the Agent-General and his council, five young factors, one officer, two sergeants, a surgeon, a chaplain and forty-seven soldiers – assisted by some thirty 'castle-slaves'. At Accra there were only seven Europeans and four slaves, and at Commenda a chief factor, a second-in-command, three soldiers and four slaves. As the trade expanded and more factories were set up, the complement of Europeans naturally increased also, until the Company's establishment reached a peak aggregate of 'well over three hundred white men besides castle-slaves'. Not in themselves especially memorable, these figures form all the same an interesting contrast to those of the number of African captives the Company delivered annually to the West Indies. In the early sixteen-eighties, for instance, when the Company's manpower was minimal, this handful of white officials contrived to have transported to the Caribbean colonies an average of five thousand Negro human beings a year. Not all these white employees of the Royal African Company were Englishmen; Irish, Dutch, French and Portuguese were indiscriminately recruited to replace English officials and soldiers who had died at their posts. These frequent deaths give to the surviving memo books of the coastal forts the funereal quality of a dirge.

## IV

Massive yet inchoate, the Royal African Company's castle at Cape Coast forms a rather tumbledown contrast to the brisk elegance and order of the old Portuguese and Dutch head-quarters at Elmina, eight miles west along the coast. Rendered impregnable from the sea by the smooth black rocks on which it stands and over which the breakers toss and thunder, the castle has a small landing beach below its eastern flank. From the town side it was entered by a high gateway, now as always undefended by drawbridge or ditch. The leading authority on the coastal castles and trade forts, Professor A. W. Lawrence, has characterized the modern condition of Cape Coast Castle as archaeologically 'disgusting' – and it does indeed require imagination to visualize the castle in its prime, for nineteenth-century alterations and accretions (including a clutter of shoddy lean-tos which shelter an overspill from the population of the town) scar the walls of the vast paved inner court, which, irregular in shape, slopes towards the sea.

The Company's foreign guests of long ago would comment on the 'slovenliness' of the English officials at Cape Coast, and on their regard for 'nothing so much as enriching themselves at the expense of their masters'. An isolated outpost above the castle, named Fort Royal, and intended to protect it from land-ward attack, had, by 1699, been so neglected for years that it looked 'more like a desolate country cottage than a fortress; its shattered walls being mended with clay, and its house within covered with reeds, as those of the negroes'. Six pieces of enemy cannon on this hilltop could have reduced the great castle to rubble, and it was not until 'some well meaning officer' des-cribed to the London committee of the Royal African Company Fort Royal's derelict state that orders were given to rebuild it. Bosman was shown the scale model for the little fortress, and also saw builders actually at work upon the hill: 'I dare engage when it is finished the English may safely depend on it' he noted; 'but the building advances so slowly that Heaven knows when that will be.' All the same, foreigners were struck by the size and strength of Cape Coast Castle itself in its pristine state – by the lofty living quarters lined with brick, the arcaded out-door balcony to which 'handsome staircases' gave access from the court, by the 'stately' central hall, the comfortable apart-ments for the Agent-General and his factors, the counting houses, store-rooms and shops. Equally impressive were the vaulted slave-dungeons, hewn from the heart of the rock, and capable of containing one thousand slaves at a time: 'the keeping of slaves thus underground' noted a French seventeenth-century observer 'is a good security to the garrison against any insurrection'. These dark, capacious caverns, dim prisons that reek of bat-droppings and decay, curiously combine the musty with the damp. That they were situated underground seems to make them symbolic as well as secure, for here lay coiled the sad and sunless roots of the prosperity for which the Company's officials strove in their chambers and their offices above. As you emerge from them back into the bubbling heat of the paved courtyard the African sun and even the African rain seem welcome.

As a respite from the sun-scorched Castle yards and battlements, successive Agents of the Royal African Company planted private gardens, constantly extended and fresh with groves of orange-trees, lemon-trees and limes. Criss-crossed by long, trim walks and policies, these gardens stretched northward of the castle, not far from the sea-shore, into an area now covered by a part of Cape Coast town. The sea-winds made the gardens airy, and in a little summer-house amidst them *al fresco* dinner parties would be held. Adjacent to these pleasure-gardens lay the burial-ground, crude with its perennial, lumpy harvest: the crimson earth-mounds of new graves.

If we take the entries in the castle 'writer's' records for any single year – January 1703 to January 1704, for instance, when Sir Dalby Thomas was Agent-General for the Royal African Company – we get some idea of the sense of mortality pervading life within the castle walls: 'died, Mr Richard Woosley, factor . . . died John Gonsalvo, a soldier . . . died John Smith, gun-smith . . . died Mr Alexander Nicols, factor', runs the record for the comparatively healthy six weeks, late January to late February 1703. In the first week of May a soldier named Anthony Guilding, James Walkden, a cook, and Mr Parsons, a Company writer, all died. For the remainder of May four further deaths are recorded – those of John Wilkie, a barber, William Pack, a soldier, John Ancketill, factor, John Hunt, surgeon's mate. Summer deaths began with that of a young Company apprentice, Thomas Watts, and continued with those of seven soldiers – Leonard Rademaker, Richard Walkden, Thomas Crawfourd, Thomas Evans, Francis Fry, William

Rouse, Robert Adamson – as well as with the death of Mr
Murray, the Company factor from Dixcove. In September a
Dutch soldier, Cornelius Decker, found dead, was thought to be
a suicide; another Company apprentice and a Welsh soldier
named Evans were buried a week later. In November there
were eight deaths – four soldiers, another apprentice, a carpenter, the Scottish barber's widow, Mrs Wilkie. There were
three more before the end of the year. Since the factories down
the coast seldom or never had a medical attendant, invalid
Europeans were sent by canoe to Cape Coast to recover or to
die: 'John George Rine, soldier, came from Dixcove for his
health.' Health, we may think, was not so easy a commodity
to come by at Cape Coast.

As we have seen, European officials on the coast died young,
thus clearing the way for the promotion of underlings. This was
particularly true of the red-coats (the European soldiers in the
Company's pay), and presumably of the gromettos or freeborn
Negro soldiers who supplemented the regular garrison, had
their own scarlet uniforms and their own officers, and were likewise on the Royal African Company's payroll. Whereas the
Company's agent, his immediate entourage, and the military
officers under him ate good provisions sent out from Europe, or
purchased from passing ships, or presented by attentive African
traders, the soldiers lived on fish and scrawny fowls. Their
superiors obtained good poultry, well-salted meat, gammon,
tongue, fine flour, olive oil, preserves, fruit, pickles, French
wines and Madeira, old brandy and, in their frequent need, the
best available medicines and restoratives. The soldiers, labourers
and canoemen, who worked long hours in all kinds of filthy
weather, had no other real resource in sickness or in health than
palm-wine, brandy and rum punch; in serious illness they were
at the mercy of amateur surgeons, who doled out 'wretched
medicines'. These soldiers were, naturally, men without education and without aim in life, often the riff-raff of the coast who
had drifted into the Company's service to replace the dead.

Alcoholism reigned at all levels of the Cape Coast hierarchy,
the factors and officers providing bowls of punch for themselves
and their guests on any and every occasion. The English
officers and men who managed to elude death looked yellowish
and prematurely wizened. At night the drunken soldiers would

fling themselves down to sleep in the open air, wearing nothing but a shirt. Nobody took heed of the strange unwelcome advice of foreigners like the Frenchman Barbot, who had an elementary medical knowledge and warned 'some of the principal men' at Cape Coast of the unwisdom of their ways: 'nothing is more pernicious to the constitution of Europeans than to lie in the open air . . . Thinking thus to cool, but, on the contrary, they murder themselves'. Barbot considered that his own good health was in part due to the fact that he kept his bed 'as warm as I could well bear it', and that beneath his clothes he wore a dressed hare's skin next his belly. To this stuffy prophylactic Barbot attributed his immunity to the fevers, fluxes, cholics, worms and dropsies which riddled the inmates of the English forts. He wore his hare's skin for two solid years together and declared that this measure kept his stomach 'in a good disposition, and helped digestion very much; though I must own it was sometimes, and especially in the excessive hot nights, very troublesome and occasioned much sweating'. Although a Huguenot refugee in English employ, Barbot, like his Dutch contemporary Bosman, found a distinct source of *Schadenfreude* in his belief that Englishmen on the coast of Africa were even more careless of their health than the men of other nations. He criticized the English soldiery for expending too much money and energy on the local African women, 'whose natural hot and lewd temper soon wastes their bodies, and consumes what little substance they have'. He asserted – quite probably with truth – that English officials had five or six Negro mistresses apiece, and also that Agents-General made money on the side by selling brandy and rum to the soldiers of the garrison, penalizing those who did not use up the bulk of their meagre pay on these costly spirits. Punch, Barbot thought peculiarly dangerous: 'It is incredible how many are consumed by this damnable liquor . . . which is not only confined to the soldiery, but some of the principal people are so bigotted to it, that I really believe for all the time I was upon the Coast, that at least one of their agents and factors innumerable died yearly of it.'

And so the Cape Coast graveyard, like the pleasure-gardens, grew.

# V

It would be ridiculous, however, to regard Cape Coast Castle in these early years of the reign of Queen Anne as nothing but a costly necropolis. The faces peering from the battlements might be emaciated by fever or flecked scarlet with the blotches and the pustules of debauch. The impatient sound of the coffin-maker's hammer might echo through the yards, and the new graves in the sunshine lie ominous and raw. But all the same the routine of life at Cape Coast trudged steadily onwards. European recruits turned up to fill the places of Rademaker and Walkden, Gonsalvo, Fry, Evans and the other soldiers and factors who had enlisted in the ranks of Death. Company ships and 'ten per centers'* swarmed in the roads. They would drop anchor for a night or two, fill up with slaves and set sail once more for the open Atlantic and the West. Other ships laden with building materials – oyster-shells from Winnebah, boards and nails – would call in on their way to some tottering factory down the coast. Timber-ships would stop off for provisions, their enviable destination a healthy port at home. The Company's Agent-General would preside over palavers between local potentates, persuade them to take a fetish oath not to trade with the Dutch at Elmina, and, later, entertain these kinglets at his board. Protests and counter-protests to the Dutch authorities would be concluded by ceremonial courtesy visits, marked by insincere speeches and ending in carouse. Deserters from the garrison would be pursued, runaway company slaves dragged back from freedom and made to suffer the usual penalty of a lopped ear. Young Company Negroes would be trained to master the art of horn-blowing. At reveille the high gates would swing open to the dawn bustle of the town. At curfew they would close, and serious drinking would begin.

Against this swirling background, the Agent-General daily dealt with problems which were often intricate, sometimes

* One result of the Glorious Revolution of 1688 had been the loosening-up of the unpopular system of royal monopolies. Thus, in June 1698, Parliament had passed an Act 'to settle the trade to Africa'. By this, for a period of ten years, private traders were permitted to send their ships to and from Africa, on payment to the Royal African Company of a tax of ten per cent on the value of their merchandise. This Act, a compromise disliked by the Company, was hard to enforce, but the 'ten per centers' soon became a major feature of the African trade.

dangerous and in almost every case elusive. His perfectly thankless job demanded both flexibility and talent: from moment to moment he was expected to switch roles – now the strict Governor and disciplinarian, now the merchant or the diplomat, the intermediary, the adviser, the arbiter, the king-maker or the judge of appeal. Probably Sir Dalby Thomas, and perhaps some few of his successors, made an effort to live up to these ideals; but the majority of Governors-General at Cape Coast became notorious as corrupt autocrats. They treated their underlings like 'white negroes', a phrase used by the surgeon John Atkins, author of the popular *Voyage to Guinea* published in London in 1737. Atkins had sailed as surgeon in a naval expedition sent from England in 1721 to chase off the coast of Guinea the pirates who were yet another menace to the Company's limping trade. His account of the state of affairs at Cabo Corso (as Cape Coast was frequently called) was not encouraging to the shareholders.

'The Factory' (wrote Atkins):

consists of merchants, factors, writers, miners, artificers and soldiers; and excepting the first rank, who are the Council for man-aging affairs, are all of them together a company of white negroes, who are entirely resigned to the Governor's commands, according to the strictest rules of discipline and subjection; are punished (gar-rison fashion) on several defaults, with mulcts, confinement, the dungeon, drubbing or the wooden horse; and for enduring this, they have each of them a salary sufficient to buy canky,* palm-oil and a little fish to keep them from starving; for though the salaries sound tolerably in Leadenhall Street (50 to 90 l. per ann. a factor; 50 an artificer) yet in the country here, the General (for the Company's good) pays them in *crackra*, a false money which is only current upon the spot, and disables them from taking advantage of buying neces-saries from ships coasting down . . . so that for the support of Nature, or perhaps indulging youthful follies, these thin creatures are obliged to take up of the Company and in effect by it sign over their Liberty; none being admitted to depart till he has adjusted his accounts. When a man is too sober to run in debt, there are arts of mismanagement or loss of goods under his care, to be charged or wanting. Thus they are all liable to be mulcted for drunkenness,

* Canky or conky was a staple food made of fermented corn, and still, under its native name of *kenki*, eaten throughout Ghana today. The English baked it, while the Negroes boiled it and made little buns or rolls.

swearing, neglects and lying out of the Castle, even for not going to church (such is their piety); and thus by various arbitrary methods their service is secured *durante bene placito*.

He added that the town Negroes were encouraged to run into debt in the same way for goods and drams, and so became Company pawns 'i.e. liable to be sold when the General thinks fit'. Factors at some of the out-forts were allowed a percentage on the trade they secured; but 'at others again, Anamabu, or Dixcove, they find a great deal of trouble, wet lodging, scarcity of provision and no profit'. Atkins noted the inevitable deterioration in morale and physique of these European slaves of the slave trade: 'I observed most of our factors to have dwindled much from the genteel air they brought; wear no cane or snuff-box, idle in men of business, have lank bodies, a pale visage, their pockets sewn up or of no use, and their tongues tied. One cause of their slenderness indeed is a scarcity of provision; little beside plantain, small fish, Indian corn and a great deal of canky, to be bought at market.' He also describes the slave-vaults at Cape Coast: 'in the area of this quadrangle are large vaults, with an iron gate at the surface to let in light and air on those poor wretches, the slaves, who are chained and confined there till a demand comes. They are all marked with a burning iron upon the right breast, D.Y. Duke of York.'*

Within the Castle walls the power of the Agent-General at Cape Coast was absolute; outside the ramparts it was ill-defined and was based more on diplomacy than on gunpower. He had neither the means nor the men to combat the host of privateers, nor to prevent the cheating in which the 'ten per cent men' freely indulged. Keeping face was therefore a major factor in successful trading. The quality of his men was low, and the size and strength of the garrisons both at the Castle and the out-factories were consistently slashed by orders for economy from the Company's governing body in Leadenhall Street. Further, there was the fundamental anomaly of the European presence on the Coast – the ownership and maintenance of forts, the sites of which were never Company property but held on ancient verbal grants and leases, which meant in reality held on

---

* The Royal African Company's factors were evidently still using the old brand dating from the original formation of the Company under James, Duke of York in 1672.

sufferance. In time of war, enemy ships might attack from the sea, but at any moment a mass of discontented Africans might launch a surprise onslaught from the land. Despite what was then called 'the custom of the Coast' – a traditional, unwritten code governing European relations with the leading Africans and the dues levied by these – one bitter fact stood out: the slave trade was ultimately controlled by a clutch of local kings and caboceers (head-men), who could sell or withhold slaves at will, raise the prices as they wished, lie, intrigue, and set one group of European nationals against another. Adroit and greedy for gain, these Africans might likewise suddenly demand protection and support in local wars. They had to be kept sweet by bribes and hospitality.

At Cape Coast Castle only the chief African traders were invited to 'go above stairs for drams' and then they were asked to stand at the door while drinking; but at small stations like Commenda Fort and other out-factories we are told that:

the traders use more freedom than at Cape Coast and will ask drams as oft as they come into the Castle for them and all their people, and sometimes several times at one visit; besides if they see any beer, they'll be sure to ask some, which is an extravagant charge for a chief [factor] to bear, since the Company will not allow it on their own trade, which is to be carried on for their sole benefit and advantage without allowing the merchant any, at least very inconsiderable, profit to himself.

Africans trading in slaves with the out-factories were consequently in a formidably strong position, of which they took advantage to the full: if the local factor did not hand out to them sufficient dashes and drams they would hawk their human wares to the factory of some more generous European national, or sell them secretly to privateers who sought to evade the shipping tax of ten per cent. 'The Gentlemen' as these disgruntled small-station factors called the members of the Royal African Company's Council at the Cape Coast headquarters, grew sour and plaintive if the supply of slaves, ivory and gold diminished; but the sole way of trying to keep up an even flow of such merchandise was by the factor's spending most of his own salary on presents and free drink for the caboceers. Cajolery was at a premium.

At Cape Coast the Agent-General, like the Dutch commander at Elmina, strove to establish a feudal and entirely fictive theory of African liegedom to his Royal Company. In April 1703, for instance, Sir Dalby Thomas summoned the 'grand' and 'petty' caboceers (or leading native traders) to a conference in the palaver hall. Here he told them that he regarded them as 'vassals to the Royal African Company of England and as long as they behaved themselves faithfully towards the Company he would not suffer them to be ill-used, and if any did attempt anything against them he would look upon it as done against the Company'. The assumption of a moral obligation that these fine words implied was, in the immediate neighbourhood of European forts, almost as much a part of the price paid for slaves as were the actual guns, iron bars, brassware, beads, calicoes and cowrie-shells for which the captive Africans were bought. In this sense White Power along the coast was little more than an uncomfortable and precarious myth, wholly dependent on the good-will and the cupidity of the coastal Africans engaged in the European trade. Together with the eternal demands for rum and brandy, the requests for armed support in tribal squabbles formed, indeed, one of the only constants in the bemusing business of the slave trade. The 'fanciful and various humours of the negroes' would make them reject one month the very commodities they had 'itched after' the month before. To young and inexperienced traders and ships' masters these whims proved exasperating and could even ruin their prospects of trade. The answer was high-pressure salesmanship, aimed to persuade the Africans to accept goods they did not really want; or else an excellent system of intelligence reports on what was or was not fashionable at any given moment up and down the coast. This was called 'the timing of a cargo'; the 'sorting of the cargo' followed, on the whole, certain established rules. Old Africa hands knew better than to offer iron bars on the Leeward Coast, although these were highly valued to Windward. Crystals, corals and brass-mounted cutlasses were only wanted on the Windward Coast. Brass pans were in demand from Rio Sestos to Apollonia. Cowrie-shells from the Maldive Islands were essential for trading at Whydah, where they were used internally as currency. At Calabar and in the other Oil River ports iron bars had to be supplemented with bars of copper. Spirits were in demand everywhere, and so were arms, gunpowder, tallow and brightly coloured cottons. Yet in this confusing world of bribery, caprice, alcoholism and largely unenforceable European threats, the representatives of the chartered companies could rely on one stable element, in itself a tribute to African character. This was the Negro leaders' wholehearted respect for any agreement sealed by fetish oath.

Examples of this reliance on the absolute validity of the fetish oath occur again and again in the history of the chartered companies. We may take as one example an exchange, in June 1703, between Sir Dalby Thomas and the messengers sent to him by a group of anglophile African caboceers of Sekondee. They had appealed to the Agent-General because the Dutch were 'disturbing' them. These Dutch traders were then well established at Fort Orange, some one hundred and fifty miles west of Cape Coast Castle, and looking down over Sekondee Bay. Within gunshot of Fort Orange stood a dilapidated English fort which the caboceers friendly to the Royal African Company now wished to see restored as a protection against the Dutch. Sir Dalby sent word that the Company would neither rebuild nor garrison the fort, nor indeed have anything to do with the people of Sekondee at all, unless the caboceers took a fetish oath 'to be true to the interest of the Royal African Company of England and promise they will use their endeavours to bring all the trade they can to the English fort'. They were also asked to swear that should the Dutch, or any Sekondee people loyal to them, attack the English fort or try to damage English interests, they would themselves at least stay neutral even if they could not actively assist the tiny English garrison.

This conception of the binding quality of the fetish oath was the nearest to that of a gentlemen's agreement which the companies ever reached with Africans. So long as the shareholders could afford to employ men like Sir Dalby Thomas, who was paid £1,250 a year and did a longish stint upon the Coast, such agreements worked. But with the gradual impoverishment of the companies, and their defeat by the swarms of separate traders* the tone of the trade declined. In the last two years of

---

* In the eight years after the passing of the ten per cent legislation in 1698 it was estimated that the Royal African Company imported into the West Indies only 17,760 slaves, while the separate traders shipped 71,268 in the same period.

the seventeenth century the directors of the Dutch West India Company decided to entrust the trade at their forts of Mouri and Cormantin to ships' masters instead of resident factors, an experiment dictated by economy but which Bosman (who knew what he was writing about) believed to be a mistake – 'for the commanders of ships, though very expert in all sea affairs, yet being unacquainted with the negroes will not be able to succeed very well: besides that some of them are of such a boorish nature that they hardly know how to preserve the honour of the Company amongst the negroes . . . and I cannot believe it will turn to the advantage of the Company'. A typical instance of ignorant behaviour on the part of such a ship-captain – in this case an English master, one Thomas Meale – is recorded in the Cape Coast Memorandum Book to which I have been referring. Meale, who commanded a ten per cent ship, the *Queen*, had seized one of the Negroes sent on board by the caboceers of Cape Coast to demand the usual fee for watering, whereupon the caboceers had 'panyared' (or kidnapped) the surgeon and certain others of the *Queen*'s crew who had gone ashore. Sir Dalby Thomas intervened, and Captain Meale sent him a letter of apology 'to pardon his error in carrying off the man, occasioned only about some words he had with him, he not knowing the custom of the Coast'. He sent the man back with the money owed to the caboceers. The surgeon and the crew were then released. Such arrogant contempt for the custom of the Coast soon ceased, amongst eighteenth-century slave-traders, to be the odd exception and became the rough-and-ready rule.

A further potent reason for the collapse of the Company system were the rivalries of the slave-trading nations – English, Dutch, French, Danish and Portuguese. The most mutually damaging was the rivalry of the English and the Dutch. From the bastion at Cape Coast the strutting English factors could watch by telescope the ships congregated in the Elmina roads. From Elmina, equally, the Dutch could keep an eye on Cape Coast. All down the shoreline of the Gold Coast, Dutch and English stations and forts were scattered. In a few places, such as Sekondee and Commenda, a Dutch and an English fort stood within gunshot of one another. Between these a wary fraternization would take place.

## VI

The proximity of the Dutch headquarters at Elmina to the English headquarters at Cape Coast was naturally fruitful of suspicion and ill-will. Dutch deserters would flee from Elmina to enlist in the English garrison; sometimes they were accepted, sometimes they were turned away at the gates. It was tacitly agreed in theory that the Dutch traders should not sell slaves to the English ten per centers, and that the English should not help the Dutch interlopers. In practice this theory did not work. The English view was that, with the boorish Dutch, you never knew where you were. In March 1703 a Captain Valentine, commanding the ten per center *Mayflower* from London, arrived at Cape Coast and 'complained at dinner that, his boat going to the Mine, the Dutch did refuse to give a glass of water to drink to two of his people that went ashore'. At other times the Dutch General would do all he could to undercut the Royal African Company by supplying the English ships with slaves: 'He is the ten per cent men's Diana' Sir Dalby Thomas wrote to his London employers in May 1705 'and they pay all adoration, with great presents, to him. In a little time, not a man of them will come out without presents for him. Captain Prince, in the *Marlborough*, stopped there the 25th instant, and stayed with him two days; and he bragged to Mr Brown he had plenty of beer, wine, etc. and a silver punch-bowl from thence'. Captain Prince was evidently one of the new breed of slaving captains, who had little use for the Royal African Company: 'He passed by us, and in his passing he was so civil as to salute the flag, which was more than he did last voyage, and then stopped a day at Morea [a Dutch fort] I suppose to take in slaves and corn.' Quarrelling with the Dutch authorities and attempting to outwit them had long been a pastime at Cape Coast. Yet, on serious occasions like a French threat to Elmina, the English would warn their rivals, courtesy visits would be exchanged, salutes fired, toasts drunk and eternal friendship would be sworn; but soon the habitual atmosphere of mutual recrimination would once again prevail. These conditions of jealousy and friction gave the African rulers and their caboceers yet one more advantage over the white traders, which they were agile to exploit.

At Cape Coast, as at Elmina, frustrating rumours were

always rife. There was, for instance, a report that the King of
Aquaffo was about to grant the Dutch permission to build a
fort on a hilltop westward of the English station at Commenda
– a hilltop over which the English felt they exercised some implicit form of jurisdiction. The King denied that he had made
any such grant, and said, rather mysteriously, that all that had
happened was that 'the Dutch general had some time ago asked
him leave to dig a large stone out of the hill, which he had
granted him and nothing else. He professed further that as long
as he lives he will never permit the Dutch so much as to walk
upon the hill, whereof he did offer to take a fetish, promising
upon all that is sacred to be faithful to the Royal African
Company of England's interest'. Sir Dalby's emissary, Mr
Brown, told the King of Aquaffo 'to remember who had done
him more good or harm of the English or Dutch, and consider
that those who had been capable to do him most good were
capable still to do him most mischief if he was not true to their
interest, he owning that the English had done most good'.

These haphazard spheres of English or Dutch influence were
maintained as much by bribery as by threats. A typical case
with which Governor Thomas had to deal was that of the
Queen of Auguina, on the foreshore of whose kingdom the
Royal African Company had built the useful fort of Winnebah,
valued in 1709 at £12,000. The position of Winnebah offered a
number of advantages: it provided a threshold to the trade in
gold and slaves with the land-locked inland kingdom of Akim,
it stood at the mouth of a freshwater river handy for watering
ships, and its forests produced timber and its estuary oyster-
shells essential for repairing other forts. The monopoly of the
Akim trade was of great value to the Royal African Company,
and was envied by the Dutch. This the Queen of Auguina
naturally knew.

The Queen of Auguina was a famous and remarkable personage in the disparate array of coastal monarchs. For long the
only female potentate to rule her own kingdom, she was a
woman 'of great wisdom and courage', and she was, at the turn
of the eighteenth century, about forty years old. To keep
political power in her own hands the Queen had never married,
but ruled her 'fertile and pleasant' land as a spinster autocrat.
As we may remember, it was she who was reputed to purchase

lovers: 'that she may not remain a perfect stranger to the soft passion, she generally buys a brisk jolly slave, with whom she diverts herself; prohibiting him, on forfeiture of his head, to intrigue with any other woman; and when the youth hath lost his charms, or her passion palls, he is exchanged for another; though some will not allow her so honourable as to be satisfied with one at a time . . . she is so perfectly a mistress of her favours that she may confer them on whom she pleaseth without fear of scandal.' This competence in conducting her private life, the Queen seems to have extended to public and foreign affairs. An ally of the English, her port of Winnebah was a thriving centre of trade. In April 1703 it was reported to the English headquarters at Cape Coast that this West African Catherine the Great had been flirting with the Dutch West India Company, and was allowing the Dutch to set up a trading station of their own on her territory at Barraco. This news at first gave rise to some fairly idle talk of 'raising war' against the Queen and people of Auguina 'for their treachery to the Royal African Company of England'. Subsequently, through the good offices of the son of another local chieftain, the Brasso Fanteen, the Queen proved amenable to the Company's wishes and agreed that 'for a small acknowledgement of something presented to her she would turn out the Dutch from Barraco'. This 'something' comprised two cases of spirits and some bolts of trade cloth. These despatched and acknowledged, a further demand for free goods was made. These also were sent down to Winnebah, and the negotiations ended in a fetish oath by the Queen and her advisers. By this they promised to evict the Dutch from their new settlement at Barraco. The English monopoly of the Akim trade was saved, and at a small price. Many such instances of semi-blackmail could be cited – jabbing little reminders of who was really in control of gold and slaves alike. The European forts and castles might have the banners and the bugles, the guns and sentries, the pompous heraldic achievements carved in stone: but it was the Africans in their thatched houses who could make or break the trade. The Queen of Auguina was but one of a small army of Guinea potentates who called the tune.

# VII

This dependence for trade on the goodwill of the kings and of their caboceers forced the chartered companies from the very outset to involve themselves in local politics. However desirable a policy of non-involvement may have seemed, it could never be pursued. Although the European theory of the innate mental and moral superiority of white men over black was never accepted by the Africans, there were many delicate occasions in which appeals to European arbitration were made. One example, that of the Fetu succession, will suffice.

The kingdom of Fetu, which lay in the immediate hinterland of Cape Coast Castle and town, was one of the richest and most powerful on the Gold Coast. The king's palace, the largest on the Coast, was reported to contain more than two hundred rooms. It stood in the midst of an open *piazza* in the centre of Fetu town, and whenever the King left it he went attended by a throng of officials, guards and slaves, and preceded by drums and trumpets. Like his neighbour the King of Commenda, the King of Fetu was carried in a hammock on the backs of slaves, and seldom, if ever, put foot to ground.

The relationship of the Fetu monarchy with the Royal African Company headquarters was extremely cordial, and the occupants of the Fetu stool cultivated a high sense of honour in all that concerned their English allies. In 1681, in the reign of Charles the Second, the King of Fetu, who was then sixty years old and wore an European-style coat of black velvet, had even offered himself as a hostage for some runaway castle slaves who had been given shelter by the townsmen of Cape Coast. The quarrel between town and castle over the slaves had provoked an armed attack on the fortress by a body of townspeople nearly a thousand strong, and had ended in slaughter on both sides. Hearing of this, the old king had immediately left his capital of Fetu with a minimal bodyguard of twelve men, and had taken up his station beneath the branches of a sacred fetish tree, half a gunshot from the castle batteries. Here he entreated the spirit of the tree to reveal the hiding-place of the castle slaves, launched an appeal to the townspeople and 'did declare solemnly he would not stir from that place till the English were satisfied in their just pretensions'. His mission successfully ended, the King made a new alliance with the English Agent, who had sent him food and drink all the time he was seated in the shade of the fetish tree.

In 1703 this remarkable man (or possibly, since Fetu genealogy is hard to establish, his successor on the stool) died. Messengers to announce his demise descended on Cape Coast: 'Came notice in the afternoon that the King of Fetu was dead, and in the evening came the Dey of Fetu to acquaint himself the General of it, and with him a woman, mother to one whom they are about to make King. The Dey was welcomed with five guns.' Five days later the King of the adjacent country of Sabo arrived at the Castle, to confer with the Agent-General and an influential old caboceer, John Kabes, as to who should succeed to the Fetu stool. 'After some conference . . . the General named Aquabrafo, the woman who came with the Dey of Fetu, to be Queen, and it was accordingly so agreed upon. She and the Dey went away that night to Fetu.' Some months after her enthronement, the Queen of Fetu and her counsellors were summoned to Cape Coast for a solemn palaver with the King of Sabo and his caboceers. There, in the presence of Sir Dalby Thomas, they swore 'to live in concord with one another, and not to make war against one another on any account, and to be true to the interest of the Royal African Company of England'.

The Agent-General followed up this king-making episode by sending the Queen of Fetu some private and personal advice: 'as to trade she must take care of herself not to give away her goods. She must trade like an Englishwoman . . . She must consider that taking yams and corn for goods ought never to be paid beforehand, nor none but she shall be paid beforehand. She must sell for Arkanian gold and slaves and make trade that way, and then she will make herself rich, and in this way she shall never want my assistance.' Urged to trade like an Englishwoman, the Queen of Fetu was soon a frequent visitor at the Castle: 'came by on Tuesday the Queen of Fetu', or 'The Queen of Fetu came and stayed eight or nine days'. These unexpected royal visitations became a feature of life at Cape Coast Castle, and seem to throw upon that bone-white scene a friendly and genial light. Nor was the accession of Aquabrafo to the stool of Fetu the unique occasion on which the local nobility sought and accepted European advice.

To make alliances with local monarchs was beneficial to Company trade. To be asked to adjudicate between candidates for a vacant stool was fortunate indeed. But, around and below the kings or queens of the coastal territories there moved and muttered the thirsting, hierarchic swarms of caboceers – forceful and devious underlings, with flashing alcoholic eyes and pale-pink outstretched palms. If you wanted to slave well these men had to be treated with cordiality, indeed, however much it went against the grain, with a species of respect. The caboceers were the bane of the European traders' lives, and so they are the people we must reflect on next.

# Chapter 10

# Who Sold Whom?

## I

WHILE working on the subject of this book I have often been admonished (and in places as far apart as London and Lagos, as Charleston and Gstaad) to 'make it quite clear that it was the Blacks who sold each other'. Implicit in this statement of the obvious lies the unspoken question: 'And so how can you blame *us* for having bought what the Africans themselves were willing to sell?'

Here is a train of thought that will carry its passengers merrily and far. Catch it, snuggle down, draw the blinds, and, like some little mountain railway in the Bernese Oberland it will rattle you safely along through many a sombre defile and pitchy tunnel of human history. For this convenient theory that the Africans primarily have themselves to blame for the slave trade can find a multitude of fellows. How could the guillotine have been a painful instrument when its use was advocated by a qualified medical practitioner? How can the iniquities of child labour in the Industrial Revolution be laid at the factory owner's gates, since it was the parents who allowed their children to be sent to the mills and the foundries, or down the Yorkshire mines? A recent book has tried to demonstrate that the Jews in Nazi Europe were largely responsible for their own deaths because they shuffled to the gas-chambers without a protest. Such methods of exoneration would provide a happy trip through history and an endless one as well. All the same, the question white people dare not voice about the slave trade deserves an answer. Who, in point of fact, sold whom?

To quote once again the words of the freed slave Ottobah Cugoano, who was writing in the later eighteenth century, we find the answer: 'But I must own, to the shame of my own countrymen, that I was first kidnapped and betrayed by my own complexion, who were the first cause of my exile and slavery; but if there were no buyers there would be no sellers.' Except in the case of children like little Ottobah, who was captured while picking fruit and chasing birds with his cousins in the woods outside Assinee and bundled through three lots of African hands before being sold at an European fort for one gun, one piece of cloth and a small quantity of lead, the kidnapping of free men or women was in many areas alleged to be rare. 'With regard to the natives' we read in John Newton's *Thoughts upon the African Slave Trade* 'to steal a free man or woman, and to sell them on board a ship would, I think, be a more difficult and more dangerous attempt in Sherbro* than in London. But I have no doubt that the traders who come from the interior parts of Africa, at a great distance, find opportunity, in the course of their journey, to pick up stragglers, whom they may meet in their way. This branch of oppression and robbery would likewise fail, if the temptation to it were removed.'

Now the question of temptation is crucial to any discussion of African 'guilt' concerning the slave trade. We have seen that, before the advent of the Europeans, domestic slavery, in a mild and feudal form, had always existed in West Africa, and that it continued to exist. Much of the time of Sir Dalby Thomas and other agents and factors was spent disentangling complicated cases of slave-ownership – had Quashoo, a black carpenter at Cape Coast, the right to sell his wife's son, Braboo, to a ten per center, when Quashoo's wife and her three children by a former husband belonged to 'a woman in the town'? Was a freeman who 'consan'd' – that is to say lived with – a slave-woman still a freeman or did he automatically become a domestic slave? These matters of slave status were delicate and important, since most of the slaves owned by Africans were debtors who had volunteered to pawn themselves and their families either in lieu of repayment or as guarantees for money borrowed from someone else in order to pay back the original debt. These 'pawns' could under certain conditions redeem themselves and their families, but at the very height of the slave trade even they were liable, like Quashoo's stepson, to be sold clandestinely to the ships.

* Sherbro River, Sierra Leone.

The other reasons for African slavery were, as we know, a certain number of anti-social crimes, such as adultery or theft. There was also, of course, slavery as the fruit of military conquest. But, until the Europeans came upon the scene, slaves were regarded inside Africa as useful and helpful people, whose ownership carried with it specific obligations – to feed, to clothe, to shelter and protect. To kings and noblemen they were also a status symbol, and necessary to the maintenance of rank. This theme of the protection afforded by a great man to his slaves resounded throughout town and village life, and formed a parallel to the serf system of feudal Europe. Such mutual loyalties were strong, but they were immediate and confined; strangers and enemies were natural prey, and so soon as it was discovered that they, like gold-dust and tusks of ivory, had a solid commercial value, there was no traditional moral or religious impediment to their being sold. The phrase 'Blacks selling Blacks' has therefore neither pertinence nor meaning, for in those days the concept of African solidarity could not and did not exist.

'If there were no buyers there would be no sellers' – that is the crux of the matter, and the final word that can be said on African 'guilt'. It was the European traders who assiduously taught Africans to sell other Africans; and, moreover, taught them to sell slaves, as they taught them to sell gold and ivory, for trash. In so far as they studied African psychology at all, the white traders studied it from a shifty street hawker's point of view. Peddling their wares with deftness and contempt, they created an artificial market for cheap brassware and old clothes, faulty iron bars, cottons, gewgaws and aged flintlocks that frequently blew up on use.* Certain items, such as the cowrie-shell currency at Whydah and at other places on the Coast, had always had a recognized rarity value in African eyes; but to arouse or instil a desire for the shoddy or second-hand products of European industry the traders made use of means as insidious as those now current amongst detergent manufacturers com-

* Several witnesses giving evidence before the Select Committee of the House of Commons enquiring into the African slave trade (1790-1) referred to the notoriously shoddy quality of trade guns. 'I have seen many of them with their barrels burst,' Lieut. Richard Storey of the Royal Navy declared before the Committee: 'and thrown away. I have seen many of the natives with their thumbs and fingers off, which they have said were blown off by the bursting of the guns.'

peting with one another on commercial television. The patronizing European attitude towards Africans – which culminated in the educational experiments of the nineteenth-century colonial powers – stemmed largely from the conclusion that people who would hand over gold-dust in return for copper basins, or valuable slaves for bolts of cloth and chintz, must be either childish or asinine. Indeed, until the second decade of the twentieth century the Africans have usually been fobbed off with the second- or third-rate : inferior trade articles in the slaving decades, inferior and deceptive educational facilities in those that followed.

The attractive analogy between slave trade methods and those by which small children were drafted to die of disease and deformity in English mines and factories during the Industrial Revolution does not, ultimately, hold. For in the world of English industry greed throbbed on one side only – that of the owners and managers, thirsty for gain. The little children, on the other hand, and their parents, worked simply and solely to keep alive, albeit at a degraded and starvation level. Since such real poverty hardly existed in Africa it was not an incentive to the slave trade, except in parching times of local famine : generally the motive of both sides, of African and European traders alike, was the same – commercial greed. Open and unbridled, this greed created at all levels a secret system of bribery as layered as the leaves on an artichoke and far more difficult to strip away. The European companies' minor employees, as well as their *laptos* or castle-slaves, cheated their immediate superiors with considerable cunning to sell human merchandise to 'separate traders' or interloping ships. The African traders and caboceers cheated their own kings and masters by demanding bribes and dashes, and by obstinately raising slave-prices already fixed at summit palavers between ship-captains and native kings. Both European Agents-General in their castles, and African kings in their sun-baked palace courtyards would strive to circumvent these underhand activities. They would issue edicts and orders to warn their underlings that the cheating had to stop. But did it?

## II

We have envisaged the slaving organization of the chartered companies as an effort to confine within a cordon of decency and order a trade essentially indecorous and by its very nature turbulent. Similarly, the African kings from whom bulk purchases were made sought to negotiate by protocol and precedent, and on set terms. The leaders on each side were much deceived – the Agents-General by their factors and their *laptos*, the Kings by their caboceers. 'Mr Dudley was removed before my time, and the account of his crimes sent you' an Agent-General wrote to the Royal African Company's London offices in 1704. Factor Dudley's crimes had been to sell nearly eighty Negroes for his private gain, contrary to the strict instructions of the act of 1698 which forbade any servant of the Company to trade in slaves for his personal benefit. Even Bosman's old friend, the hospitable King of Whydah, was more or less powerless in the hands of his caboceers. A detailed account of the slave-trading structure at Whydah is given by our previous acquaintance, Captain Thomas Phillips, who commanded the slave ship *Hannibal*, chartered to, but not owned by, the Royal African Company.

Anchoring off Whydah in May 1694, Captain Phillips went ashore with his colleague Mr Clay, the captain of the *East India Merchant*, a ship likewise chartered to the Company. Phillips had just spent a month at Cape Coast Castle, a fortress which he much admired – 'I believe there are no better barracks anywhere than here, each two having a handsome room allowed them'. Handsome perhaps, but not healthy; for of the thirty soldiers he had brought out on the *Hannibal* to replenish the Cape Coast garrison more than half were dead within two months. For Phillips the English factory at Whydah formed a sorry contrast to Cape Coast: 'Our factory, built by Captain Wiburne, Sir John Wiburne's brother, stands low near the marshes, which renders it a very unhealthy place to live in; the white men the African company send there, seldom returning to tell their tale.' It was surrounded by a six-foot wall of baked mud, with a gateway to the south – 'within is a large yard, a mud thatched house, where the factor lives, with the white men; also a store-house, a trunk for slaves,* and a place where they bury their dead white men, called, very improperly, the hog-yard; there is also a good forge and some other small houses'. This factory had, however, its uses: 'The factory proved beneficial to us in another kind; for after we had procured a parcel of slaves and sent them down to the sea-side to be carried off, it sometimes proved bad weather, and so great a sea, that the canoes could not come ashore to fetch them, so that they returned to the factory . . . we sometimes shipping off a hundred of both sexes at a time.' The specific aim of captains Clay and Phillips was to buy thirteen hundred Negroes, to complete the slaving of their own two ships. The negotiations took in all nine weeks.

Once ashore Phillips and Clay, who were accompanied by their respective surgeons and pursers, and protected by a naval guard of twelve sailors, were carried to this English factory in hammocks – 'we were soon trussed up in a bag, tossed upon negroes' heads and conveyed to our factory'. The Royal African Company's factor at Whydah, a Mr Pearson, proved brisk and capable. He was on good terms with the King, apparently understood the Whydah people, and ran his factory with Negroes from the Gold Coast – 'who are very bold, brave and sensible, ten of which would beat the best forty men the king of Whydah had in his kingdom; besides their true love, respect and fidelity to their master, for whose interest or person they will most freely expose their lives'. Resident factors like Pearson, lonely and isolated men, could cultivate the cheerful loyalty and affection of their own slaves in a way which those transients, the ships' captains, obviously could not.

As soon as he heard of their arrival, the King of Whydah sent two of his caboceers to welcome them. He later sent two more to bid them come to his palace at once, 'saying he waited for us, and that all former captains used to attend him the first night'. They therefore took again to their hammocks and were carried to 'the king's town, which contains about fifty houses'. There they complimented the King in the name of the Royal African Company, and told him (untruthfully) that they had rejected many offers of Negro slaves upon their way because the Company preferred to deal with him. They expressed the hope

* Houses for storing slaves were known as 'trunks'.

'that he would oblige his cappashiers to do us justice, and not to impose upon us in their prices; all which we should faithfully relate to our masters, the Royal African Company, when we came to England'. The King replied through his interpreter that 'the African company was a very good brave man; that he loved him; that we should be fairly dealt with and not imposed upon'. He enquired what goods they had brought with them, and how many slaves they wished to buy. The next morning was appointed for a formal palaver about prices. After a banquet rendered stormy by the King's sudden rage on learning that the *Hannibal* and the *East Indian Merchant* had not brought the silks, muskets or pictures promised him as a gift by another English captain, the guests took their leave in fairly optimistic mood. They soon found, as others had before them, that the generous King of Whydah was less powerful than he seemed, and quite as capable of lying as they themselves: '. . . he did not prove as good as his word; nor indeed (though his cappashiers show him so much respect) dare he do anything but what they please'.

Next day they were given apartments and store-houses inside the palace compound; none of the rooms had doors until the sailors made them, and fitted keys and locks. Clay and Phillips had agreed to go each of them to the slave trunk on alternating days, to avoid any sign of competition – 'the blacks well knowing how to make the best use of such opportunities, and as we found make it their business and endeavour to create and foment misunderstandings and jealousies between commanders, it turning to their great account in the disposal of their slaves'. Phillips felt queasy inside the trunk: 'I could hardly stand or go to the trunk without assistance, and there often fainted with the horrid stink of the negroes.' At Whydah he was also subject to violent headaches.

Once prices were agreed on, the King commanded that the gong or bell be beaten to advise the people of Whydah that they should bring their slaves down to the trunk for sale. This bell Phillips describes as a hollow piece of iron shaped like a sugar loaf. It was carried around by a man who beat upon it with a stick – 'which made a small dead sound'. Before the common or garden slaves could be sold, the Europeans were obliged by tradition to purchase first the slaves of the King, known as *Reys*

*Cosa.* These royal things were usually the worst in the trunk, and the most costly. Then followed the caboceers, each according to his rank, with their own slaves to sell. A minute scrutiny by the ships' surgeons was necessary at this point, as the caboceers shaved their slaves so closely that it was only possible to tell their age by their teeth. They also polished their bodies with palm oil to make them look sleek. Slave-owners were paid by promissory note, specifying the goods agreed upon for each sale, and to be redeemed upon the following day. Purchased slaves were then branded on shoulder or breast with the first letter of the ship's name, 'the place before being anointed with a little palm oil, which caused but little pain, the mark being usually well in four or five days, appearing very plain and white after'.

When fifty or sixty Whydah slaves had been collected, they were sent to the ships under the supervision of two caboceers who bore a title which the English translated as 'captain of the slaves'. Another caboceer was 'captain of the trunk', and yet another 'captain of the sand'. The responsibilities of this latter official were to take charge of the trade goods as they were brought ashore by canoe, and to see that cases left all night upon the sands because of a shortage of porters were not rifled. If any slaves were lost in the passage to the ships, or ran away from the trunk, the caboceers in charge were bound to replace them. Phillips lost twelve of his slaves by suicide off Whydah: 'The negroes are so wilful and loath to leave their own country, that they have often leaped out of the canoes, boat and ship, into the sea, and kept under water till they were drowned, to avoid being taken up and saved by our boats, which pursued them.'

The cowrie-shell currency of Whydah was used by the Africans for ornamental as well as financial purposes. Called by the French traders *bouges*, and so by the English *bougies*, the shells were gathered amidst the rocks and shoals of the Maldive Islands, off the coast of Malabar, transported as ship's ballast to Goa, Cochin and other Far Eastern ports, whence they were despatched to Dutch and English factories in India, sent in packages to Europe and there crammed in small barrels for the Guinea trade. They were of all sizes, but the smaller they were the more valuable they were considered. These milk-white shells, which one French trader describes as looking like olives, were bored and threaded by the Whydah Negroes, forty to a string or *toque*. The Africans of Whydah prized them far above gold-dust, and rated a man's rank and power by the number of cowries and the number of domestic slaves that he possessed. Other trade goods popular in Whydah were thin brass basins, which were afterwards sliced up to make bracelets, leg ornaments and collars; lawns, chintzes, iron bars, gunpowder and brandy. The King of Whydah, who asked more for his slaves than his caboceers were permitted to demand, further exacted a tithe – usually a dishful of cowries – on every sale a caboceer made in public. This understandably led his caboceers to send secretly for European traders after nightfall, and sell them two or three slaves at a time in the privacy of some house. It was reckoned that, at the close of the seventeenth century, the King of Whydah was making the equivalent of four hundred pounds sterling from each foreign trading vessel, and there were often as many as fifty ships off Whydah in a year. All the same, he could not circumvent the underhand ways of his caboceers: 'In short' writes Willem Bosman, 'if the King were not cheated he would have a vast income, and be a potent prince, considered as one of this country-kings; but, compared with the oriental or other kings, he makes indeed but a wretched figure.' A peculiarity of trade along the Whydah coast was the absence of local canoes, so that slavers had to pick up canoes and kroomen at Cape Coast or some other centre, and bring them, with a skilful boatswain, down to Whydah. None the less, Phillips and Clay lost several barrels of cowries, over one hundred iron bars and some other trade goods by canoes upsetting in transit to the shore. Phillips explains that they could not protest, and were obliged to be amiable about these little accidents, lest the kroomen should play them 'more such tricks'.

It was not only of kings, caboceers, newly bought slaves and kroomen that the Europeans on this coast were chary. The majority of slaving captains were considered by each other to be dangerous and dishonest, men who 'commonly undermine, betray and out-bid one the other; and the Guinea commanders' words and promises are the least to be depended upon of any I know use the sea; for they would deceive their fathers in their trade if they could'.

These were some of the difficulties of slave-trading on the Windward Coast. Further eastward and southward, beyond the

Bights of Benin and Biafra, the Portuguese were supreme; and here, on the Leeward Coast, the inexperienced trader ran into yet another complex problem – that created by the influence of the Portuguese missionaries and, through them, of the Roman Catholic Church.

## III

After the Dutch capture of Elmina in 1637, the Portuguese abandoned any pretence of keeping up permanent forts or factories on the Windward Coast, with the solitary exception of their small station 'São Joao de Ajuda' at Whydah which survived in Portuguese hands until 1961. Up and away to the north-west in the region of Senegambia and the Rivers of the South, where long ago they had been the first white explorers, the Portuguese had retained a couple of factories, at Cacheu and at Bissau, below the mouth of the Gambia River; but for the main trade in ivory tusks, and in slaves shipped direct to Bahia, Pernambuco, Rio, Maranhao and other Brazilian ports, they now concentrated on the vast stretch of the Leeward Coast to the north and south of the Congo River. This gloomy littoral, the borders of which were not then defined, came to be loosely known as Angola, and, so far as the trade in slaves went, was in the seventeenth and eighteenth centuries virtually a Portuguese preserve. The slavers of other nations found Congolese Negroes difficult and expensive to buy, for the Portuguese monopoly was so complete that few slaves were likely to be available for random purchase. Writing from London to the King of Cacongo in February 1688, the Council of the Royal African Company told him: 'We have frequent complaints by every ship we send thither that the slaves cost one third part more there than at all other places in Guinea and that there trade cannot be driven with that security and faithfulness as we find in other places.'

The voyage to Angola was, in any case, inconveniently long, and involved calling in at a Portuguese-held island for refreshment – Fernando Po in the Bight of Biafra, São Tomé, with its mist-laden valleys, dead equatorial heat and chattering half-breed population, or, further south still, the island of Annaboa off Cape Lopez. This eastward journey down the monotonous

African coast, past fort after fort and factory after factory, is the one which Joseph Conrad has described in his sinister tale of the Congo River, *The Heart of Darkness*. 'The edge of a colossal jungle' he writes 'so dark-green as to be almost black, fringed with white surf, ran straight, like a ruled line, far, far away along a blue sea whose glitter was blurred by a creeping mist. The sun was fierce, the land seemed to glisten and drip with steam. Here and there grayish-white specks showed up clustered inside the white surf, with a flag flying above them perhaps. Settlements some centuries old and still no bigger than pinheads on the untouched expanse of their background.'

To the little ports at the mouth of the Congo slaves were brought down in coffles from far up country and, in the Portuguese manner, baptized before shipment to Brazil. For although it was the Portuguese who had initiated the slave trade, the old crusading ideals of Prince Henry the Navigator and his soldiers still survived as a humanizing force. The slaves on Portuguese ships were not chained together on the Middle Passage, and they slept on mats which were kept clean. Miscegenation was the order of the day, and the Africans, though bought and sold, were still regarded as undeniably children of God. This attitude baffled English, Dutch or French traders who made landfall on the coast of Angola, and added one further complication to the arduous business of collecting slaves.

In August 1700, for example, there anchored in the mouth of the River Congo the ten per cent ship *Don Carlos*, English despite its name and bound for Jamaica out of London. The master's aim was to buy slaves at the town of Sonho, which lay concealed up a twelve-mile creek, and then a further six miles inland. Sonho was to the south of the river; Cabinda and its bay, another slaving-port sometimes used by the Dutch or English, lay to the north. On board the *Don Carlos* was James Barbot, a nephew of Jean Barbot, the French Huguenot who had taken refuge in England and afterwards wrote his *Description of the North and South Coasts of Guinea*. Young Barbot was travelling as supercargo. In collaboration with another Frenchman, Jean Casseneuve, first-mate on the *Don Carlos*, he wrote an account of his Congolese adventures which his uncle, who had never penetrated so far south, printed as a supplement to his own book.

Once the *Don Carlos* had anchored, the captain sent the
pinnace to the dock to bring back two natives who spoke broken
Portuguese. These men told them that the only ships within
range were one English and one Dutch slaver, filling up with
Negroes at Cabinda. With these interpreters, the captain and
the mate made their way to the town of Sonho, where they were
kept waiting in the usual way. They were received by the King,
to whom they presented six yards of chintz, in return for which
he had a chicken killed and served up on a dirty pewter platter.
This King of Sonho, who had a shaven head and was quietly
dressed in a very short black cloak and a black loin cloth, cut a
very different figure from the gold-plated monarch of Benin, or
the cheated King of Whydah. He and his noblemen wore necklaces of beads from which a cross, or an *agnus dei*, was suspended,
and his first question when told that the Englishmen were after
slaves was to enquire whether the captain would promise to
have them instructed in the faith of Christ and whether he and
the mate had yet called upon the Portuguese friar resident
in the town. He then gave them a goat and six hens and dismissed the captain but retained the mate as a hostage for some
noblemen, one of them a caboceer known as 'the Receiver of the
Whites', whom he sent down to the English ship. On their
second visit to Sonho, the King announced that he could not sell
the Englishmen slaves without a licence from the Portuguese
friar. When interviewed in his turn, this priest objected to slaves
being sent to Barbados 'to the heretics, where he was sure the
poor wretches should never be instructed in the Christian
faith' – an argument which the master of the *Don Carlos* seems
to have combatted by suggesting that the slaves would be taken
to Jamaica and there sent on to the Catholic colonies of Portugal
and Spain. At further prolonged palavers, the King of Sonho
offered his guests palm-wine, which he himself drank from a
great silver cup, and began a serious argument to fix the prices
for slaves. Barbot, Casseneuve and the ship's master were by
now convinced that trade would never be good at Sonho, as the
natives kept on bringing up the Catholic question and even
accused the English of planning to sell slaves to the Turks. They
therefore moved on to the bay of Cabinda. By the time they
set sail on the morning of New Year's Day 1701 they had
assembled four hundred and seventeen men, women and children

for shipment to Jamaica on what proved an inauspicious voyage.

The air of Cabinda 'being very unwholesome' six seamen and the third mate died; the Captain, the supercargo, the first mate and several others of the seamen fell sick. On realizing the weakness of the crew, the male slaves organized a mutiny, killed one seaman outright, cut the cook's throat, badly wounded the boatswain and three seamen, and almost succeeded in taking over the ship. In the mêlée, nearly thirty slaves were killed or drowned themselves. The mutiny was put down by firearms, and the ringleaders were whipped by all the seamen 'that were capable of doing that office'. The outbreak had been made possible by carelessness as well as by sickness, since the slaves had been issued with knives, had been able to rip iron off the forecastle doors, and had in many cases broken free of their fetters.

What seems most arresting about young Barbot's account of the voyage of the *Don Carlos* is not the mutiny – a constant threat and a too-frequent occurrence on slave ships still within sight of the sombre shores of Africa – but the King of Sonho's insistence on Christian baptism, and the power in his territory of the Portuguese missionaries. Alone amongst the slave-trading nations of Europe, the Portuguese recognized that the Africans had souls. During the very brief moment – 1679 to 1683 – in which the Portuguese took over the great Danish fortress, Christiansborg Castle at Accra,* they built a chapel there, under the charge of an African priest ordained by the Bishop of São Tomé. Portuguese respect for spiritual values did not prevent their buying and selling slaves in larger quantities than any other European nation; but they did at least treat their captive Africans with some semblance of humanity. Their attitude was surely influenced by the geographical fact of Portugal's proximity to Africa, as well as by the centuries of Moorish occupation of large parts of the Iberian peninsula, which produced over the generations a mixed and only semi-European race. In modern Brazil most of the old families have Arab, and

---

* Christiansborg is said to have been sold to the Portuguese by the Danish commander's Greek assistant, who allegedly instigated his superior's murder in 1679. The Portuguese found its possession uneconomic, and sold it back to the Danes four years after.

many of them Negro, blood, neither is such a confused ancestry considered shameful nor, generally, a thing to be concealed.

## IV

I have already lamented the fact that the white traders and factors can only be, from our standpoint in time, a throng of faceless men. The African caboceers and middlemen are even harder to picture. With a snobbery not unusual in diarists, the appearance, clothing and mannerisms of many a petty Guinea royalty have been recorded in detail by memorialists such as Bosman, the Barbot family, Atkins, Falconbridge, Dr Houston and others; but with rare exceptions even the names of the leading caboceers have been lost. Sometimes the power or eccentricity of a caboceer caught the Europeans' fancy – there is the example of Santi, who organized the slave trade for the King of Lay, a place near Accra. Santi functioned in the sixteen-eighties, but he is very vaguely characterized as 'a famous black'. On the whole the influence of the caboceers, though great, was limited and local – and their names died with them in the wailing funeral rites.

Some of the most efficient slave-traders of African blood were mulattoes and, like the ostentatious Edward Barter of Cape Coast, could read and write and might, to inspire added confidence, even profess to be Christians. Barter (of the apt surname) was reputed, in the last decades of the seventeenth century, to exercise more power around Cape Coast 'than the three English agents together (in whom the chief command of the Coast is vested jointly) who by reason of their short stay here are so little acquainted with the affairs of this coast that they suffer themselves to be guided by him, who very well knows how to make his advantage of them'. Barter, who was legally married in England, had eight other wives and a quantity of mistresses on the coast. He could raise a substantial private army from his own slaves and his freemen followers. No one, in Barter's lifetime, could negotiate with the Cape Coast English without his aid. A half-black selling whole-blacks to the whites, this betwixt-and-between personage had grown rich in his profession.

Africans working at the heart of the slave trade could, if they were skilful and wary, acquire a nuisance value exasperating to native kings and Europeans alike. One well-documented native who had thriven in this pimpish role was a caboceer of Commenda on the Gold Coast, in the first decades of the eighteenth century. He was called Kabes, and known to the English and the Dutch as 'John'. From an ingrained hatred for the Dutch, whom he felt had done him an injury, Kabes had deliberately invited their trade rivals the English to build a castle in one of his salt villages, a stone's throw from the Dutch fort at Commenda. This neat battlemented building, with bastions and a square tower from which the flag of St George fluttered in the wind from the sea, was a source of great annoyance to the Dutch, who detested Kabes in consequence. John Kabes was paid a retainer and given protection by the Royal African Company but, while pretending to have influence with the up-country kings who ruled in the hinterland of the Gold Coast, he managed to alienate both the English, who needed him, and the mighty Asantehene, or King of the Ashanti, who did not – and who went so far as to return Kabes' rich gifts to him with the injunction 'to compose his roguish palavers before he sends his presents'. The traders from Ashanti who wended their way down the tracks through the rain-forests with gold-dust and coffles of slaves, disliked John Kabes too and 'had generally conceived an ill opinion of him'. Kabes' chief victim, William Baillie, the English factor at Commenda from 1713 to 1718 was soon hoping for Kabes' death: 'He is not likely to live much longer, being now old and beginning to grow sickly and infirm; and till his end comes I am afraid the Company trade will never flourish.' The actual date of Kabes' demise is, of course, not known, but his would seem to have been a lengthy and an angry life: he would end some quarrel by cutting off a few of his enemies' heads and was responsible for at least one suicide – that of the mother of a Cofferoe boy unjustly pawned to Kabes' cousin Apeo, and reluctantly redeemed by Kabes too late. A glance at Kabes' inconsequent yet wily behaviour will further illustrate, if in miniature, the part played in the Atlantic slave trade by the Africans themselves. It will also once more emphasize the Europeans' and Africans' enervating lack of confidence in one another.

'The traders came into the Castle to trade, along with John

Kabes, who came in bawling.' This tired entry in Baillie's Commenda diary was made in March 1715 and at once sets for us Kabes' hectoring tone. White traders and resident factors were always complaining of the sheer noise made by the Africans with whom they haggled for slaves, and of their 'saucy' manners. Anyone acquainted with West Africa knows those sudden cannonades of loud but short-lived anger, and the louder laughter which follows it, making the heated air seem to crackle and quiver in the market-place. An old man in Baillie's period of office, John Kabes remained as argumentative and wily as when he had crossed swords with the Dutch Company in his youth. His courtesy or business visits to the Agent-General in the Castle at Cape Coast tended to finish in a row. Rampaging homewards, his followers would *panyar* (or kidnap) free townswomen, and in reply to a remonstrance from the Castle Kabes would send the ladies back later with a curt message that it 'had been done without his knowledge'. A paid employee of the Company he would charge them for every service he did them – for hiring them canoes, for instance, to fetch shells and lime when the western flank of Commenda Castle fell down after a spectacular thunderstorm: 'he not perceiving' wrote Baillie 'any obligation he's under to serve the Company at the expense of his own pocket'.

Sometimes Kabes seemed to be on the Company's side, sometimes to have 'an aversion' to working for them. His perpetual intrigues with inland tribes endangered the trade at Commenda by interrupting the flow of slaves to the English fort, or diverting it for purposes of his own to interloping ships. Baillie, who loathed 'John' for his roguery could only issue weak warnings on 'the ill consequences of his palavers in the country and how prejudical they are to the Company's interest, and that if he be resolved to continue disturbing his neighbours and consequently stopping the Company trade, we must find out new means to govern him that the Company may not suffer by his villainy'. When Kabes was busy watching his corn being planted, he would totally ignore the most urgent summons to the English fort. When he heard through his grape-vine of a caravan of slaves trudging down to the coast he would say nothing to Baillie, borrow trade goods from the English warehouse, send these up-country, intercept the traders and secretly buy their slaves cheap. He ordinarily aimed to sell these to interloping slave ship masters, in a hurry to set out across the Atlantic, and willing to pay higher prices than the Company's men. If, however, the watch-ships which the Company rather unhopefully posted here and there along the coast made such an operation hazardous, he would bring the slaves into the Castle, dress up as northern traders some of his own people whom Baillie did not know by sight and pretend to negotiate with them to sell Baillie at a high price slaves he had himself bought for a low one. Sick slaves Kabes would pick up for little or nothing, and he tried to use these worthless specimens to refund his debt to the Company warehouse: 'Upon my refusal' Baillie noted 'he demands liberty to carry them aboard an interloper, which he certainly does.' But when his vanity was aroused, Kabes would prove most cooperative, giving his advice on the knotty matter of the Fetu succession, informing on Dutch plans to send armed slaves from Elmina to Sekondee fort, bringing in to Cape Coast in chains a couple of 'English negroes' who were to be sent to Barbados as punishment for creating trouble at English Sekondee. He would go on modest English embassies to such local grandees as the King of Aquaffo to find out, for instance, about that mysterious Dutch request that the King allow them to dig up a large stone on a hill near Commenda. Kabes was maddening, but he was indispensable.

A part of the strength of the position of John Kabes and other Africans like him lay in the weakness of that of the English factors at the out-forts. The Cape Coast Council stinted Baillie of trade goods, which meant he could not always buy slaves; and when he did have goods, slaves became suddenly scarce. The garrison at English Commenda was derisorily weak, and yet 'the Gentlemen' as Baillie called the Council, were mean about essential gunpowder – which was also used to salute visiting Dutch officials, and on such occasions as John Kabes' 'dancing days and customary'. 'The Gentlemen' tried to remove the eight black soldiers of the Commenda garrison and they refused Baillie rum and brandy to befuddle African traders. Poor Baillie had many other troubles apart from a shortage of trade goods and gunpowder; his health was about as bad as that of most of the Europeans in the region, and he often suffered from stomach disorders – stoppages and 'a violent evacuation of blood' which necessitated journeys to see the surgeon at Cape Coast, or inspired an appeal to have that medico sent down to Commenda by canoe. Then there was the collapse of the castle wall, cutlass fights between English soldiers (one of whom nearly severed his opponent's hand) and other accidents like that of a domestic slave falling into the cookhouse fire.

Thus, in one sense, the Company trade in slaves at Commenda proved more lucrative to the African Kabes than to his European employers. He seems always to have had the upper hand, and would on occasion resort to such prima-donna-ish tactics as threatening, since the Company 'was so hard on him', to 'go and live in the Bush'. This dependence on a leading African gave, to the out-station trade, a tangled uncertainty that was very damaging. The English, Dutch, French or Portuguese interlopers, who made descents upon the coast in small swift ships, hid up the creeks or anchored in some sheltered bay along the coast, could treat with greater flexibility and speed. It mattered little to them what Africans they offended, so long as, by offering higher prices, they could get more trade. With none of the overhead expenses of castles, forts and factories, and anxious to set out over the Atlantic with the minimum of delay, they could fill their slave-holds quickly, pay more or less what was asked, and make a smart get-away from the unwholesome coast on which the Companies' men were left to argue, drink and rot.

It is easy to see how native caboceers like John Kabes possessed, and made use of, the whip hand. Theirs was, by and large, a position bringing with it a pleasing sense of power. But what of the sensations of the powerless – of the slaves collected by hirelings and inferiors for caboceers and kings to sell? How did it feel to be a newly captured slave, stored, chained and whipped in the castle pens and dungeons, and then branded and packed for export over the vindictive, restless sea? Up-country Africans had never seen the ocean. Coast-dwellers knew it to be governed by bevies of evil spirits. The brutish white-faced seamen were all too clearly the personifications, or at any rate the cannibal minions, of these.

# Chapter 11

# Night Thoughts

## I

IT WAS then almost night, and the land breeze making down the river – we were then employed in getting sail upon the vessel, and making all ready to purchase our anchor. In the mean time, a canoe came along side of us; the men came on board to bid our Captain farewell. Our captain ordered some rum and tobacco and pipes to be given to these men. As soon as they had got these few articles they went again into the canoe and made the best of their way to shore. Then the captain ordered us to weigh anchor, and we got out to sea.

This was at dusk in White Man's Bay, at the mouth of the Sierra Leone River. The ship was an English slaver commanded by a Captain Strangeways, and its nocturnal departure from Sierra Leone was recalled by Mr John Bowman, who had served as mate on many slaving vessels from 1765 to 1774. Mr Bowman was one of many men with long experience of the African trade who came forward to give evidence before the Select Committee of the House of Commons, enquiring into the slave trade during the early days of the Abolitionist agitation. This Committee, which succeeded a committee of the whole House convened in 1789, sat during 1790 and 1791, and heard numerous witnesses both favourable and unfavourable to the continuation of the trade. This corpus of verbatim anecdote and recollection, of conflicting opinions and emotions, provides a kaleidoscopic and intensely personal view of the slave trade at its zenith in the latter half of the eighteenth century. Captains and factors, kings and middlemen and kidnappers, surgeons, seamen, mates, slaves abject or heroic, all jostle one another for a moment's attention, and seem then to fade back again into that soft tropical night which was, on the coast of Africa, the slave-traders' sole really reliable ally.

'Did your vessel leave the coast in the day or the night?' The question was put by a member of the Committee to Dr Thomas Trotter, who had served as surgeon on board the Liverpool slaver *Brookes** between Cape Palmas and Anamabu in the years 1783 and 1784. 'In the night, after dark, and when all the slaves were secured below, to prevent them from murmuring or showing any signs of discontent at leaving the coast' Dr Trotter answered. 'Every ship that was in the [Anamabu] road when we came there, or that sailed before our ship, left the road in the same manner; the custom I apprehend is general from what I have heard.' Although silence in the slave-holds could thus be bought for the first few hours of the voyage, while the captain slept in his cabin and the seamen sprawled under the booms,† the endless nights that followed on the long Middle Passage offered no such respite. Many witnesses have described 'the signs of extreme distress', the 'looks of despair', 'the gloomy pensiveness' on the puckered faces of the slaves as they were thrown on board the slave ship, chained, and slung into the holds; but once they realized that the vessel was under sail, their sadness became horrifyingly vocal. 'The slaves in the night were often heard making a howling melancholy kind of noise, something expressive of extreme anguish' (related Trotter). 'I repeatedly ordered the woman, who had been my interpreter in the latter part of the voyage, to enquire into the particular causes of this very melancholy sort of noise.' The answer came back that it was because the slaves had been dreaming that they were in their own country again, amongst their families and friends; when they woke up to find themselves in reality on a slave ship they began to bay and shriek. 'This exquisite degree

* The *Brookes*, which was owned by Captain James Jones of Liverpool (who reckoned that on slavers five females could be reckoned as four males, and three boys or girls should take up the space allotted to two grown persons) became famous through the diagram of it distributed in Great Britain by Clarkson and the Abolitionists. In Paris Mirabeau had a model made from it, which he kept in his dining-room, and nearly four thousand copies of the diagram were sent to Philadelphia. The *Brookes*, a vessel of 320 tons, had been known to carry 609 slaves on the Middle Passage. [The diagram is reproduced as the end papers to the present book.]

† The seamen on Guinea ships usually slept on the exposed deck, which did further harm to health already impaired on the coast; many would reach the West Indies with swollen and ulcerated legs. On the voyage to Africa trade goods were stored in most of the available space below-decks, and, on the Middle Passage, slaves.

of sensibility was particularly observable among the women'
(Dr Trotter emphasized) 'many of whom, in these situations,
I found in violent hysteric fits.' A younger witness, the twenty-
five-year-old Surgeon, Isaac Wilson, who, before he entered the
Royal Navy, had served on a slaving voyage during which one
hundred and fifty-five slaves out of a total of six hundred and
two had died on the Middle Passage, had been told by his
Captain that 'the mortality of the slaves was owing to their
thinking so much of their situation'.

The finality of a slave ship's leaving, and of the dark coastline
of Africa receding into the mist, was even more morally
devastating than the cruelties that had gone on in the slave pens
and dungeons immediately after a slave's capture; and these
were bad enough. Ottobah Cugoano, the freed slave on whose
published reminiscences I have already drawn, has written of
his departure from a coastal fort. When a boat came in shore
to take the slaves on board ship for Cape Coast Castle (Cugoano
writes):

there was nothing to be heard but the rattling of chains, smacking
of whips, and the groans and cries of our fellow-men. Some would
not stir from the ground, when they were lashed and beat in the
most horrible manner. I have forgot the name of this infernal fort;
but we were taken in the ship that came for us to another that was
ready to sail from Cape Coast. When we were put into the ship we
saw several black merchants coming on board, but we were all drove
into our holes and not suffered to speak to any of them. In this situation we continued several days in sight of our native land; but I
could find no good person to give any information of my situation to
Accasa at Agimaque.* And when we found ourselves at last taken
away, death was more preferable than life, and a plan was concerted
amongst us that we might burn and blow up the ship and to perish
altogether in the flames; but we were betrayed by one of our own
countrywomen.

The inability of Ottobah Cugoano to plead with the African
traders who came aboard the ship as it lay off Cape Coast
Castle is not surprising, for it was an absolute rule that none of
these visitors were permitted so much as to see the main deck,

* Ambro Accasa, with whose children Ottobah had been brought up, and who
is described by him as king 'of that part of Fantee known as Agimaque and
Assinee'.

where the men slaves crouched in chains, 'nor even to speak to the women abaft'. A carpenter named James Towne was another witness who spoke of this ban before the Committee. As always, it was fear that dictated the prohibition – fear that the free Africans might encourage some rebellious plan, by signal, with the slaves. 'Nor are the slaves on the main deck allowed to look over the sides, when any canoe or boat is coming to the ship' Towne reported. 'There are always two officers on the main deck to prevent such matters, with each of them a cat to flog them if they should attempt to look over the sides. This sufficiently prevents them from ever attempting to get redemption.' The after-part of the ship was separated from the main deck by a lofty barricade – 'as strongly put together as wood and iron can make it' – so that male and female slaves could not look at or talk with one another, for no contact between them was permitted for so long as the ship was moored off the African coast. To the terrors of slavery and the fear of the white faces, of the ship, of the unknown sea and of the unimaginable future was added the agonizing sense of being so near and yet so far from friends and home.

## II

By the middle of the eighteenth century the kidnapping of children like Ottobah Cugoano was a frequent occurrence. It followed on the whole a set pattern. He himself was captured when playing with some other children in the forest. By an odd prevision Ottobah had not wanted to go out on this fatal day, and had only joined them when taunted with cowardice, one boy suggesting that young Cugoano was afraid to run any risk because he formed part of a king's household, or because he was afraid of a *bonsam*, an evil and predatory spirit which lurks along the forest paths. Two hours after they had entered the forest, a number of men suddenly appeared and accused them of trespass – '[they] said we had committed a fault against their lord and we must go and answer for it ourselves before him'. Ottobah and his companions tried to run away, but, threatened with pistols and cutlasses, they were soon captured. One of the kidnappers now assumed a friendly role, telling the children that he would plead for them personally with his chief. By a series of stratagems, the little group of captives was taken from place to place, sub-divided and then bartered piecemeal. Ottobah ended up staying for six days with a stranger who swore that he would 'do all in his power' to return the child to his uncle at Agimaque. By this time the boy's suspicions were aroused, but he still thought that, if his uncle knew where he was, a search party would be sent out to claim him. One evening yet another stranger came to the house, chatted with the owner and told Ottobah that, being a friend of his relations, he would take him back to Agimaque next morning. They travelled together for two days. The man carried a bag of gold-dust, and explained that they were going to the sea to buy goods to take back with them to Agimaque. In the evening of the second day they came to a town where Ottobah saw his first white men – 'which made me afraid' (he writes) 'that they would eat me, according to our notion as children in the inland parts of the country'. Next morning the kidnapper took Ottobah, under guard, into the European castle; when the child asked why he had been brought there he was told it was 'to learn the ways of the *browfow*, that is the white-faced people'. The man exchanged Ottobah for a gun, a piece of cloth and some lead, and then left. Crying bitterly, Ottobah was put into the slave prison for three days, after which he was shipped down to Cape Coast and loaded on a slaver bound for the West Indian island of Grenada.

In another published account, that of Olaudah Equiano, a native of Benin who was captured along with his sister while they were minding their absent parents' house, the kidnappers are described as having climbed over the compound wall. These were two men and a woman, who hid the children in forest huts and took them by hidden paths towards the fatal coast. They tied and gagged Olaudah and his sister and ended by carrying the squirming boy in a large sack. Brother and sister would lie weeping all night in each other's arms, until a morning came when they were forcibly separated and never saw each other again. 'I cried and grieved continually' Equiano remembered 'and for several days did not eat anything but what was forced into my mouth.'

The slaving captains bought these kidnapped children without asking any questions. The evidence shows that children from eight to thirteen years old – and, indeed, often younger than that – were almost invariably brought on board without any of their family. Dr Trotter recalled a little girl of about eight who was bought for the *Brookes* by its commander, Captain Clement Noble, and who had been snatched from her mother by the man who sold her to the ship. The plight of these bereft boys and girls sometimes touched the more humane members of a slave ship's crew, though never, of course, to the extent of setting the children free or of trying to trace their families. Mr Ecroyde Claxton, who had been surgeon's mate on the *Garland,* and then served as surgeon on the *Young Hero,* both of which were slaving in Bonny in 1788, afterwards said he was moved by the 'afflicted' state of their human cargo – 'one in particular, a girl who, when she found she was sold, clung fast about the neck of her disposer, and eagerly embraced him – he did all that laid in his power to make her easy under her situation; but notwithstanding his exertions, accompanied by ours, it was impossible, though a child of ten or twelve years of age, to give her any comfort'.

For generations the ordinary man in Great Britain, in so far as he thought about the slave trade at all, assumed that slave-cargoes were composed solely of convicted criminals or prisoners-of-war. One single voyage on a slave ship was sufficient to dispel this illusion. William Dove, owner of a Plymouth tanyard, who had sailed to West Africa in 1769 as cooper aboard the Guineaman *Lilly* of Liverpool, was typical of men who found their ideas on slaving methods change radically with experience. One day, when the *Lilly* was anchored off a point of land called the 'Piccanini Sisters', a canoe approached her bringing an African who styled himself 'Ben Johnson, Grand Trading Man'. Mr Johnson carried with him a small, kidnapped girl for sale. Once paid, he set off promptly homewards in his canoe; but within ten minutes a second canoe came alongside the *Lilly,* paddled by two natives who hurried aboard to ask the captain whether he had not just bought a little girl. Captain Saltcraig showed them the child, and they precipitately left the ship to return half an hour later with Ben Johnson tied up in their own canoe. Lugging him aboard and shouting 'teeffee! teeffee!' – 'which' explained Mr Dove 'implies a thief' – they offered the protesting kidnapper for sale in his turn. 'What, Captain? Will you buy me, Grand Trading Man Ben Johnson from Wappoa?' their incredulous prisoner screamed; but Captain Saltcraig showed a Liverpudlian sense of business, as well as one of poetic justice. Declaring that 'if they would sell him, he would buy him, be he what he would', he summoned the boatswain to bring irons, and in a trice Mr Johnson of Wappoa was pushed through the wicket gate in the main deck barricade, and fettered to another Negro whom he may perhaps himself have already sold to Captain Saltcraig.

William Dove, who was of a loquacious turn, told the Committee that this episode had altered his notion of the mode of getting slaves:

for the notion I first entertained was that they were taken in war principally . . . but I was then led to think that they were taken by surprise or kidnapped from that circumstance of the girl's being brought on board; and what further confirmed me in the opinion was that I have seen children brought on board separately by themselves and men and women brought on board without any marks or wounds fresh on them or any that I could see had been made of old wounds; these were my reasons for thinking that they were obtained by kidnapping and taken by surprise.

He added that the *Lilly* carried between thirty and forty unaccompanied children, besides four or five babies born on the Middle Passage.

Kidnapping of adults as well as of children was, like local wars and village raids, encouraged by the white traders. In the more deserted coastal stretches – notably in the region in which the French *Compagnie du Sénégal* operated – the natives would always go armed whenever a slave ship was lying in the vicinity. At such periods it was unsafe to go down to the shore to look for shell-fish to market, or even to go down to the river to bathe. The boatswain of the *Warwick Castle*, who was at Bonny in 1771, saw one such blatant case of kidnapping. 'I went ashore at Bonny Point' he related 'with a boat to haul upon the beach to be cleaned, and I saw a young woman come out of the wood to bathe; afterwards, I saw two men come out of the wood, who seized the woman, secured her hands behind her back, beat her and ill-used her on account of the resistance she made, and brought her down to me and desired me to put her on board, which I did. For it was the Captain's orders to the ship's company, whenever anybody came down with slaves, instantly to put them off to the ship.'

When a Guineaman anchored off shore along the Gold Coast, it was the established custom for five or six of the 'gold-takers' to attend constantly on board. These were African freemen, who acted as 'black brokers' between the ships' masters and those who had slaves for sale, and were interpreters as well as trade overseers. Gold-takers were urged by impatient captains to get slaves by any means they could. 'Fat Sam', a gold-taker at Anamabu, would send his private canoe after any fishermen he saw working in the neighbourhood of the *Brookes,* aboard which he was then arranging details of trade: 'they were immediately brought on board, put in irons and about a week afterwards he received payments for them'. This delay in payment was customary in such circumstances, for the families of these random captives would sometimes come out to redeem them, usually at a higher price than that for which the men had originally been sold. Fat Sam would send fresh slaves to the ship after nightfall, a security measure fashionable along the coast. At Bonny the king's slave-cargoes would be delivered openly by daylight, but the small slave-peddlers would 'come on board in the evening, with one or two slaves bound hand and foot, lying in the boat's bottom, covered over with mats'. This preference for secrecy and for the night clearly shows that, to the general run of Africans, slaving was neither a popular nor a respectable pursuit.

## III

Nor was it just Africans kidnapping Africans. In these riper times, when the power of the chartered companies had flagged before the hasty determination and the voracity of slave-traders from Liverpool and other big European ports, white captains would even try to kidnap the very freemen who came to them to trade. When the *Gregson* of Liverpool arrived in Bonny River in 1771, those of her crew who came aboard the *Warwick Castle* upon a friendly visit, boasted that they had already kidnapped thirty-two Negroes on their voyage down the coast. Even in the vicinity of Cape Coast Castle, where some sort of old trade decorum was supposed to reign, the freemen traders became very wary of going on board a stray Guineaman. Here it was the custom for native traders, on sighting a new ship, to send up smoke signals from the shore to show that they had merchandise available. The Guineaman would then stand in, and the canoes would come skimming towards her through the surf. 'We got pipes, tobacco and brandy on deck, in order to entice them on board' runs one boatswain's account 'unlaid the gratings, cleared the slave room and made every preparation to seize them, had they come on board. They would not come on board though we so endeavoured to entice them.' On this occasion only two of the Africans dared come up the ship's side, and stand in the main chains; but when the seamen tried to grab them they leaped nimbly overboard.

These attempts at direct, as against indirect or inspired kidnapping, had several and obvious advantages. The Negro thus ensnared was all for free. No trade goods were wasted, no haggling was involved and a captain and his crew could happily exercise their guile and slake their taste for fun. The choice moment for these attempts would be when a new or unknown trader came on board to present his 'book' for the captain's inspection. This book formed his credentials and was in fact 'only a bit of paper, specifying their character and behaviour' and written out by any European ship's master with whom a native trader had had satisfactory dealings. Of these books the Africans were pathetically proud, since they hugely prized their own reputations for honesty. They would carry the certificates in a small wooden box strung round their necks to preserve them in case of one of the accidents to which canoes on that squally, surf-torn coast were all too prone. Captain Hugh Crow, of Liverpool fame, tells us in his *Memoirs* how he once amused himself when becalmed off Las Palmas on his way to the Oil Rivers in the winter of 1801. A native and his son came from the shore in a small canoe, and the man, after clambering on board the *Will* and swallowing what was called 'a washmouth' of spirits presented Captain Crow 'with great self-satisfaction . . . some certificates of his good conduct which he had procured from captains who had at various time employed him'. Crow says that on being handed the 'book' he determined 'to amuse myself at his expense, and though I found their contents highly favourable to his character, I returned them with affected coldness'. He told the book's owner, who went by the name of Tom Goodhead, that the papers contained warnings against his character, and that they advised ships' masters to watch him narrowly. Goodhead stood 'for a moment petrified with astonishment', and then jumped right over the quarter-deck rails into the sea. He swam underwater for some distance and then, surfacing, demanded in the pitiful broken trade lingo current on the coast, whether what the captain had said was true: 'Capy! booky speaky that mouth?' Fearing that he had a potential suicide on his hands, Crow soothed the man down, invited him back on board and gave him 'a small present'. He felt that the incident placed 'in a strong point of view the high estimation in which a good name is held by the poor Africans'.

Tom Goodhead got off lightly as the victim of a mere bad joke, for Captain Hugh Crow would never have stooped to personal kidnapping. He preened himself on running ships humanely and well – 'We sailed from Bonny with a cheerful crew and our complement of healthy negroes' he writes in another passage, and he quotes with complacency a Kingston saying: 'Crow has come again and, as usual, his whites and blacks are as plump as cotton bags.' Other ships' masters were less scrupulous. James Morley, a young gunner in the Navy who had made six slaving runs to Africa between 1760 and 1766, the first of them as a cabin boy at the age of nine, had watched one of his captains give an African glasses of brandy laced with laudanum until he fell insensible on to the deck. This particular Negro had come to the ship with a friend in their canoe. The friend had wisely stayed below, while his companion climbed on to the gunwale to present his book. The captain invited him to come down on to the deck, which he refused to do and remained perched on the netting; but after two tumblers of brandy and laudanum he collapsed, and was carried down to the slave hold and put in chains. In another contemporary case, off the Sierra Leone River mouth, the captain sent his mate on shore to invite aboard two African 'gentlemen traders' to take their leave of him before he set sail down the coast. He ushered the guests into his cabin where he gave them so much to drink they could not stand. When the ship had put out to sea the captain summoned the mate and, pointing to the sail-case, told him to look into it and see what a fine prize he had got. In the case lay the two traders, stupefied with drink; when they woke three hours later they were dragged up to the deck, put in irons and sent forward amongst the men slaves. At the end of the voyage they were sold with the rest of the cargo, in Antigua. 'What did the two men say when they came to themselves and discovered their situation?' Bowman, the former mate, was asked. 'They made lamentations, and were sorry that white men should be such great rogues to take them from their own country as they were free men' he replied.

The coastal Africans did not take these thefts of their friends quietly. There are many recorded examples of ships' crews, gone ashore in a pinnace for food and water, being attacked or 'panyared' themselves in retaliation for the crimes of the white men from some previous ship. On the whole, these Africans exercised a certain justice in revenge; for they would often either wait for the return of some particular ship on its next voyage, or else they would attack, or refuse victuals to, a ship from the same European port. Occasionally, by appealing to some other and more fair-minded captain, they might succeed in getting back their kidnapped relatives should the ship on which they were captive not yet have left the coast. Such instances of release were, however, rare. Rarer still were the cases of Africans who had been taken away into transatlantic slavery and then had managed to return home. A once famous example was that of two princes, brothers of the King of Old Town, Old Calabar, who as the result of one of the periodic massacres in which the people of Old Town and New Town mutually indulged were shipped off in a slaver in 1767. These youths were sold in the West Indies, and escaped to Virginia (where they found slave conditions better than in the Caribbean). After three years there, they made their way across the Atlantic to Bristol, where a merchant involved in the trade to Old Calabar got them taken off the ship by a writ of Habeas Corpus. This merchant, Mr Jones, sent them back to Old Calabar in one of his ships. This is hardly, perhaps, a typical case, since these two young Calabaris were clearly men of spirit as well as persons with, from a Bristol merchant's point of view, interesting and influential connections in their native place.

When slaves were hard to come by, certain captains would organize their own regular white raiding parties on shore. Boats from a number of ships would put off together, 'to take whomever we could catch', as one member of such an expedition put it. They would steal into a native town or village, snatch up any human being they saw and throw their victims, bound and their mouths stuffed with oakum, into the bottoms of the boats, which would be lying at a grapnel in the river. On these adventures the sailors all went armed; the villagers would retaliate 'with a scattering fire', and a few white men would often be wounded or lost. 'I knew nothing of the expedition till I was ordered to take command of the boat which I then was but too ready to do, thinking it a piece of sport to go on shore' one English participant related 'but which afterwards I was sorry for having done. The slaves I had taken were made part of the cargo and afterwards sold in Charles Town, South Carolina'. He added that he had known other seamen who had been on similar sprees: 'Several, who have told it to me themselves, and have made a boast and laugh of it, and who have been wounded also.'

This piecemeal ravaging of the coast is symptomatic of the lengths to which, in lean times, eighteenth-century slavers would go to assemble their cargoes; but for real bulk-buying they always depended on encouraging local potentates to embark on raids which they dignified by the title 'war with their neighbours'. These 'wars' were indeed nothing more than pillaging expeditions for human loot. Like the bringing of the slaves on shipboard, and like the surreptitious sailing of the full ships out to sea, these operations were mounted under the protective shelter of the night.

## IV

'He asked me first: "Parker, will you go to war with me?" I said: "I did not care".' This very English expression of assent was elicited from Isaac Parker, a runaway sailor hiding in New Town, Old Calabar, by his host, Dick Ebro, son of a New Town king. Isaac Parker had been serving as a sailor before the mast on board the Liverpool ship *Latham*, which was commanded by an unpopular captain, George Colley, known for starving and ill-treating his crew. The *Latham* had gone to Old Calabar in 1765, had slaved, and had then been temporarily becalmed upon the bar. Although she was what Parker called 'homeward bound' – by which he meant bound with a cargo of slaves for the West Indies – he had decided to desert and had sought sanctuary with Dick Ebro, an African slave-trading acquaintance in the town, who locked him up in his house for three days until the ship had sailed. Parker stayed in Old Calabar five months, fishing, shooting parrots in the swamps, and cleaning the Africans' muskets, cutlasses and blunderbusses. When Dick Ebro asked him to go along with him to war there had been no disturbances involving the Calabaris and the up-river or 'creek men', and no rumours of attack. There was, however, a shortage of slaves to sell: 'slaves' Parker believed 'were very slack in the back countries at that time'.

Preparations for the 'war' began. The great war canoes of Calabar, which sported, when armed, two three-pounders on wooden blocks, one astern and one in the bow, were brought out and filled with ammunition, cutlasses, pistols, powder and ball. By day they paddled up the river creeks, over smooth water the colour of zinc, walls of pale mangrove towering on either hand, and over them the startling sky. At dusk they would draw their canoes on to the bank, leaving two or three Negroes in charge of each. The raiding party would then swiftly rush a village, handcuff anyone they could seize, and take them back to the canoes, which would set off rippling in the darkness for another village higher up the river. Parker reckoned that in this one expedition they had got forty-five slaves, who were clapped into the various slave-pens of New Town and there sold to the ships. A week or two later Parker went with his hosts to villages even further up the river; in eight days they seized about the same number of people. These were again promptly divided amongst the captains 'when news was given them as before'. Men, women and children were captured indiscriminately and then sold. No heed was taken to see that families were kept together – 'they were divided, some in one ship, some in another, except the sucking children who went with their mothers'.

John Bowman, a former mate on a number of slave ships, with experience of trading on the Sierra Leone, Scassus, Junk and Cape Mount Rivers, and a contemporary as well as a compatriot of Isaac Parker, had been on many such native raiding parties in a more official capacity, indeed in the frank role of instigator. On one of his voyages he had been sent up to the head of the Scassus River by his captain, and instructed to set up a factory 'with ten slaves money'. His orders were that, once settled, he was 'to encourage the town's people, by supplying them with powder, ball and ammunition, to go to war and to give them all the encouragement that laid in my power to get slaves'. He therefore sent for the king and his caboceers and told them of his mission. They replied that they would 'instantly go to war in two or three days' time'. Some days later they returned, 'all dressed with some kind of skins, and with great caps upon their heads and with their faces painted white in order to make them look dreadful'. They asked for rum, tobacco and ammunition; and set off. There were between twenty-five and thirty of these warriors, some of whom came back at the end of five or six days with the somewhat paltry booty of two women and a six-year-old girl whom they had seized in bed asleep. Later, some men were brought in by the rest of the party.

Under Bowman's auspices, these raids would take place once or twice a week. The Englishman would sometimes march out with the raiders for about a mile or so, but 'was afraid to go any further'. He once waited on the bank of a small river, with four men to guard him, for the triumphant warriors' return. From this vantage-point he could hear the war-cry and he asked his companions what it meant: 'They told me that they had got to the town and were making war'. Bowman saw the town in flames and professes to have been affected by this as well as by the wails of the twenty-five or thirty captives of all ages who were soon being tugged towards him along the forest paths, hands tied and with ropes round their necks. They reached home by mid-day, when the slaves were 'carried to different parts of the town'. Up the Scassus, and in other places where he had traded, Bowman had often come across deserted or ruined towns and villages – some of them depopulated by slave-raiders, others prudently abandoned by their inhabitants 'for fear the white men should take them . . . The traders informed me it was war that had destroyed all the villages, and the inhabitants taken out and sold to the white men'. During his terms of duty in the Sierra Leone region, Bowman incidentally formed a very high opinion of African honesty and industry. He found the

Negroes friendly and hospitable and, in their commercial dealing 'just and punctual'. He liked the 'trading-men' better than 'the war-men', and bought from them ivory and camwood, as well as ample food supplies for the ships. When he first arrived at the head of the River Scassus, the village contained less than thirty souls, living in six or seven houses; when he left there were forty or fifty houses and well over an hundred villagers. This increase was entirely due to the news that 'a white man was come to live with them and had brought a great deal of goods'.

European observers, as well as European slave-traders and participants, were well aware of the artificial nature of these so-called war missions. Charles Berns Wadström, the scientist who had been sent by the King of Sweden to Senegambia in 1787 for one year, gave precise and disinterested evidence before the House of Commons Committee. Asked in which ways he thought that slaves for European ships were obtained in the region lying between the Senegal and Gambia Rivers he stated that these ways were three in number – 'general pillage, which is executed by order from the King, when the slaving vessels are on the coast; the second, by robbery by individuals; and thirdly, by stratagem and deceit which is executed both by the kings and individuals'. In this country, inhabited by the pastoral, somewhat fair-skinned Fulanis, and by the blacker Jalofs, it was also possible to obtain Mundingo slaves. Across the Atlantic none of these exports of Senegambia were rated much good for hard field labour, and were chiefly bought by planters to be turned into artisans and domestic servants. In Senegambia the slave-raids were made, as usual, at dusk; the King sent out his cavalry, armed with guns, pistols, sabres, bows and arrows and long lances, to round up any of his unsuspecting subjects they could find. The Swede blamed the French Senegal Company and the French Governor of the fort on Goree Island for stimulating and indeed exacting these semi-royal forays. He had stayed at Joal for a week, and during that time the King of Barbessin had sent out raiders daily. Wadström had reached Joal in the company of a French embassy sent from Goree to the Barbessin king.

The King of Barbessin, Wadström went on to say, did not much care for the way in which he was forced to 'harass his subjects'. It was the French officers and the mulattoes who went with embassies who 'excited' him by a policy of deliberate intoxication to send the raiding parties forth. Every morning they agreed amongst themselves to make the King drunk, but one day Wadström was privy to a conversation between the King and the French ambassadors at a moment when the monarch happened still to be cold sober. The King then told them he thought it hard that he should be continually obliged to 'distress his subjects', and that people from Goree were always bringing him presents which were trifling and insignificant in themselves and which in any case he did not want. They then came back with extravagant claims upon him, and were supported in these by the French Company. The French Governor of Goree, said the King, 'listened too readily to their complaints', and 'thought little of the sufferings of the negroes'.

In common with the majority of the witnesses examined by the Commons Commissioners, Berns Wadström emphasized the natural industry of West Africans, their kindliness, admiration for integrity, and decent, friendly treatment of their own domestic slaves. If these West Africans had any general attitude to the slave trade, they seem to have regarded it simply as part and parcel of a widespread commercial system by which they supplied quaint European wants – gold, slaves, camwood, ivory–in return for valuable articles like brass and copper which they coveted or required themselves. Captain Hugh Crow's executors, who edited the memoirs of that hard-headed yet jocose slave-trader, pointed out that their author had shown that 'the general negro character is full of gentleness, mingled with a sprightliness and good humour which incline their possessors to innocent mirth and mutual good offices'. Although, in the patronizing way then fashionable, they wrote of the 'ignorance and superstition' of Africans, they did attribute 'the practice of trafficking in their fellow men' to the initiative and encouragement of Europeans. Captain Crow himself we shall consult further, for he was one of the most literate – one might even say literary – of the English traders in slaves. Crow believed strongly in the slave trade as an economic necessity for the colonies, as a 'nursery for seamen' and as improving the lot of the Africans who were transported. His last assumption is comprehensible when we realize that he drew his conclusions from a limited experience of West Indian ports where he saw well-dressed, domesticated Negro servants and artisans who, as his editors remark, 'experience a treatment very different from that of their fellow blacks on the plantations'. Some of the Negroes of Kingston concocted a calypso about their friend Captain Crow, who had fought off enemy ships during the wars with France. Sung *con spirito* the first lines go:

> Capy Crow da come again
> But em alway fight and lose some mans,
> But we glad for see em now and den,
> Wit em hearty joyful gay,
> Wit em hearty joyful gay,
> Wit em tink, tink, tink, tink, tink, tinkara,
> Wit em tink, tink, tink, tink, tink, tinkara.

In his mind's eye Crow compared the gaiety of these tinkara-ing 'blackies' with what he personally knew of the African scene. But Crow's scene in West Africa was the eerie swampland of Bonny and Old Calabar, a world all its own, a world of islets, creeks and mangroves, a world which had spawned a strange, strong-minded, dreaded people famous for witchcraft and human sacrifice. These malevolent towns and their outports were unique on the Coast, in that they had been created by and were wholly dependent upon the slave trade to the west. Fishing hamlets had been transformed by the trade into rich and powerful slaving states, where families and factions vied for power and prosecuted hereditary feuds with blood-lust and with zest. In these Oil River ports life was wholly guided by slaving. To those who sold the greatest numbers of slaves went the power and the glory – political power and the glory of material things.

# V

We have so far drawn on European records and reminiscences of slave-trading, and on the memoirs of a few literate slaves. Would it not be interesting if we had at our disposal a third and most improbable category of documentation – the diary, say, of an eighteenth-century African slave-trader himself? And this, by one of those chances of survival, is exactly what we have. Until the bombing of the offices of the United Presbyterian

Church in George Street, Edinburgh, in the last war there existed a stout folio volume, perhaps an old log-book, which contained a very curious diary, written in pidgin English by a leading Efik slave-trader and senior member of the Egbo secret society of Bonny, named Antera Duke. During the bombing of Edinburgh this diary, together with other books and records in the George Street offices, was destroyed; but excerpts had already been made from it, have been transposed into modern English, and expertly edited. The diary covers three years of the later eighteenth century – 1785 to 1788.

Perhaps because he was familiar with ships' log-books the diary of Antera Duke begins each day with that reference to the weather which makes the diaries of King George the Fifth and Queen Mary seem initially uninspired: 'About 6 a.m. at Aqua Landing and a very foggy morning', 'About 6 a.m. at Aqua Landing with a fine morning'. But, the weather once dismissed, Antera Duke goes on to record little daily happenings and small routine events for which there are no parallels in English journals, royal or commoner's. 'I saw Jack Bassey come and bring one woman slave to be beheaded in honour of my father' . . . 'We heard news about a new ship. Three more heads were cut off' . . . 'At midnight Captain Brown's tender goes away with 430 slaves' . . . 'My fisherman came home with slaves and Robin sent me one girl' . . . 'Potter and his tender went away with 350 slaves' . . . 'After nine o'clock at night I sent five people to go to Yellow Belly's daughter, the mother of Dick Ebro's sister, to stop one of her house women from giving any slaves to the ship, because her brother gave one of my fine girls, which I gave to my wife, to Captain Fairweather who did not pay me' . . . 'I walked to Henshaw's town to see my mimbo wife' . . . 'A foggy morning, so I was to work in my little yard, but at the same time we and Tom Aqua and John Aqua joined together to catch men' . . . 'At 8 o'clock at night Long King Aqua sent one of his gentlemen to be killed by our hands so we sent that gentleman by Long Duke to the river to be killed'.

And there are even more interesting activities for us to watch, these foggy, foggy mornings at Aqua Landing.

# Chapter 12

# Foggy Mornings at Aqua Landing

## I

As A slaving centre, Old Calabar had been frequented by Europeans for more than three centuries. Off Aqua Landing in Duke Town, or at any of the other slimy townships – Old Town, Creek Town, Guinea Company, Henshaw Town, Big Qua Town, Hickory Cock – that clustered up the estuary of the broad Cross River big ships could find anchorage in good, deep water. Since these trading settlements were generally known to white men as 'Old Calabar', the main tributary of the Cross was christened by them Old Calabar River; it was where these two rivers mingle their dun waters that the high-rigged sea-going ships could lie. For safety, health and comfort captains and crews would live on board while conducting negotiations with the Efik traders of Old Calabar for slaves and elephants' tusks, as well as for Middle Passage stores of bananas, yams and corn. Slaving parties could also be sent out by long-boat, upriver to the hamlets of Tom Ekrikok and Old Ekrikok, further water-logged villages which owed their prosperity to the European trade.

To slave at Calabar could take a twelvemonth, but with luck and bribery a ship might be filled up in a far shorter time. Moreover, in this remote and tenebrous region of the Niger Delta, the rules of conduct half-heartedly assumed to govern European traders on the African coast were almost totally abrogated. Rivalry between the people of Old Town and those of its flourishing offshoot, New or Duke Town, had for instance, reached in 1767 a stage of mutual hostility which impeded foreign trade itself. The masters of seven European ships therefore entered into a secret agreement with the Duke Town leaders, promising to invite the unsuspicious chief men of Old Town to a palaver on board and then betray them for execution to their enemies. The sanguinary result of this intrigue is known as the Massacre of Old Calabar. Three or four hundred Old Town men were slaughtered, and the less eminent members of their retinues seized and shipped as slaves. On another occasion in this same year a distinguished refugee from Old Town, found hiding behind a chest on board the *Canterbury*, was dragged up on to the quarter-deck and handed over to a principal Duke Town trader named Willy Honesty. An eyewitness reports that Willy Honesty exclaimed: 'By God, Captain Parke, if you give me that man to cutty head, I'll give you the best man in my canoe [as a hostage] and you shall be slaved the first ship.' The captain picked a man from the canoe and ordered the captive to be handed over to Honesty. 'I recollect very well that he asked for a drink of water' the witness continued 'whether it was given to him or not I cannot say; he was supported down the ship's side into the canoe; and immediately taking of him by the hair of his head one of the black people in the canoe held him over the gunwale of the boat, struck off his head, I believe with one stroke, and then holding his head up there were great shouts in the canoe. This I saw with my own eyes.'

In less exceptionally dramatic circumstances, much hospitality was dispensed by Europeans and Africans in Calabar, on ship as well as shore. Many of the Efik traders could read, calculate and write in pidgin English, and their attitude to Europeans was jocular and lacking in respect. Between kings and ships' captains those insincere, familiar-seeming friendships in which businessmen delight were long established and, year after year, renewed. The steamy days and nights were whiled away in drinking. On protracted visits to Old Calabar, masters would spare their anchor cables by mooring the great sailing ships to forest trees on the banks of the Cross River.

The density of growth, and the extreme variety, of these massive trees are the most lasting visual impression which you carry back with you from a journey by the squat ferry boat up the Cross River from Oron to Calabar, a city which now ranks as, but in no way seems, a major modern West African port. It is as if each tree in these forests were engaged upon a struggle for survival with others more powerful or more predatory than itself; and they make of the Cross River a wide green corridor. There are gay-looking trees with parasol tops, others from which cataracts of creepers wildly fall, others so high that they thrust assertively up above the ragged skyline, and everywhere are crooked palm-trees lunging out, as it were, for sun and air. The whole effect is sombre and brooding – a riverscape that does not charm but threatens, with that most frightening and impersonal of all the threats that Nature wields: indifference. These delta forests seem as immune to humanity as the desert sands. You could stumble into their rank-smelling depths and die there, and it would make no difference to anything or anybody at all. Was it, perhaps, this atmosphere of stark detachment that gave the delta people their astounding disregard for human life?

From Oron the ferry moves over to the right bank of the Cross River and sets off northward, past Parrot Island, another former rendezvous for slavers, and Seven Fathom Point. The open sea at the river mouth is visible from Parrot Island, and so, when trade was scarce and foreign ships were few, the elders of Duke Town would conduct an albino child to the shores of the island and there sacrifice it to the white men's god who ruled the ocean and who sent white men's ships and white men's goods to benefit the populace of Calabar. This was but one of the 'bad practices' for which the Oil River tribes became notorious; for nowhere on the coast were there so many spirits to propitiate, and so many complicated ways of evading misfortune. The birth of twins, for example, was in this region rated an unforgiveable calamity; the babies were immediately put into an earthen pot and thrown away to die in the bush, while their mother was reviled and outlawed for her crime. Twin-murder was officially suppressed by the efforts of the heroic Scottish missionary Mary Slessor (whose Victorian monument stands in the Presbyterian graveyard on the heights of Calabar), but the wholesale sacrifice of slaves at the death of a great man, or in his memory, was given up more slowly. Antera Duke's diary records the death, in July 1786, of Duke Ephraim, the head of Duke Town, and the executions of slaves that followed it: 'About 4 a.m. I got up' Antera notes: 'there was great rain, so I walked to the town palaver house and I found all the gentlemen here. So we got ready to cut heads off, and at

5 o'clock in the morning we began to cut slaves' heads off, fifty heads in that one day. I carried 29 cases of bottled brandy, and 15 calabashes of chop for everybody, and there was play* in every yard in town.' Plays enacted in honour of the dead likewise involved executions: 'We saw Robin Tom, King John and Otto Ditto Tom; King John sent them to come and make a play in honour of Duke and my father and Egbo Young's mother; so they cut one woman's head off for Duke and seven Bar Room men to be beheaded for my father. So they played all night.'

These constant decapitations distressed certain of the European captains, who would sometimes unsuccessfully try to buy the victim off. A contemporary of Captain Crow has described how the selected slave was pinioned to a stake driven into the ground, which held him or her in a sitting position. A rope was wound round the head and over the eyes. The ends of this were held by by-standers who, immediately the head had been severed from the trunk by a single blow with a leaden-handled sword, would tug on the rope and toss the dripping head into the air, playing with it like a ball. 'If the executioner fails to strike off the head at a blow, the spectators set up a laugh of scorn and disappointment' our informant explains. The death of any great leader was the signal for a positive holocaust of murders. The widowhood of such a man's favourite wives was brief but nerve-racking; summoned by the once enticing words 'King calls you' they would tidy themselves hastily, swallow a mug of rum and trot to the place of execution where they were strangled with a piece of silk. Their fate was at least better than that of the chief's immediate retinue, some of whom were usually buried alive in his tomb beneath the earthen floor of his own palace or of the palaver house. Poisoning or witchcraft was usually assumed to be the cause of great ones' deaths. Inquests and investigations, which took the form of forcing suspects to 'drink doctor' (*esere* or Calabar beans pounded in water and believed by the Efiks to be a truth-revealing drug), accounted for many more corpses. The bodies of those who died during the test were chucked into the 'bad bush' once the eyes had been removed.

* 'The Ibibio are noted for their masked dancers, puppet, and stilt dancers' writes the editor of Duke's diary. The Efik are a branch of the Ibibio peoples.

It was such rather spectacular antics as these that had earned the Ibibio a baddish name with the tribes west of the Niger, and that persuaded men like Captain Crow that a West Indian or American plantation offered slaves from Calabar an alternative distinctly preferable to staying at home. Efiks and Ibibios, however, were not well liked by the planters, who found them fierce and moody in the cane or rice fields. In Calabar the Efiks only enslaved their own people for adultery or theft. They never sold their domestic slaves to the European traders, whom they supplied with war-captives, and with persons either snatched on raids like those which Isaac Parker witnessed, or obtained by purchase from nearby tribes. Except when it came to the frenzy of a funeral the Efiks treated their own slaves affectionately and well.

It was on such facts as these that I was ruminating one hot, late afternoon on the ferry bound for Calabar. A clumsy, two-decked boat, it nudged its way evenly up the river, past islet, mangrove swamp and tangled forest. There were far too many passengers for the benches, and people kept strolling and skipping from side to side of the decks to crane out over the rail – Nigerian ladies who would have looked willowy had they not been bundled up in their robes, their tall bright turbans tilted at a jaunty angle; a couple of self-important chiefs attended by boys bearing their striped umbrellas of state; flirtatious, ogling youths in clean white shirts and jeans. This was a kindly holiday atmosphere, Coca-Cola bottles chinking and a lot of light-hearted laughter. But, gazing down from the deck at the misty river-water sliding by, and out at the forest walls upon its banks, that laughter seemed to me to be about as suitable as laughter on the Styx.

# II

The exact position of Aqua Landing,* where Antera Duke and his friends spent busy mornings in the fog, is no longer identifiable, but it clearly formed part of the foreshore of Duke Town, today the major component of modern Calabar, a port of

* From *akwa*, the Efik word for big or large.

125,000 inhabitants. The wharf of sandy cement on which the Oron ferry sets you down is one of a series of wharves with warehouses and cranes lining a road most misleadingly called 'The Calabar Marina'. The true centre of Calabar – that is to say the squawking market-place, the post office, government buildings and churches – lies uphill on a dry plateau of heath or scrub dotted with straggling trees. Here, likewise, is the Progress Hotel, a group of cement bungalows with air-conditioning machines that do not work. Calabar is not a welcoming place.

In the time of Antera Duke and on into the nineteenth century, Duke Town consisted of low, thatched huts, that were so scattered pell-mell amongst the trees that bewildered strangers often lost their way. On the shore, facing out over the river, were a quantity of large guns, badly mounted, risky to fire, and on the whole used only for courtesy or ceremonial occasions connected with slaving ships: 'I saw that Coffee Duke sent his son to tell me news about a new ship.' (Antera Duke noted in a typical entry.) 'After a little time I heard 5 great guns fired at Seven Fathoms Point and we saw the ship come up. It was John Cooper's tender arriving, so we fired three great guns for him.' The firing of these aged guns was also a form of hospitality: 'Great morning fog' (Antera recorded on Christmas Day 1787) 'and at 1 o'clock we had Captain Fairweather, John Tatam, Captain Ford, Captain Hughes, Captain Potter, Captain Rogers and Captain Combesboch and Eyo Willy Honesty and Willy Tom Robin. We had dinner in Duke's house and supper. At 8 o'clock at night they went on board, and we fired three guns.' Four days after Christmas Captain Fairweather set sail with a cargo of three hundred and seventy-seven slaves; three weeks later, Captain Combesboch got two hundred and eighty.

Apart from being used to mark genial occasions, to welcome new ships or salute departing ones laden with slaves, the rusty guns at Aqua Landing were fired at European funerals: '7 o'clock at night we hear that Captain Aspinal is dead and hear all the town cry out' wrote Duke in June 1787, and (next day): 'All the Captains came ashore to bury Captain Aspinal with much ceremony. So we fired 6 great guns ashore'. The guns also lent dignity to magic rites: 'I went to my back cabin to plant some mimbo trees* and all our family walked up to the new palaver house and took one young boy slave to make doctor,† and two guns to be fired for the doctor; one gun fired and broke Long Dick Ephraim's hand. Dick must lose one of his hands by that gun.' Such accidents were not, in Calabar, confined to guns manned by Africans. In March 1787, when Antera Duke and some of his colleagues had gone on board Captain Aspinal's ship to discuss 'comey' (or slaving customs dues) they came back on shore with 'all the Captains. Then every ship fired guns. One gun came up and cut one of Captain Tatam's white men's head off.' A few weeks later there was another mishap: 'At three o'clock after noon Captain Hewitt and Combesboch and one little ship belonging to Hewitt came for 60 slaves, and Aspinal's mate lost both hands by the firing of guns.'

The winding streets of old Duke Town were really sand paths, which became so hot in the mid-day sun that they scorched your feet. A main thoroughfare, Duke Street, ran from the shore to the market-place and ended at the mansion of Duke Ephraim, head of the House of Duke. This important residence was large, and raised off the ground on pillars. Inside, the house displayed a welter of European objects accumulated over many generations of friendships with the white slave-traders: clocks, watches and other mechanical devices lay about amongst the greasy family fetishes and there were European beds, sofas, tables, cabinets, pictures and china. Most of these acquisitions were neglected, broken or decayed, but it was the fact of possession more than the condition of the object that primarily mattered to its owners. This taste for European things was widely spread in Calabar. In a letter of 1773, written in trade English by Grandy King George of Old Town to the Liverpool merchant Ambrose Lace, the immense list of trade goods required for slaving is followed by a terser list of the King's personal requirements – a six-foot square looking-glass in a strong frame,

* *Mimbo,* a white and not wildly intoxicating drink made from the liquid of a species of palm-tree. Duke's Town had a mimbo market, and Antera Duke a 'mimbo wife' – i.e. a country wife who lived on and tended his plantation of mimbo trees beyond the town.

† 'To make doctor' – to be slaughtered. Decorated by shelf upon shelf of painted skulls, Calabari and Bonny palaver-houses were considered unattractive by European slave-traders who were, however, at times invited to listen to debates and trials within their walls.

one red and one blue coat with gold lace 'to fit a large man', a table and six chairs for the King's house, an armchair for himself, a case of good razors, a gold-mounted cane, a close-stool and two pewter chamber-pots. Calabari ideas of European elegance were clearly based on what they saw in captains' cabins; and, indeed, the upper floor of any two-storied Efik house is still called a '*dek*', though spelt without the 'c'. These two-storied houses were of wood, and were built with materials which wealthy Efiks ordered all the way from Liverpool. White carpenters and joiners from the ships would help put the houses together in the squelch and sand of the Cross River settlements. On a fine November morning of 1786 Antera Duke records that he 'went down to the landing to look for a place to make a dwelling house'. The materials for his new house reached Duke Town next summer: 'I had Captain Potter come ashore' he notes in August 1787; 'after 11 o'clock Potter sent his tender and his ship to bring 35 white men and at noon they began to put up two sides of the house; and after 2 pm I have all the Captains to dinner and supper with me.' The floor was laid a month later, and no doubt Antera was soon entertaining European captains in his new residence.

Apart from the serious business of slaving, the Efiks and their white friends seem to have spent a very great deal of their time in entertainment – eating, drinking 'fine mimbo' or brandy, acting plays, and dancing. There were dances on shore every night, after which the white seamen usually stayed on, 'sleeping in the dew during the night . . . after being heated with spirits, and were consequently soon carried off'. The Dukes of Duke Town kept a very good table, complete with European crockery, glassware and cutlery. One or other of the Duke's quantities of wives would be detailed to prepare a luncheon in her own house, to which all important foreign visitors would be bidden. She would usually serve a 'yam chop', a dish of boiled yams and boiled fowls served up with sweet palm oil and pepper, and washed down with mimbo, rum or brandy. Generally, these wives wore little, but they would dress up in 'a very grand way of their own on holidays', wearing brilliant colours, with rings of burnished copper on their arms and legs, and with their hair twisted tightly into a cone one or two feet high. Like their arms, their faces were striped by tribal cuts. In Calabar, as elsewhere on the West African coast, it was the women who did agricultural as well as household work; strangers to Calabar were, on first landing, 'struck with the indolent, careless, yet cheerful appearance of the men, who saunter about the streets, sometimes strumming a musical instrument made like a child's money box with holes in the top' which made 'a sober monotonous tink-tink sort of jingle'. The kings and dukes of the region moved about in great state, preceded as well as followed by thirty or forty attendants, their regalia, which in one case included a human skull mounted on a baton, carried before them. These chief men were on the whole simply dressed, except for spectacular occasions; but they always wore 'a gold-laced round hat, like those worn by gentlemen's servants', sometimes set off with plumes.

The fact that so many of these great men up the Cross River, as well as those of Bonny, spoke and wrote English added one more peculiarity to the slave trade in this region. The peoples of other river settlements trusted entirely to their memories, which (a contemporary of Crow's remarked) 'necessity and use have enabled them to cultivate and strengthen to an extraordinary degree'. It also meant that these literate traders could lodge complaints direct with Liverpool owners if English ships' captains behaved in a way they did not like. A perennial source of friction was the fate of 'pawns' – hostages who were usually the children or other close relatives of a king or a duke, and who were lent to anchored ships as guarantees of safety and to make sure that thousands of pounds' worth of European trade goods entrusted to the Efiks for the purchase of slaves up-country would not be stolen or misappropriated. Some of the less couth captains thought it clever to carry away these high-born pawns and sell them as slaves in the Indies; at such times the old guns on the shore were used in earnest, and volleys were exchanged between, say, Old Town and the ships. In one of the interesting eighteenth-century Calabari letters preserved at Liverpool,* Grandy King George of Old Town – who would sign himself 'your best friend Grandy King George' – refers to such a rumpus:

* These pidgin-English letters from Calabar were printed *in extenso* by Gomer Williams in his *History of the Liverpool Privateers* (1897). I have here modernized spelling and punctuation.

I hope you and merchant Black wont let us want for encouragement or the other merchants of that place [Liverpool] that has a
mind to send their ships. They shall be used with nothing but civility
and fair trade. Other Captains may say what they please about my
doing them any bad thing, for what I did was their own faults, for
you may think, sir, that it was very vexing to have my sons carried
off by Capt. Jackson and Robin's sons and the King of Qua's son –
their names is Otto, Imbass, Egshiom, Ogen, Acandom, Ebetham,
Ephiyoung, Aset. And to vex us more the time we were firing at
each other they hoisted one of our sons to the yard-arm of Bishop
and another to Jackson's yard-arm and then would carry all of them
away and cut off my head if it had not been prevented.

There were, of course, faults on both sides, nor did the pawns
provide unlimited security. In a letter to his owners from Captain James Berry, of the brig *Dalrymple*, which lay off Old
Calabar in the spring of 1763, this ship's master reports being
kidnapped opposite Old Town. He had gone 'down the river
to get a little air thinking there was no danger of being molested'
because of the presence of pawns in his boat, but this had not
prevented Rouge Ephraim, Robin John, Robin John Tom and
Captain John Ambo from sending out two war-canoes to capture him. Berry was held on shore for a month, forced to pay
his captors whatever they pleased, and to surrender one big gun,
several muskets and 'two jackets of the black boys' before he was
released. He was also obliged to make out for them a worthless
set of good conduct certificates or 'books'. Some days later Duke
Solomon Henshaw 'and the rest of the gentlemen of the other
party' – that is to say Duke Town people – came on board the
*Dalrymple* to apologize and to sell Captain Berry ninety-eight
slaves, of which he bought forty-seven 'all of which was good,
only one woman'. Berry declared that he never would forgive
'the Old Town Scoundrels' or 'the injury Ephraim and the rest
did me till I have satisfaction'.

Despite such affronts and affrays the relations of the grander
Efik traders with the merchants of Liverpool remained urbane.
In return for presents from England, they would send personal
gifts of their own. In the summer of 1773, for example, Robin
John Otto Ephraim of Parrot Island sent a small Negro boy for
Joshua Lace, one of Ambrose Lace's young sons, and Robin
John's mother sent Mrs Lace a tusk of valuable ivory. Another

note to Lace, this time from an Old Town functionary, written in 1776, acknowledges the receipt of a picture, a book, a gown, an ink cake and some wafers for sealing letters. It adds that the writer had had to pay the Egbo men the day before.

# III

The diaries of Antera Duke contain many references to Egbo men, and to 'blowing' Egbo. Similar allusions occur in the Liverpool letters of the Calabari traders, in the memoirs and testimonies of Europeans who had been up the delta, and in ethnological studies of the Ibibio and the Efik peoples. Anyone upon whom Egbo was blown was shunned by his fellows and was obliged to stay within the confines of his house, which, if he did not make amends for his misdemeanours, was pulled down over his head – a head, moreover, as like as not itself in danger. Egbo could be blown on a ship's Captain if he had made himself unpopular with the Efiks; until the ban was lifted after a palaver he could buy no slaves and find no trade. An eighteenth-century slave-trader defined Egbo as 'a national bailiff and executioner'. In a modified form, Egbo still exists in Nigeria, but its interest to us here is the extent to which it affected the slave trade. What, precisely, was Egbo?

Stripped of the magic and terror that cloaked it, Egbo* was the all-powerful secret society which organized and protected the river settlements of the delta. A Leopard Society, Egbo had nothing in common with the cannibal Human Leopard Societies of, say, up-country Sierra Leone. Egbo's official reason for existing was to propitiate the potent local spirit from which it took its name, and who was personified by the Egbo himself – a tall, robed figure with a horrifying mask, long raffia hair, a hide whip in one hand and a sharpened sword in the other. The identity of the individual inside this Egbo costume was unknown and dangerous to speculate upon. When the Egbo drums were beaten, and Egbo himself emerged from the palaver house with his alarming band of attendants, the women of the town rushed to lock themselves into their houses. Like lepers in the

---

* *Egbo* was the European corruption of the Efik word *Ekpe* meaning Leopard.

Middle Ages, Egbo had a bell – in his case attached to his back – to warn loiterers of his approach. After important funerals Egbo visited the families of the deceased in their houses, and whipped them; but his chief preoccupation was punishing anyone who was behind with the Egbo tribute-money which every man had to pay. His usual punishment was whipping, but he was quite as likely to slice off the defaulter's head. Captain Crow's contemporary, Grant, was on the river-bank one day when Egbo, silencing his bell, stealthily crept up behind a fisherman: 'before the poor fellow could, after starting round on hearing his footsteps, make his escape to his canoe, his head rolled upon the beach. The dread [Grant continues] in which he is held is such that fishermen and others will even leap into the water, and swim across the river, though endangered by the sharks, to escape him'. Captain Snelgrave records that in the year 1734 he managed to buy a boy slave about to be sacrificed to Egbo by the King of Aqua; but such salvage operations were, as we have seen, rare.

Since Calabar lacked a recognizable political system, Egbo supplied the want by a set of complex rules and rites. It was supported by so-called voluntary contributions, contained many grades of fellowship and was directed by a counsel of the leading men. Egbo's ramifications remain complex and arcane. No foreigner has ever fathomed all its implications and traditions, but it has always been a fairly competent means of keeping order, and of, however summarily, settling disputes by discussion. For its chief members it was a way to wealth, the dues paid being divided amongst themselves. It seems also to have been an outlet for the African passion for dancing, playing musical instruments, and acting symbolic plays. But Egbo's rule was one of fear and not of love. Egbo struck terror into the villagers and shocked the European traders. Nor can we blame the latter for finding Egbo both mysterious and abhorrent.

For Europeans, Egbo was one more manifestation of that perplexing subject – the African's attitude to death. Many of the slaves they bought were able to will themselves to die on board the slave ships, while slaves executed at smart funerals or buried alive with their master's corpse often seemed strangely resigned to their fate. An ignorant seaman – even indeed a literate captain – could not be expected to understand about the shadow-world into which the dead were believed to with-draw, and which a great man must enter surrounded, as proof of his authenticity, by numbers of dead wives and dead servants, bringing with him his ceremonial stave and other signs of power. Sailor-boys from some snug West Country village connected death and funerals with a parson reading prayers over an open grave in a leafy churchyard; with the tolling of a church bell; with a throng of sorrowing relatives supporting the widow through the old lych-gate. Funerals in Calabar or Bonny were, on the contrary, a signal for wild and almost indiscriminate slaughter. Instead of comfort at the hands of their nearest and dearest, African widows faced immediate strangulation. Instead of a pension, ancient and trusted retainers were hurled living into the master's tomb. Instead of the reading of the will by a country solicitor, the bereaved family received a dawn visit from Egbo and his followers, on whipping bent. To young Jem or Willy, to Raoul or to Heinz, this was a perfectly incomprehensible and, consequently, perfectly despicable state of affairs. And once the funeral rites were over recriminations, as we have seen, set in. There was no country doctor in tie-wig and gaiters to send in, after a discreet interval, his heavy bill. Instead of this there were screaming-matches presided over by the witch-men in an effort to find out who, and how many, had poisoned the deceased or used magic to bring about his death.

Clearly, in European seamen's eyes, these Africans had no respect for life or death, and were thus suitable only for export to the plantations.

# Chapter 13

# The Great Column of Blood

## I

CALABAR because of its deep water anchorage and efficient and obliging native traders might be popular with European ships' masters, but the actual export product of this eerie region – Calabari Negroes – were not always in demand on the other side of the Atlantic. In the West Indies, planters could not on the whole afford to be choosy, and would accept Calabaris or anything else reasonably young and healthy that they could get. On the great rice and indigo plantations of South Carolina, however, Calabaris were not wanted. 'There must not be a Calabar amongst them,' the eminent Charleston slave trader Henry Laurens wrote to the St Kitts merchants, Smith and Clifton, when indenting for a fresh stock of slaves in 1755. 'Prime negro men of any country except Calabar bring great prices with us, £40 stg. and upwards,' Laurens wrote in September of the same year to another St Kitts middle-man. Apart from the fact that the chief demand in and around Charleston was for Gambians and other tall races, and that he refused to handle what he termed 'a scabby flock' of new slaves from the Delta, Laurens gave an interesting reason for the prejudice against the natives of Calabar: 'Stout healthy fellows sell to most advantage with us,' he wrote to Peter Furnell, of Jamaica; 'the country not material if they are not from Calabar which slaves are quite out of repute from numbers in every cargo that have been sold with us destroying themselves.' The Calabaris, in fact, carried with them over the sea their inborn contempt for the value of human life, and their longing for the African nether-world the gate to which was death.

Henry Laurens was partner in the firm of Austin and Laurens, which aimed to sell not more than seven hundred

Negro slaves a year. There were some dozen firms handling the
retail slave trade in Charleston, but in the mid-eighteenth
century, Austin and Laurens were the largest and most successful of them all, with one quarter of the whole Charleston trade
in their hands. In 1748 Laurens had gone to England to make
business contacts. His surviving letter-books form a corpus of
extremely detailed and immediate information on the American
end of the slave trade and show once again how risky, if profitable, this trade could be. International wars, or the possibility
of them, affected slave-prices in Charleston, as did the state of
the crops of rice and indigo on which the wealth of the southern
planters then depended. His correspondence was widespread –
he would write to Devonshire, Reeve and Lloyd of Bristol, to
Samuel Touchett of London, to Lascelles and Maxwell of
London, to Smith and Clifton of St Kitts and to Barbados firms
such as Law, Satterthwaite and Jones, or Gidney Clarke. Henry
Laurens was one of the leading citizens of Charleston and one of
the greatest plantation owners in South Carolina. Apart from
slaves, he dealt in rice and indigo, rum, beer, wine and deerskins.
On most of his goods he charged a five per cent commission,
but for slaves he raised this to ten. Apparently alone among the
merchants of Charleston, Laurens felt personal doubts about
slavery – 'You know, my dear Sir, I abhor slavery' he once
wrote to his eldest son; and after the Declaration of Independence he made elaborate plans to manumit his slaves.
Through no fault of his own he was unable to put these plans
into effect. Henry Laurens was in no way typical of the merchants and planters of the Low South, nor were his liberal views
shared by his fellow-citizens in Charleston.

And now, with the fine and hospitable city of Charleston,
South Carolina, and the allied vista of the columned plantation
palaces and the superb gardens and parklands of the South we
are entering a realm of conflict – a conflict between aesthetics
and morality which is, to say the least of it, disquieting. Pacing
the brick pavements and the cobblestones of Charleston, peering
through wrought iron gateways at the tall town-houses, at the
spacious porticoes and at the yards abloom with camellias and
jessamine, with gardenias, azaleas and the coral vine, it is hard to
recognize that all this civilized beauty has its roots in the sacked
villages of West Africa, and in the slave-dungeons of the coastal

castles and forts. How connect with these latter Gaddesden House on East Bay Street, or the Nathaniel Russell House on Meeting Street or any of the other mansions built by the planters to escape, in summer-time, from the malarial swamps in which their Negroes toiled and died? Yet all these houses, town and country alike, are the product of the dungeons of Elmina, the slave-pens at Whydah, the stinking ships lying off Anamabu, the night-raids by long-boat upriver at Sierra Leone. Middleton Place and Marshlands and Boone Hall owe their existence to hard bargaining for human flesh in the Gambia or Benin.

Ouspensky once wrote of the two histories – the history we all learn at school, the official history, which he called the history of crime; and the real history running on simultaneously with quiet persistence and which he took to be represented by medieval cathedrals such as Notre Dame de Paris. It is tempting but not possible to try to wrench this theory round to apply it to the marvellous houses of the Old South, but these form in fact a bloody chapter in the history of crime. The builders of Notre Dame were anonymous but they were free. The plantation houses of America stand on slave-dug foundations, are built of slave-baked bricks and slave-cut stones and slave-felled timber. Public buildings, moreover, were often financed by a tax on the importation of slaves: 'I am in hopes that this year, please God, there will come in a good many negroes' (Governor Nicolson of Virginia wrote to the Council of Trade and Plantations in London in June of 1700) 'so that there may be money enough in a year or two to build a house for his Majesty's Governor, as also the Capitol'. By the seventeen-twenties there were indeed enough Negroes to produce money as well as labour for such purposes and, in the words of the author of *The Mansions of Virginia 1706–1776* 'the new economic system was showing its effects and the era of great houses in the new style had begun'.

In *The Air-Conditioned Nightmare*, Henry Miller has asserted that 'the days of the great plantations bequeathed to the brief and bleak pattern of our American life a color and warmth suggestive, in certain ways, of that lurid, violent epoch in Europe known as the Renaissance'. But does this really hold? The standard of elegance and comfort in the country houses of the

Old South was usually far higher than that of the learning of their owners, and it would seem ludicrous to compare life on the old rice plantation with that which, in Italy, produced the Baptistery at Florence or the Venetian *palazzi*. Furthermore the masons and the bricklayers of Tuscany or the Veneto were neither lashed, nor bought, nor sold. In America, as Miller reminds us, 'the great houses followed the great crops; in Virginia tobacco, in South Carolina rice, in Mississipi cotton, in Lousiana sugar. Supporting it all, a living foundation, like a great column of blood, was the labour of the slaves'.

Travelling down the eastern seaboard of the United States in a search for material for this book, I was interested by the difference of attitude to my subject as one ventured further and further south. Up in Boston, and despite clear evidence to the contrary, people will deny that Bostonians ever had anything to do with the slave trade, and the Massachusetts Historical Society has even gone to the pains of publishing documents to show that the New England slave trade was centred on Newport, Rhode Island. In Newport itself the clapboard town's complicity in the trade cannot be ignored, but emphasis is laid on the leading part played in it by immigrant Portuguese Jews like Aaron Lopez, who lie buried there in the calm and shady little graveyard of the first American synagogue. In Charlottesville, Virginia, you get embarrassed replies if you ask how it came about that the venerated Thomas Jefferson who wrote against slavery still owned slaves and constructed Monticello with slave labour. When you get down into the Carolinas some of the descendants of the planters and merchants, some members of the old and charming aristocracy of Charleston and elsewhere, can scarcely understand why one thinks the old days of slavery were bad at all. They will refer to Roman slaves, to Saxon slaves, even to the building of the Egyptian pyramids, as well as, of course, to slavery as mentioned in the Bible. I got the uneasy feeling that I recall having had many years ago in Montgomery, Alabama – that to certain nostalgic Southerners it is the abolition of slavery, rather than its original existence, that constitutes the real crime.

In the Old Slave Mart Museum on Chalmers Street in Charleston – a building which in fact, was probably never a slave-market at all – a leaflet assures the tourist that the wooden stalls on the second floor of this converted barn were places in which 'prospective buyers could inspect slaves offered for sale. This again gives the lie to the popular image of the slave tied in chains standing before the public and subject to every indignity'. We are further told that surviving handbills show that slave-families were sold together and not, as every Northern and foreign eye-witness has recorded, ruthlessly split up. 'Thus,' the writer of this curious leaflet concludes, 'we have a record of a *business* – a sad and unfortunate one, yes – but still a business and not, as some may say, a mere exercise in cruelty.' The implication of this sentence beggars comment.

In the Southern States what I have earlier termed the *Myth of the Merry and Contented Slave* is still very much alive. In places like Charleston, inhabited by some of the most winning and civilized people I have ever met, it goes hand in hand with paternalism and with the cloying conviction that Negroes are quaint and sweet. In the museum there are collections of old Negro proverbs such as: 'If you knock de nose de eye cry', for example, or 'as de ole crow fly, so de young one too' or

> Sick chicken got de pip
> I see it in her eye.
> Stand back, nigger boy,
> And let dat chicken die.

Family tales of Negro cosiness and loyalty have been handed down, and when I was impolite enough to mention *Uncle Tom's Cabin*, a respected Charlestonian friend replied tartly: 'Mrs Stowe knew *nothing*. How could she, *coming from Cincinnati*!'

Back volumes of the *South Carolina Gazette* contain, however, many items which contradict the *Myth of the Merry and Contented Slave*. 'The negroes it seems have again begun the hellish practice of poisoning,' runs a news paragraph for January 1761 which records the hanging of a male and a female slave on Wadmalah Island. The number of advertisements for runaway slaves in the *Gazette* and other Southern papers do not suggest contentment either. In 1761 a Negro man is sought and may be recognized by '*his country marks* on his face and down his breast and belly'; or (in 1749) 'Sarah a lusty black wench with a very remarkable child of brick colour, has white curl'd hair and a twinkling in its eyes'; or 'a new negro from the Papaw country, his country name Arrow'; or 'a Mundingo negro with his country marks on his temple and cheeks'. Thus did the proud tribal cuts made in childhood as a sign of family and station become a means of identifying runaway Africans who were then handed back to the plantation overseer with his lash. If several slaves were on the loose, their owners would combine in volunteer bands which held a form of meet on horseback before the hunt began.

In the streets of Charleston a curfew for Negroes was enforced. Any Negro found walking about after dusk without a written permit from his master or mistress was arrested. Owners often made extra money by hiring out their domestic slaves, who were then given a copper identity disc bearing name, date and occupation to wear. Albino Negroes and mulattoes were exhibited for money as freaks or curiosities – a *Gazette* advertisement for May 1743 announces one such exhibition at the house of Mr Joel Poinsett in Charleston. Mr Poinsett was showing for a week in June, and for five shillings a head entrance fee, 'a WHITE Negro girl, of Negro parents, she is as white as any *European*, has a lovely blush in her countenance, grey eyes continually trembling, and hair fisled [*sic*] as the wool of a white lamb'.

The position of domestic slaves on the Southern plantations was as privileged as in the West Indies. They were nattily dressed, the footmen chosen for their height and looks, the ladies' maid rustling about 'in the scarcely worn silks of her young mistress' and, according to the freed slave Frederick Douglass (who escaped from the Lloyd plantation in Maryland in the year 1838) 'they resembled the field hands in nothing except their colour, and in this they held the advantage of a velvet-like glossiness, rich and beautiful. The hair, too, showed the same advantage'. But even these favoured beings lived on a knife edge and could at any moment be given a flogging for some trivial or imaginary offence. Douglass records many unsavoury incidents of his boyhood, one of the worst of which was watching the aged Colonel Lloyd thrash his old and trusted Negro coachman, who had been with him all his life, and whom he forced to take his unmerited punishment kneeling. Writing of the Lloyd plantation as 'secluded, dark and out of the way' Douglass explains that, even in Maryland, such estates were run as total tyrannies. The constant use of the cow-hide whip was, he points out, contagious, and Negroes in positions of slight authority over others would lash their fellow-slaves mercilessly. 'Everybody in the South' (he concludes) 'seems to want the privilege of whipping somebody else.'

Life on the old plantation was certainly lurid and violent; but there, we may think, its resemblance to Renaissance Italy most distinctly ends.

## II

'Our orders are that you embrace the first fair wind and make the best of your way to the coast of Africa, and there invest your cargo in slaves. As slaves, like other articles, when brought to market, generally appear to the best advantage; therefore too critical an inspection cannot be paid to them before purchase.' These instructions to a ship's master in 1785 were issued not in Charleston, South Carolina, but in Salem, Massachusetts.

Except for the famous witch trials of 1692,* there has never been anything very lurid and violent about Salem. The quiet Sabbath atmosphere of Salem, the gabled houses, the surrounding woods of birch and maple, the brisk New England air with the tang of the sea would seem the antithesis to that of the Carolina mansions and plantations, mysterious with Spanish moss swaying from the branches of the live oaks, and ostentatious to a degree which the Founding Fathers could never have envisaged. Yet it was from Salem, as well as from Boston and from Newport, that the slaving ships set sail for the coast of Guinea. One of the grievances of white Southerners in the nineteenth century – probably even a covert grievance still today – was that the Yankees who had become so vociferously humanitarian over the evils of slavery were the direct descendants of the chief American traders in slaves.

This is not to say that there had not always been voices raised in sonorous protest against slavery in the Northern and Middle States. The Philadelphia Quaker, Anthony Benezet, published

---

* An expression of public hysteria which only lasted four months, resulted in nineteen hangings and one pressing to death, and had its origins in an accusation that a West Indian slave named Tituba who belonged to a local Congregationalist clergyman had helped two other women bewitch ten young girls.

tracts upon the subject in 1762 and 1767, calling Negro slavery 'a lamentable and shocking instance of the influence which the love of gain has upon the minds of those who yield to its allurements' and condemning the slave trade itself as 'a trade which is entered upon from such sensual motives and carried on by such devilish means'. Writing in 1783 to a young lady who had lately moved from Maryland to New Jersey, the Boston merchant, Matthew Ridley, then in Paris told her: 'Time might reconcile you to the sight of the slaves. It is however a painful reflection to a generous mind and ought never to have been introduced. It is one of the evils that it will be very difficult to correct. Of all Reformations these are the most difficult to [? ripen] where the roots grow as it were in the pockets of men.' Actual Negro slavery in New England was never as prevalent as in the South, largely because there was no economic need for slaves, no plantation life, and a climate then considered far too cold for African survival. All the same, a French visitor to Boston in 1687 recorded that there was scarcely a household of any consequence in Boston city which did not possess one or more Negro slaves. Boston slaves were thus wholly domestic; in a letter of February 1738 from Peter Faneuil of Boston to Captain Bulkeley of the ship *Byam* this Bostonian merchant asked him to purchase in Antigua 'for the use of my house, as likely a strait-limbed Negro lad as possible you can, about the age of 12 to fifteen years, and if to be done, one that has had the smallpox'. The New England attitude to their own slaves was, we may surmise, more humane than that of most Southerners, and we might take a random inscription from a New England gravestone as representative of this:

*In memory of Caesar.*

Here lies the best of slaves
Now turning into dust;
Caesar the Ethiopian craves
A place among the just.

His faithful soul has fled
To realms of heavenly light,
And by the blood that Jesus shed
Is changed from Black to White.

Jan. 15 he quitted the stage
In the 77th year of his age.

1780

But the fact remains that it was the New Englanders who, on that side of the Atlantic, were most busily and thriftily engaged upon the Triangular Trade.

Theirs was the Triangular Trade with a difference. Slave ships out of New England, which were smaller than those out of Bristol, London or Liverpool, out of Holland or Metropolitan France, were known as 'rum-boats' because instead of the conventional copper bars and brass basins, bright cottons and glass beads, their sole cargoes were kegs of rum. It was with this beverage that slaves were bought up and down the Guinea coast. For instance, in the accounts of the Newport ships *Titt-Bitt* and *Cassada Garden*, lying off Anamabu in 1756, African men are recorded as fetching one hundred and fifteen gallons of rum each, and African women ninety-five gallons apiece. New England's particular contribution to the spread of alcoholism in West Africa was to encourage the drinking of rum instead of brandy. Until 1723 the favourite drink on the coast had been French brandy, but in that year the Rhode Islanders introduced the novelty of rum. This caught on quickly and (according to a tax protest by the Colony to the Board of Trade dated 1764) 'from small beginnings increased to the consumption of several thousand hogsheads yearly, by which the French are deprived of the sale of an equal quantity of brandy'. In 1764 the consumption of rum was 'annually increasing upon the coast', and the Rhode Islanders looked forward 'a few years' to the satisfying probability that 'the sale of French brandies there will be entirely destroyed'.

Most New England ships took their slaves to sell in the West Indies – whence great numbers were sent up to the colonies in America – and with the profits made they bought molasses, which they took back to New England to be made into rum for the West African market. It has been stated that by 1750 there were sixty-three rum distilleries in Massachusetts alone, turning out some 12,500 hogsheads a year, with another thirty distilleries in Rhode Island. In the year 1752 a Yankee captain, trying to stock up quickly with rum so as to get away to the

231

African coast, was informed by his agent that there was not
enough rum to go round, and that his hope of loading his sloop
with it in five weeks was not realistic: 'We cannot give you any
encouragement of getting that quantity of rum these three
months, for there are so many vessels loading for Guinea, we
can't get one hogshead of rum for cash.'

Nicholas Owen, whom at the beginning of this book we
found peaceably making a shell picture on the Sherbro River,
tells us that 'our old Europeans' thought the Yankee captains
comical. He explains that in an eighteenth-century New England
seaport, 'if a man is esteemed for his honesty in public, let him
be what profession so ever, he is to be preferred in a ship to these
and other parts of the world, if he can take an observation and is
acquainted with that part of navigation called plain sailing
without any of the practical part of seamanship'. New England
butchers, carpenters or farmers might turn up on the Guinea
Coast in charge of a rum-boat, and Owen suggests that they
returned safely home 'more by chance than art'. But he himself
did not think European factors and ships' masters right to laugh
at 'the great many remarks of simplicity laid to the charge of
these people'. He admired the Yankee captains because they did
not swear and were 'an industrious honest people, who despise
the gaudy toys of the foolish for things more substantial and
necessary for the life of man'. The eager involvement in the
slave trade of these sober, and sober-minded, persons who loved
God and eschewed profanity may well make one ponder. A
modern historian of Rhode Island has even suggested that a
slaving voyage made under such a captain must have been the
making of many a likely New England lad. 'Think of the effect,
the result of a slave voyage on a youngster starting in his teens'
(wrote H. W. Preston, Director of the Rhode Island State
Bureau of Information in his *Rhode Island and the Sea*, published
in Providence in 1932). '. . . What an education was such a
voyage for the farmer lad. What an enlargement of experience
for a country boy. If he returned to the farm his whole outlook
on life would be changed. He went out a boy; he returned a
man.'

# III

Whether the blithe country boy off a farm outside Concord, or the fisherman's son from Gloucester, Massachusetts, returned from Guinea men or brutes is open to conjecture, but certain it is that their restricted New England outlook would have been sharply widened by their experiences on the Gambia or amidst the flying human heads of Old Calabar. The authors of *Black Cargoes* believe that the conditions of seamen serving on the New England slavers were better than those of seamen on European ships. Yankee captains did not usually carry a cat-o'-nine-tails, and the comparative classlessness of rural New England society prevented the captains from exercising too haughty or too absolute a power. Many of their crew might also be their relatives or neighbours 'and the captain was frequently reminded of what the neighbours might say'. These authors appositely quote Whittier's lines on the fate of an unpopular Marblehead skipper:

> Old Floyd Ireson, for his hard heart,
> Tarr'd and feather'd and carried in a cart
> By the women of Marblehead!

On the other hand, the Negro slaves on Yankee ships suffered more on the Middle Passage because the ships were so small. Slaves on these brigs and sloops were only released from their chains to work the pumps in a crisis, for many of the New England ships were so unseaworthy that 'you could see daylight all around the bows under the deck'. The eighteenth-century *Boston News Letter*, which carried frequent advertisements of slaves for sale on Beacon Street or Summer Street, also recorded melancholy details of successful ship-board mutinies – as, for example, an uprising on board a Rhode Island ship, Captain Beer commanding, which was lying off Cape Coast Castle in the winter of 1746. This ship was already loaded with 'a number of negro slaves, and a considerable quantity of gold dust on board; the said slaves found an opportunity to rise against the Master and men and killed the said Master and all the crew, except the two Masters [Mates] who by jumping overboard and swimming ashore saved their lives. What became of

233

the vessel and negroes afterwards the letter* does not mention'.
On another occasion, in 1765, a Captain Hopkins from Providence was obliged, while on the Middle Passage and owing to
the sickness of many of his crew, to call upon a certain number
of slaves to help run the ship. These slaves managed to release
the rest, and the whole drove of them attacked the crew; they
were overpowered in the end, but eighty of the valuable people
were either killed, wounded or thrown overboard during the
tussle.

Such was the enthusiasm with which New England merchants
plunged into the rum trade that sometimes they unintentionally
created a glut of that spirit on the Guinea Coast. The *Boston
Gazette* for 12 September 1763, reports 'the very discouraging
accounts' of two Rhode Island captains on the Guinea Coast,
who complained of the shortage of slaves and that prices in rum
were consequently rising. Twenty more vessels were setting out
from Newport, carrying nine thousand hogsheads of rum all
told – 'a quantity much too large for the places on the coast
where that commodity has generally been vended'. Agreements
could sometimes be made with English ships on the coast,
whereby they exchanged trade goods with the Yankees for so
many gallons of rum, but all the same a glut was not unusual.
In 1736 a Captain Cahoone, writing from Anamabu to his
owner, the merchant Ayrault of Newport, Rhode Island, said he
had never seen so much rum on the coast 'at one time before',
and that there were also swarms of French slavers – 'never seen
before for number, for the whole coast is full of them'. He reports
that there were seven sail 'of us rum men' at Anamabu alone –
'we are ready to devour one another, for our case is desperate
. . . I have got on board sixty-one slaves and upwards of thirty
ounces of gold, and have got thirteen or fourteen hogsheads of
rum yet left on board, the trade is so very dull it is actually
enough to make a man crazy.' But as always, the fortunes of the
coast fluctuated; forty years later a second mate, Peleg Green,
from Newport, was writing to Aaron Lopez, one of the leading
Jewish slave-merchants there, that he had reached Anamabu
and found 'times to be very good, thanks be to God for it, there
was only one rum man, that is Captain Johnson of Boston and

* i.e. a letter 'from the coast of Guinea' which was dated 14 January 1747 and
reached Boston *via* Barbados.

he had almost done before we arrived'. But, in general, as we know, slaving on the coast was a long and tedious business, made all the worse by sickness and by the rains that began in May and lasted till October. As at Cape Coast Castle and the other forts on shore, alcohol was both a necessity and a menace to the seamen on board their anchored ships.

And what of our country boy, fresh from the sea-winds of Cape Cod and the quiet and ordered beauty of the trim villages of New England, snug and Breughel-like in the snow, a mass of lilacs and of linden trees in summer? Everyone has perhaps his own conception of what constitutes manhood, but might we not legitimately suppose that a career begun on a Gloucester fishing schooner would be more likely to turn our boy into a man than service on even the best-run slave ship? Even if we picture all New England slave ship masters to have been as stern and religious as Captain Ahab himself, we must assume that, once on the coast of Guinea and engaged in the frantic febrile search for slaves, they had not too much time left over to inquire into the morals of their crew or to shield some rustic mother's lad from the riveting realities of life on the African coast. On board many of the slave ships, the captains did make some effort to limit the crews' drinking habits. But expeditions by open boat, either down the coast or upriver, with the aim of picking up slaves piecemeal or in small 'parcels', were impossible to control. On these trips, kegs of rum and brandy formed a natural part of a longboat's cargo; men soaked to the skin by tropical rain for days together could hardly be expected to refrain from cracking such kegs open and replacing what they drank by river-water. 'The blacks who buy the liquor' wrote John Newton 'are the losers by the adulteration; but often the people who cheat them are the greatest sufferers'. Further, the sailors would inevitably swill palm-wine in great quantities, either sold them by the Africans or offered by kindly black acquaintances. And then there was the problem – one on which no New England mother would have cared to dwell – of the African women. 'Problem' is in fact the wrong word. The real difficulty lay in the apparent availability of African women on the coast, and in the danger that voluntary liaisons or attempted rape would often lead to a seaman's death either by knife or poison. For the captains it was irritating enough to have their men sick or dying of fever. That they should risk being murdered for their pleasures was too senseless and capricious altogether. Newton remarks that many captains did make efforts to keep their seamen under control, but that many more did not mind how their men spent their spare time so long as they did their jobs properly on board.

The hunt for and purchase of the slaves was degrading in itself, but, for a neophyte, the intense sexuality of life on the Guinea Coast was irresistibly alluring and corruptive. Amongst West Africans virility was, and remains, a status symbol. A chief was often chosen for the number of his wives, which meant for the number of his children; and in order not to lose his power and perhaps his life it was essential for him to be surrounded by living and squalling proofs of his sexual potency. Outwardly, Negro girls and women of good families behaved with discretion; but white lovers and the gifts they brought were popular with them, and many of the seamen, like the garrison soldiers in the forts, were thought to have literally worn themselves away copulating in the night dews on the coast: 'and lewdness' (John Newton sententiously reminds us) 'too frequently terminates in death'.

Apart from these perilous and obvious manifestations of manhood, the Guinea Coast had much else to show the travelling boy from Beverley or Marblehead. Even the whaling ships at home could not compare in splendour with, say, the state war-canoes of the two Kings of Bonny, King Pepple and King Holiday. To old hands like Captain Hugh Crow, it was always clear that King Pepple was in some unidentifiable way the social and constitutional superior of King Holiday. They would never make state visits to anchored European ships together, although it was thought by the Europeans that they were more or less co-partners on the Bonny throne. Sometimes they quarrelled, when King Holiday would withdraw with his retinue to seek sanctuary in Fish Town, a holy place of safety far out in the mangrove swamps and which was ruled by priests. The two kings, like all the others down the coast, wore gold-laced hats, but King Pepple would sometimes sport a pair of scarlet leather boots which seemed too small for him and which caused him to topple over when he was drunk. The ceremonial canoes of Bonny were famous for their size and their construction, cut, like those of Calabar, from the log of a single giant cotton-tree.

There were fifteen rowers on each side, as well as a complement of one hundred and fifty armed men. When equipped for war – that is to say for slaving forays – the canoes shot by with colours flying, drums beating and horns blowing. Seated musicians played on other instruments and some of the retinue danced up and down the middle of the boat. The rowers kept 'admirable time' with their paddles, and the great war-canoes sped rapidly, relentlessly on their predatory course. Bonny offered other novel and interesting spectacles – not least amongst them that of the big land-crabs creeping in and out of holes in the earthen house-floors after an important home-funeral. 'Although there is no doubt the ugly creatures consume the bodies' (Captain Crow explains) 'the inhabitants eat them with a great deal of relish.'

Tales such as these, which really needed pruning rather than elaboration, would echo, months later, through the neat parlour of some weatherboarded farm cottage in Massachusetts as the boy (now a man) displayed the bright, obscene sea-shells, the live parrot or monkey, and the dried snake-skins brought back as presents to his parents and his demure sisters. Other sights and episodes would be wisely left unmentioned, to be mulled over in the warmth and privacy of an attic bed, or while milking the cows in the chill New England dusk. The temptation to go a second time to the coast of Guinea would grow until it became irresistible. For whatever Africa finally makes of you, and however incomprehensible that continent begins to seem, it does inspire you with a gnawing nostalgia, and exercises over those who have once been there a pull as strong, I think, as the more publicized and legendary pull of the East.

# IV

Of the New England ports which served as main pumping-stations to the great column of blood down South, Newport was the most active. Although the Newport slave merchants used Barbados as a main information centre on current prices, and also sold in other West Indian islands, they did a brisk, direct trade with Charleston firms, and almost regarded the city of Charleston as yet another West Indian island. Samuel and William Vernon, of Newport, traded chiefly with Austin and

Laurens, the Charleston firm already mentioned. The Vernon letter-books are as detailed as those of Henry Laurens, and show with what painstaking competence the American trade was run. In June 1756, for instance, Austin and Laurens had reported to their Newport correspondents that a Negro girl sold to a planter named Yarnold had died after the sale, and that they had persuaded him to take the matter to arbitration – the question being whether he should pay for her or not. This incident riled the Newport traders: 'we don't imagine whether he bought the girl at a public or private sale that you warranted her to be perfectly sound and well – which is not customary for new slaves, and whether we are not entitled to as much compensation as he is – or whether he can't afford to bear such a loss as well as we are we can't say. These things we think are quite foreign from the dispute.' This particular case was of consequence, for it involved a matter of principle – that slaves fresh from Africa should never be guaranteed sound – and it could have set a dangerous precedent by which the traders stood to lose a good deal, since newly arrived slaves often died from past ill-treatment on the Middle Passage, from the physical shock of plantation conditions, or from suicidal melancholia.

Charleston firms had sometimes to complain of the state of a slave ship's cargo, either because of sickness contracted on the voyage or because the Negroes had been carelessly selected on the Guinea Coast. 'We have this day sold to the amount of £7,445.12/- currency, in which two are included that sold at vendue for only £35., 12s' (Henry Laurens wrote, again in 1756, to the Vernon brothers of Newport):

They seemed past all hopes of recovery. God knows what we shall do with what remain, they are a most scabby flock, all of them full of crockeraws – several have extreme sore eyes, three very puny children and add to this the worst infirmity of all others with which which 6 or 8 are attended (vizt) Old Age – those the vessel brought last year were very indifferent but these much worse . . . We had a sloop arrived with one hundred and fifty prime slaves from the factories at Gambia and Bence Island the evening before the sale of your negroes which would not at all have injured your sale had they been good, for we did not discover what a prime parcel they were until the first day's sale was over.

The Vernons replied that although this news showed that it had been 'a very bad voyage' for them personally, they were certain that Austin and Laurens had used their 'best endeavours' in the sale.

The slave trade was, of course, only one section of the widespread shipping interests of the Rhode Island merchants, who also dealt in whale and sperm oil, in spermaceti candles, and in and import-export business with the ports of Europe. Most of these firms were family concerns – there were Christopher, George and Robert Champlin, the four Brown brothers of Providence Plantation, a large family named Wanton, as well as individuals like Philip Wilkinson and Stephen d'Ayrault, Junior. From 1790 on the slave trade was chiefly in the hands of the brothers de Wolf, the youngest of whom, Levi, is said to have 'retired in disgust after making one voyage to Africa'.

Although they were distinguished for sobriety – Newport slaving captains of the pre-Revolutionary era belonged to the Fellowship Club of Newport, the rules of which forbade gambling, drinking, quarrelling and swearing – that high moral tone on which New Englanders have ever prided themselves was not always audible in their ships along the Guinea coast. Captain Samuel Moore, of Boston, who traded in the Gambia River in the seventeen-thirties was a notorious cheat, who passed off pewter forgeries as Maria Theresa dollars, and got himself into trouble with the King of Cassan for giving him inferior trade goods. Simeon Potter, a ship-owner of Bristol, Rhode Island, issued instructions to his captains that they were to deal with African rather than European slave-traders, to make sure to water the rum as much as possible 'and sell as much on the short measure as you can'. It was Potter's theory that the heat of the sun would make the rum rise in the kegs so that it mixed with the water; and he is on record for remarking: 'Money? Why I'd plough the sea to porridge to make money!' Simeon Potter had a sister who had been given the good old New England christian name of Abigail. Miss Abigail married one of her brother's supercargoes, Marc Antoine de Wolf, a Jew from the French island of Guadeloupe. De Wolf settled down in his wife's home town of Bristol, Rhode Island, and sent several of their eight sons into the slave trade. The most famous of these, James de Wolf, was tried before a Newport grand jury in 1791, and found guilty of murder for having thrown into the sea a Negress who had contracted small-pox while on board his ship. By the time the verdict was reached he had already left the state. James de Wolf was later elected to the United States Senate, and lived on into a distinguished old age.

The de Wolfs were not the only Jews prominent in the Rhode Island slave trading ventures. We have already come across the name of Aaron Lopez, who, with his partner, Jacob Rodriguez Rivera, owned the most successful slaving business in the state. Aaron Lopez was a man with a long, ascetic, olive face who wore a white tie-wig. He has been described as boundlessly knowledgeable in commerce, of irreproachable integrity and of 'polite and amiable manners'. His characteristics, we learn, were 'hospitality and benevolence' and he was considered 'an ornament and a valuable pillar in the Jewish society of which he was a member. Thus he lived and thus he died; much regretted, esteemed and loved by all'. Aaron Lopez had a nephew, Abraham Lopez, and a son-in-law, Abraham Pereira Mendes, who made trips for the firm to Jamaica and New York. In May 1752, for example, the *New York Gazette* carried an advertisement which read: 'To be sold by Abraham Pereira Mendes, a parcel of likely young negroes, pimento, coffee etc. at the house in Smith's Fly, lately in occupation of Roger Pell, innkeeper. N.B. If any person has a mind to purchase any of the goods mentioned, they may inquire of Mr Daniel Gomez.' In 1767, when on a mission to Jamaica, Mendes reported back to his father-in-law that a consignment of Negroes was 'in such poor order' owing to being cooped up in too small a brig for him to do anything but sell them off cheaply: 'To my great surprise I found the negroes nothing to what I expected.' His father-in-law replied that it gave him 'no small pleasure' to learn that Mendes was on the spot in Kingston 'to assist Captain All in the disposal of his small cargo'. Captain All's small cargo, however, turned out as we see to consist almost entirely of 'refuse slaves', and Captain All himself fell ill. He left Kingston for Newport in November but, although the prudent Mendes had 'got the cash for the boys' he would not send it by Captain All: 'the vessel having poor rigging and going on the winter's coast would not venture to remit by him the money, but shall wait for your further orders. Could I [have] got insurance made here would have remitted.' British occupation of Newport during the Revolutionary war ruined many of the merchants there. Aaron Lopez lost all his thirty vessels, and went to live in benevolent retirement in the little Massachusetts township of Leicester.

Were we, at this late stage of our contemplation of the slave-traders, still capable of feeling either astonishment or pain we might perhaps experience both when looking at these Rhode Island Jews. Like the Jewish slavers of Jamaica, Lopez and his ramified relatives were of Sephardic origin. Persecuted in Portugal, these families had sought sanctuary in America, where they could practise their faith in freedom and grow rich respectably. You might have supposed, might you not, that a national and religious group which had chosen freedom would hesitate at making a fortune by enslaving others? You would have been sadly wrong.

But though the Jews of Rhode Island remained as unmoved by African misery as the planters of the South or as the merchants of Liverpool and Bristol, there flourished in New England one body of noble-minded persons to whom the slave trade and slavery itself had always been anathema: the Quakers. In 1773 the Rhode Island Quakers, in particular, received powerful and expert support for their views from a new recruit to their ranks in the person of Moses Brown, youngest of the four slave-trading brothers of Providence Plantation. Converted to Quakerism, Moses Brown gave up slaving to devote the remainder of his life to fighting the trade, and to trying to persuade his immediate family and other prominent Rhode Island merchants to desist from it as well. The zeal of the convert is frequently derided, yet Moses Brown in America, like John Newton in England, was specifically equipped by experience to preach the abolition of an evil trade in which he had himself for so long taken part.

# V

It is reckoned that 'articulate criticism of the trade in Negroes' began in North America with the publication of Samuel Sewall's pamphlet *The Selling of Joseph: a Memorial* which was printed in Boston in June 1700. Sewall was a jurist of distinction who kept a well-known diary, in one passage of which he recorded that he had 'been long and much dissatisfied with the

trade of fetching negroes from Guinea' and that he had determined 'to write something about it'. Expressed with tortuous-
ness, his arguments were in fact simple: if the Negroes bought
for the slave trade were, as was alleged, captives taken in tribal
wars, how could we know that these wars had been justified?
'Every war is upon one side unjust' (wrote Sewall). 'An unlawful war can't make lawful captives. And by receiving we are in
danger to promote and partake in their barbarous cruelties.'
He further suggested that if a party of Bostonian cronies had
gone down to the Brewsters to fish and had there been attacked
and captured by 'a stronger party from Hull' and afterwards
sold as slaves to an outward bound ship 'they would think
themselves unjustly dealt with, both by sellers and buyers. And
yet' (he concluded) ' 'tis to be feared, we have no other kind of
title to our Niggers.' His pamphlet met with what he called
'frowns and hard words', but also with approval in some
quarters. It was not till many decades later in that century that
the Quaker campaign against slavery began to have a real
effect. Dr Samuel Hopkins, pastor of the First Congregational
Church in Newport and an ardent abolitionist wrote to his
friend, Levi Hart, in 1787: 'We have no men of any other
denomination in these States, who appear so conscientious, dis-
cerning, faithful and zealous, in this matter, as these Quakers
do.' 'The Friends' (Hopkins wrote in 1784 to Moses Brown)
'have set a laudable example in bearing testimony against the
slave trade, and exerting themselves to suppress the slavery of
the Africans; and I must say, have acted more like Christians,
in this important article, than any other denomination of Christians among us. To our shame be it spoken!' Hopkins said that
he had 'dared publicly to declare' that the town of Newport was
'the most guilty, respecting the slave trade, of any on the continent, as it has been, in a great measure, built up by the blood
of the poor Africans'. Old Newport, with its steeply sloping
streets of clapboard houses, and its general air of having been
designed by Grandma Moses, seems today as difficult to asso-
ciate with the slave-pens of Anamabu as the more sophisticated
mansions of the Battery, Charleston. But the connection is
memorable; and direct.

While clergymen like Dr Hopkins, and members of the
Society of Friends, preached and printed pamphlets and tried

to get abolitionist articles inserted in local newspapers, Moses Brown acted as an ardent but often unsuccessful Fifth Column agent amongst the Rhode Island shipowners. Hearing, for instance, in October 1783 that the firm of Clark and Nightingale 'had in contemplation sending a vessel to Africa for the purpose of getting negroes and selling them as slaves in the West Indies' he wrote an impassioned letter of dissuasion, asserting that he had always been averse to the slave trade, but had at first let himself be over-ruled by others, and by the incontrovertible fact that he himself held slaves. He declared that the trade was 'an evil, which has given me the most uneasiness, and has left the greatest impression and stain upon my own mind of any, if not all, my other conduct in life'. This letter had no effect on Clark and Nightingale. Like Moses Brown's campaign, that of Dr Samuel Hopkins was uphill work, for a large part of his congregation were rich slave-traders. So entrenched was the slaving interest in Rhode Island that the editor of the *Newport Herald* was persuaded to refuse to print one of Hopkins' essays on the subject, although he had previously promised to do so: 'He says he has consulted his friends and they tell him it will greatly hurt his interest to do it; that there is so large a number of his customers, either in the slave trade, or in such connection with them, or so disposed with respect to it, to whom it will give the greatest offence, that it is not prudent for him to do it.'

All the same, the devotion of the Quakers to the abolitionist cause, together with the upsurge of liberal ideals during the War of Independence, did have some legislative effect. By 1778 it had been forbidden by law to import Negroes into Rhode Island, Connecticut, Pennsylvania, and Virginia, but by 1783, writes Sir Reginald Coupland, 'It was still legal . . . for citizens of New England or the Middle States to take a hand in importing slaves into the plantation-states of the South where slavery was now as deeply rooted as in any West Indian island.' At the Congress of Philadelphia in 1787 anti-slavery clauses in the new American Constitution were deleted at the behest of the delegates of South Carolina and Georgia, two states which insisted on recognition of slavery as their condition for joining the Union. This Southern blackmail injected fresh life into the slave trade, and ensured another three generations of suffering to the African slaves.

During and after the War of Independence, there was a tendency in America to blame the existence of slavery, and the conduct of the slave trade, on the British. Writing in 1776 to his son John, old Henry Laurens of Charleston (who was afterwards one of the American plenipotentiaries of the Paris peace conference which ended the war) told him, as we have seen, that he abhorred slavery:

I was born in a country where slavery was established by British Kings and Parliaments as well as by the laws of that country ages before my existence . . . not less than £20,000 sterling would all my negroes produce if sold at public auction tomorrow. I am not the man who enslaves them, they are indebted to English men for that favour, nevertheless I am devising means for manumitting many of them, and for cutting off the entail of slavery – great powers oppose me, the laws and customs of my country, my own and the avarice of my countrymen – what will my children say if I deprive them of so much estate? These are difficulties but not insuperable.

Laurens was particularly incensed by the way in which the British army and navy raided the plantations of the South 'to steal those negroes from the Americans to whom they had sold them, pretending to set the poor wretches free, but basely trepan and sell them into ten fold worse slavery in the West Indies, where probably they will become the property of Englishmen again and of some who sit in Parliament; what meanness! what complicated wickedness appears in this scene! O, England, how changed! how fallen!' As a preface to this eloquent piece of hysteria, Henry Laurens reminded his son of the loyalty of their own Negroes: 'My negroes there [in Georgia] all to a man are strongly attached to me, so are all mine in this country, hitherto not one of them has attempted to desert.' Although he had grown wealthy by buying and selling Africans, and owned large plantations where his slaves lived under the inhuman Black Code of South Carolina, Laurens became emotional on reading, in August 1776, that phrase in the Declaration of Independence which declared that 'all men are created equal'. It was this phrase which persuaded him to relinquish his ambivalent attitude to slavery, and to adopt the most ungrateful role of abolitionist; for if all men were created equal, how could any be a slave?

## The Great Column of Blood

We know that Dr Johnson, in his arguments with Boswell, was quick to point out the inconsistency of American complaints of British oppression with their sanguinary tyranny over their own slaves. In 1775 Thomas Paine published in Philadelphia a tract, *African Slavery in America,* in which he unwittingly echoed Johnson's protest, asking Americans 'to consider with what consistency or decency they complain so loudly of attempts to enslave them while they hold so many hundred thousands in slavery'.

The long and noble history of the abolition of the slave trade belongs to some other book than this; but a glance at that great, and finally successful, movement initiated by Thomas Clarkson and William Wilberforce in Great Britain will be relevant here, if only because of the cynical opposition it aroused and because of the bloody doings which its investigations uncovered and revealed.

# Chapter 14

# An Obstinate Hill

## I

IN WHAT now remains of the narrow old High Street of the city of Kingston-upon-Hull in Yorkshire there stands, still protected by its original wall of reddish brick, a pleasant, roomy, late-Elizabethan building now called Wilberforce House. This is the birthplace of William Wilberforce, the famous philanthropist, known to history as the Liberator of the Slaves, and allotted in his lifetime the somewhat unsavoury role of 'authorized interpreter of the national conscience'. The brick exterior of this old house, in which in August 1759 the national interpreter was born, is corrugated by niches and panels, but its Tudor casement windows were replaced by the Wilberforce family, and large eighteenth-century window-frames now let in the sunlight and the smell of tarred rope from the barges lying along the river-quay. A small garden separates the house from the road and is entered between tall brick gate-posts surmounted by stone balls. A kind of shallow gatehouse protrudes from the centre of the building. You can go under its archway into a large formal garden at the back of the house, stretching down to the river-side. In summer-time this garden is fragrant with stocks, rosemary and sweet-william. In the front garden a white marble statue of Wilberforce broods, and inside the house, now a museum, are his portraits and relics, as well as a remarkably life-like wax effigy of the philanthropist seated pensively at his desk.

One of the chief rooms in this admirably-kept museum is devoted to the slave trade, and to Negro slavery. There are, of course, documents in cases; but in other cases are exhibits more evocative by far – manacles, fetters, cow-hide whips, branding-tools and an example of the iron collar which was clamped round new slaves' necks to prevent their escape into the bush. From this collar (which locks) protrude four iron spikes some two feet long and each ending in a double hook. The object of this contraption was to ensure that a fleeing slave would at once become entangled in the tumultuous undergrowth of West Africa. If not recaptured, he would thus face death by starvation or from wild beasts. These collars were also used as punishments on the West Indian plantations, where they were known as 'iron necklaces' and where, together with the 'iron boots' (which had 'iron spurs') they would often be used to shackle offending Negroes one to another. 'A chain fastened about the body with a padlock is another mode of tormenting this oppressed race of beings' (wrote a visitor to Antigua in 1787). 'A boy who has not yet seen his fourteenth year passes by my house several times in a day and has done so for these six months past with no other clothing.' Such collars and such chains are still to be seen lying around in West Africa today – at Badagry on the Nigerian coast near Lagos, for example, a place of mud and creeks near which I once spent a sand-strewn Christmas, suffocated by the heat and deafened by the boom of the waves in the Bight of Benin.

But if the curios in the Wilberforce collection made me think, one sunny August morning, of the distant Bight of Benin, there is no reason to involve anyone else in this un-nostalgic reverie. Let us rather think of William Wilberforce, whose delicate face with its whimsical smile gazes down at us from the paintings and the drawings on the walls, and whose twelve-foot statue, wearing senatorial robes, stares out across his native city from the summit of 'an elegant fluted Doric column' at one end of St John Street, Hull. The health of William Wilberforce was always precarious; as a boy he was therefore sent to the nearby Hull grammar-school, where he would be 'put on a table to read aloud as an example to other boys'. Wilberforce died when he was seventy-four, and if he did not actually work himself to death in the cause of abolition – first of the slave trade, then of Negro slavery itself – he certainly worked himself into successive states of nervous collapse. A politician and a man of the world, who concealed his profound piety by a brilliant sociability and a winning charm which his friends have said defied description, Wilberforce's intimacy with Pitt and his familiarity with the power-groups at Westminster and inside London society gave this son of Hull a unique position amongst the Abolitionists.

A clause in the first draft of Jefferson's Declaration of Independence (later, as we know, struck out on the insistence of Georgia and Carolina) blamed the slave trade on King George the Third, and we have seen that Henry Laurens of Charleston likewise attacked the British for initiating the trade in slaves by which he had grown rich. We ourselves have seen how, in the eighteenth century, British slavers led the world. Is it not appropriate, then, that the greatest of the Abolitionists should have sprung from a thriving British seaport, and by his zeal and eloquence should have aroused the conscience of the honest British people until they insisted that their Government obliterate the trade? This comforting reflection will not, however, do. It must join its close relatives, the wishful thought and the obvious conclusion, in the old wicker cliché-basket. Had Wilberforce been born in bloodstained Liverpool we might then speak of poetic justice – did we wish to be so fey. But Kingston-upon-Hull was not a slaving port. It was whales, not human beings, the stalwart Hullmen hunted through the cruel Greenland Sea. Nor was Wilberforce a pioneer of the Abolition movement, but a recruit to it; and there seems to me no valid reason for regarding him as the greatest Abolitionist of them all. Were we obliged to select a candidate for this position (and I see no reason why we should) it is Thomas Clarkson of Wisbech who might seem most eligible. No one would wish to belittle William Wilberforce, but he himself was the first to deprecate invidious discrimination, and to recognize how hugely he depended for his facts and arguments upon the work of other and less socially graceful devotees of the cause. Urged on by Pitt, Wilberforce became in 1787 the Parliamentary mouthpiece of the Abolitionists. A politician himself, he well knew that politics is no more than the art of the possible. He lent adroitness and sophistication to what had begun life as a homespun Quaker cause.

Now, it is arguable that this Quaker cause would never have triumphed when it did without the labours of William Wilberforce and the Saints, and without the support of Pitt, Fox and Burke. But to what extent did the timing of this triumph – and indeed the very triumph itself – depend on economic and political factors such, for instance, as the decline of West Indian sugar prices as a result of the French wars? To the Trinidadian historian, Dr Eric Williams, the abolition of the British slave trade by the Act of 1807 is almost entirely to be explained in cynical and economic terms: the Government let the humanitarians have their way because the slave trade was no longer necessary to the economy. The Oxford historian, Sir Reginald Coupland, who cherished the old-world conviction that history is nothing but the tale of personalities, took the opposite view. Since we are here studying the slave-traders and not the abolition of the trade nor the morality of George III's government, we need not try to adjudicate in this perplexing case. Wilberforce and the great majority of his contemporaries certainly took Coupland's view and felt that good had triumphed over evil, right over wrong. But are contemporaries the best judges of their history? In our own lifetimes we have seen an Empire vanish with almost supersonic speed. Colonies have been ceremonially set free, and each one accorded the backhanded compliment of a Thanksgiving Service in Westminster Abbey. But will not historians of the future point out that we were giving freedom to territories which we could no longer economically, politically or physically afford or control? It would be reassuring to believe that the Act of 1807 for the abolition of the slave trade was a spontaneous gesture of national atonement – reassuring, but would it be true? This worm of doubt must wriggle in the mind.

## II

It took the British Parliament nineteen years to abolish the trade in slaves. The national conscience of which William Wilberforce became the acknowledged keeper had in the first place to be created before it could be interpreted or kept. Individual thinkers and writers in Great Britain as well as in France had long made lonely protests against slavery and the trade, but the public which read Defoe, Savage, Pope, Shenstone and Thomson was inevitably a limited one, and not inclined to make a political issue out of the subject. Dr Johnson might rail against it, and Horace Walpole write sarcastic reflections upon 'that horrid trade of selling negroes', but they had no effect upon the public at large, who knew nothing of the trade and cared still less. To kill the trade it obviously required more than a handful of sophisticated intellectuals. It required organization, detailed evidence, and an absolute devotion to the cause. The Quakers alone had been active and outspoken on the subject. In 1774 every Friend was forbidden, under pain of expulsion from the Society, to have any dealings with slave-traders; two years later every Friend who owned slaves was commanded to set them free. When, in May 1787 a committee of twelve men publicly dedicated to the destruction of the slave trade was set up in London, all but three of its members were Quakers. One of these three was Thomas Clarkson, son of a clergyman who was headmaster of Wisbech Free Grammar School. Thomas Clarkson was then twenty-seven years of age. He had already been an Abolitionist for two years. His sense of vocation was as strong as that of Florence Nightingale, and to the cause he had adopted in his youth he sacrificed his time, his health, his peace of mind and what the wealthy William Wilberforce once described as 'a considerable part of his own little fortune'.

Like many dedicated men, Thomas Clarkson was not always easy to get on with. Unlike Wilberforce he neither charmed nor beguiled. When conducting, at Liverpool, a series of investigations as relentless as those of a detective in charge of a major murder case, he was nearly thrown over the pier by a group of enraged slave-captains; he only escaped death by charging boldly into them as, nine abreast, they edged him to within a yard of the drop into a gale-swept sea. Even his name seems pedestrian compared to those of other members of the committee, like William Dillwyn or Granville Sharp. It was a name to defeat even major poets. A Wordsworth sonnet on the Abolition Act, in which Thomas Clarkson is addressed as a 'true yoke-fellow of Time', as 'Duty's intrepid liegeman' and as the 'firm friend of human kind' opens with the uninspired lines:

> Clarkson! it was an obstinate hill to climb:
> How toilsome – nay, how dire – it was, by thee
> Is known; by none perhaps so feelingly.

Hazlitt, who like Cobbett and all the other vocal radicals, detested William Wilberforce for his skill in running with the hare and hunting with the hounds, for his interesting combination of piety and material wealth, and for his butterfly mind, likened Thomas Clarkson's physical appearance to 'more than one of the Apostles in the Cartoons of Raphael'. Hazlitt also criticized Wilberforce for not giving Clarkson his just due of praise during the final Abolition debate: 'Mr Wilberforce said too little on that occasion of one compared with whom he was but the frontispiece to that great chapter in the history of the world – the mask, the varnishing, and painting. The man that affected it by Herculean labours of body and equally gigantic labours of mind was Clarkson, the true Apostle of human Redemption on that occasion.'

Clarkson was one of the few Abolitionists who was not a strong Conservative. He disagreed with Pitt's policy and with the war with France and he used to tell Wilberforce bluntly what he thought. The difference between their attitudes is not easy to define – one might say that Wilberforce was an Abolitionist on strictly religious grounds, Clarkson on those of general humanity. Wilberforce was on the side of authority after the Peterloo Massacre, but he did add a clause to an early Factory Act insisting that children should only be employed in cotton-mills after the age of nine. Hazlitt has called William Wilberforce 'fluctuating' and 'time-serving' and suggests that his conscience would not 'budge' unless the world went with it. Like many other enjoyable passages in the *Spirit of the Age,* Hazlitt's portrait of Wilberforce was perhaps unfair; but at any rate there was nothing either time-serving or fluctuating about Thomas Clarkson. We cannot imagine William Wilberforce sitting up night after night until two in the morning in the seamen's brothels and pot-houses of Liverpool or Bristol. As a *venue* such places were no more welcome to the Wisbech headmaster's son, but he knew where to find his witnesses and collect his evidence. Clarkson would have gone down into the sewers if they would have yielded convincing new slave-trading facts.

Thomas Clarkson's interest in the slave trade began, however, undramatically, and was the outcome of an academic exercise. Educated at St Paul's School, he went up to St John's College, Cambridge, as a sizar in 1780 at the age of twenty. He graduated as Bachelor of Arts and in 1785 won the senior bachelors' prize for a Latin essay. The subject that year was slavery: *'anne liceat invites in servitutem dare?'* – 'is it right to make men slaves against their will?' Having declaimed his essay before an enthusiastic audience in the Senate House, he set out to ride back to London, dismounting every now and then to walk and think. During this journey he was still obsessed with the slave trade, on which, for his prize essay, he had done such research as he could:

I frequently tried to persuade myself in these intervals that the contents of my essay could not be true. The more, however, I reflected upon them or rather upon the authorities on which they were founded, the more I gave them credit. Coming in sight of Wades Mill in Hertfordshire, I sat down disconsolate on the turf by the roadside and held my horse. Here a thought came into my mind that, if the contents of the essay were true, it was time some person should see these calamities to their end.

Young Clarkson decided to translate his essay and sought a London publisher. His mind naturally turned to Thomas Cadell in the Strand, the friend of Doctor Johnson and a publisher with the unusual reputation of being generous to authors. But Cadell did not wish to publish Clarkson's manuscript, now entitled *An Essay on the Slavery and Commerce of the Human Species, particularly the African.* As Clarkson was leaving Cadell's bookshop in dejection he ran into a Wisbech friend of his father's, named James Hancock. Hancock took him to Phillips, who had his own publishing house in George Yard, Lombard Street. Phillips accepted the pamphlet and then introduced the young man to Dillwyn, James Ramsay and other Quakers who were already interested in Abolition. Clarkson decided to throw up the clerical career he had planned for himself, and to devote his life to the African cause. In 1787 he had his first meeting with Wilberforce who 'stated frankly that the subject [of the slave trade] had often employed his thoughts and that it was near his heart'. In the same year, as we have seen, Clarkson joined with eleven colleagues to found the Committee dedicated to the destruction of the international slave trade. This Committee, which held five-hour evening sessions often as much as twice a week, set itself no mean task – that of arousing at first the interest and then the conscience of the nation. By using all available means of publicity the Committee began to attract the attention of thoughtful persons – bishops, clergymen, University dons, certain Members of Parliament, the educated gentry of both sexes. Soon letters were pouring in asking for further information; other letters arrived from people who had lived in the West Indies, from men who had worked as surgeons on slave ships, even from enlightened planters. The most striking of these informative letters, which gave eye-witness accounts of the slave trade, the Committee would ask permission to publish as circulars which were printed in tens of thousands. Anti-slave-trade cells were established all over the country, public meetings held and petitions sent up to Parliament. Every form of propaganda was utilized. Josiah Wedgwood gave the Committee a porcelain plaque modelled on their seal, which showed a suppliant Negro on his knees in chains with the motto: 'Am I not a man and a brother?'; copies of this were despatched all over the country in parcels of five hundred. Sympathizers set them in snuff-boxes and on bracelets, and women had them mounted on gold pins to stick into their hair.

Once the Committee got into its stride, its success was startling and swift. It provoked the massive opposition of the Liverpool merchants, the plantation owners and the patriots who believed the slave trade to be 'the nursery of British sailors'. To counteract these hostile interests, as well as to convince the public and Parliament of the truth of their assertions, the Committee's first and most patent need was the diligent collection of really reliable evidence, and this was not as easy as it sounds. Individuals – ex-captains, surgeons, seamen – were happy to dilate upon the horrors of the African trade, but they were often either too timid or too self-interested to let their names appear in public, or to come up to London to give evidence. 'When I took out my pen and ink' (writes Clarkson) 'to put down the information, which a person was giving me, he became evidently embarrassed and frightened. He began to excuse himself from staying, by alleging that he had nothing more to communicate, and he took himself away as quickly as he could with decency. The sight of the pen and ink had lost me so many good evidences that I was obliged to abandon the use of them and to betake myself to other means.' For it was on Thomas Clarkson that the Committee relied to collect the evidence it needed.

Clarkson was a man to whom that worn-out word 'indefatigable' could most precisely be applied. On one occasion, for
example, he needed some vital evidence about slaving methods
in the Bonny and Calabar rivers. In casual conversation with
a friend he heard of a sailor, 'a very respectable man', who knew
these rivers well, and with whom Clarkson's friend had spent
half an hour at an inn the previous year. The friend knew
neither the name nor the address of this invaluable tar, only
that he came from 'some ship of war in ordinary'. Now, a
warship 'in ordinary' was one out of commission, 'laid up in
the different rivers and waters in the neighbourhood of the
King's dock-yards'. Clarkson started his quest by examining the
crew of every warship in ordinary at Deptford, Woolwich,
Chatham and Sheerness. 'I had now boarded above a hundred
and sixty vessels of war' he writes cheerfully. 'I had found out
two good and willing evidences among them.' But he still had
not found the man he was looking for. At Portsmouth he
boarded more than one hundred ships, and retrieved a gunner
named George Millar who had witnessed the Calabar Massacre
of 1775, 'the only disinterested evidence living, of whom I had
yet heard'. Drawing a blank at Portsmouth, he travelled three
hundred miles to Plymouth, and there, aboard the *Melampus*
frigate which was the fifty-seventh Plymouth ship he had
investigated, he unearthed the man he sought. This man was
no other than Isaac Parker, the sailor who had jumped ship
at Calabar in 1765, taken refuge with Dick Ebro, and accompanied that native trader on slave-raids up the river. To
Clarkson's 'inexpressible joy' Parker was able to give an exact
account of these raids, and of how till night fell the raiding
canoes had 'concealed themselves under the bushes, which hung
over the water from the banks . . . They seized men, women and
children, and as they could find them in the huts. They then
bound their arms, and drove them before them to the canoes'.
Parker, who was given an excellent character and had even
sailed with Captain Cook, agreed to come up to London to give
evidence. 'I returned now in triumph,' writes Clarkson. 'I had
been out only three weeks, and I had found out this extraordinary person, and five respectable witnesses besides.' He had
also boarded between three and four hundred men-of-war.

Apart from his superhuman energy and quite obsessional

zeal, Clarkson had another qualification which came in handy : he was a mathematician, who had taken first place among the junior optimes in his Cambridge mathematical tripos. Calculating tonnages, slave-space, the Middle Passage death-rate, and the incidence of crew wastage was thus child's play to him. On his first journey in search of evidence he accumulated, from the muster-rolls of slave ships, the names and fates of over twenty thousand seamen. When a member of Parliament opposing Abolition declared that the death-rate among slave ships' crews was no greater than that in the Newfoundland trade, Clarkson merely settled down to work on Newfoundland ships' rolls, took a mean average over a certain number of years and proved the statement untrue.

He was sent on his first journey, to Bristol and to Liverpool, after the fourth meeting of the Committee in June 1787. This, his initial experience of a slaving port, shocked him to the core; but it brought him new and profitable ideas.

# III

Having laid his plans for this first experiment in field-work for the Abolitionist cause, Clarkson bade adieu to each member of the Committee. He also called on Wilberforce who was ill, a circle of admirers at his bedside. 'When I left him, I felt much dejected' (wrote Clarkson). 'It appeared to me as if it would be in this case, as it is often in that of other earthly things, that we scarcely possess what we repute a treasure, when it is taken from us.' His anxiety was unnecessary, for this particular treasure survived another four decades.

As his mode of transport into the West Country Clarkson chose horseback. He thought it would relax him after his bout of over-work in London, and he wanted to be solitary and not forced to indulge in the idle chatter of fellow-passengers on a coach. As he rode through the leafy hedgerows of late June, past meadows filled with buttercups and sheep's parsley, he reflected on the magnitude of his task. It is important to notice that at this time Clarkson and his colleagues were not aiming at slave-emancipation, but at the abolition of the trade in slaves. Further, their arguments were twofold – the wickedness of the trade in itself, and the presumption that if it were replaced by a trade in African produce as much, if not more, money would be made by the merchants. Clarkson had assembled a collection of African woods, fabrics and goldwork; he would run down and buy additions to this collection from any Guineaman that put into the port of London. He had worked out statistics to prove that a real African import-export trade would in the end be far more profitable than the slave trade had ever been. But he still had no answer to those who asserted that serving on a slave ship was the best training for serving on a man-of-war, and that to attack the slave trade was to weaken the British Navy. This answer he found, to his astonishment, in Bristol.

Turning a corner of the road a mile from his journey's end, Clarkson suddenly saw Bristol lying before him. It was eight o'clock of a summer's evening and the haze that lay over the city and the mouth of the shining River Avon made Bristol, with its church spires and fine classical buildings, look larger than it was. Church bells were ringing, but, he tells us, 'the sound of them did not strike me, till I turned the corner before mentioned, when it came upon me at once. It filled me, almost directly, with a melancholy for which I could not account. I began now to tremble, for the first time, at the arduous task I had under-taken, of attempting to subvert one of the branches of the commerce of the great place that was then before me . . . I anticipated much persecution in it also; and I questioned whether I should even get out of it alive'. These qualms passed as he approached Bristol, and he says that he entered the city 'with an undaunted spirit, determining that no labour should make me shrink nor danger, nor even persecution, deter me from my pursuit'. His first contact was with a Quaker convert, Henry Gandy, who had made two voyages on a Guineaman and now wished to make reparation 'for the indiscreet and profane occupations of his youth'. Through Gandy he met other leading Quakers, and his researches began.

Clarkson found that Bristol people 'talked very openly on the subject of the slave trade . . . everybody seemed to execrate it, though no one thought of its abolition'. In the first week of July he learned that the captain of the slave ship *Brothers*, then lying in the King's Road preparing for an African voyage, could not get a crew. A party of men who had been sent on board her had fled back to shore. On inquiry he found that, on the previous voyage, the captain had ill-used the seamen brutally, and that thirty-two of them had died. He also learned that 'the treatment of seamen was a crying evil in this trade, and that consequently few would enter into it'. This was a revelation to Clarkson: 'The relation of these circumstances made me acquainted with two things, of which I had not before heard: namely, the aversion of seamen to engage, and the bad usage of them when engaged, in this cruel trade; into both of which I determined immediately to inquire.' He had come to Bristol intending to investigate the treatment of African slaves; he now found that he must investigate the treatment of British seamen as well. If he could prove that seamen were worse used on slave ships than on any others, he and his Committee would have a new and invaluable weapon in their hand. He would show that the famous 'nursery for British sailors' was not a nursery but a torture-chamber, not a cradle but a tomb.

By the rather devious means which soon became essential to his task, Clarkson obtained the muster-roll of the ship *Brothers* and found that thirty-two of the seamen had indeed died. He next came across the case of one of the ship's crew 'which, as it was reported to me, exceeded all belief'. John Dean, a free Negro, had, for 'a trifling circumstance for which he was in no way to blame', been fastened by the captain to the deck. He was laid out on his belly, and the captain had poured hot pitch over his back and torn at the flesh with heated tongs. A London attorney had taken up the case, and the captain had been fined; but the ship's owners, perfectly aware of the case, had continued to employ 'this monster'.

Clarkson soon found that Dean's was not an isolated case. Almost every slaver coming into Bristol during his sojourn there had on board victims of their captains' brutality. A young man named Thomas, surgeon's mate on the Guineaman *Alfred* which had just come into port, had, after being repeatedly knocked down by the captain, become so distraught that he had tried to commit suicide three times. After the third attempt to jump overboard he was chained to the deck day and night, and was now thought to be beyond hope. With some difficulty Clarkson found out where young Thomas was living – or, rather, dying. He found him delirious, with his legs, thighs and body swathed in flannel. He was too far gone to give any coherent account of what had happened, and at one moment he mistook Clarkson for an emissary of the captain sent to kill him. His image haunted Clarkson, but just as he was deciding how best to help Thomas he heard that he was dead.

Clarkson was not one to leave matters there. He next cross-examined Dixon, another seaman from the *Alfred* who had been put in irons, and had had his underlip split in two by the captain. Dixon's friend, Matthew Pyke, stated that he had had his arm broken by the chief mate in Black River, Jamaica, and that he had also, contrary to the practice in merchant vessels, been severely flogged. He showed Clarkson his lacerated back and broken arm. Dixon and Pyke declared that, on board the *Alfred*, all of the crew were abominably treated, with the one exception of 'a person of the name of Bulpin'. The next stage was clearly to interview this favoured being. Clarkson caught up with James Bulpin just as he was stepping out to stay with friends near Bridgewater in Somerset. He proved to be 'a young man of very respectable appearance and of mild manners'. This mild person 'gave a melancholy confirmation' of the three cases of Thomas, Dixon and Pyke, and added, for full measure, that a certain Joseph Cunningham had been notoriously badly used on board the *Alfred* and that another of the crew, Charles Horseler, had been so severely beaten on his chest with the knotted end of a rope the size of a large ball and 'made on purpose', that he had died of it. Bulpin added that the *Alfred*'s captain, when mate of a slave ship, had been tried in Barbados for the murder of a seaman but had been acquitted after bribing the relevant witnesses to disappear.

Clarkson's first reaction was to want to issue a writ against the captain of the *Alfred*. He was dissuaded by his friend, the Deputy Town-Clerk of Bristol, who explained to him that since seamen could not afford to stay on shore once they had spent their wages, he would, if he really wanted to mount a trial, be obliged to keep the whole crew at his own expense for an indefinite length of time. Further, the slave ship owners would lure these witnesses away by making them boatswains and inferior officers in other ships. When the trial came up, the witnesses would have vanished. 'To which' Clarkson remarks 'he added that, if I were to make a point of taking up the cause of those whom I found complaining of hard usage in this trade,

I must take up that of nearly all who sailed in it; for that he only knew of one captain from the port in the slave trade, who did not deserve long ago to be hanged. Hence I should get into a labyrinth of expense, and difficulty, and uneasiness of mind, from whence I should not easily find a clue to guide me.'

The case of the slave ship *Alfred* is but one single example of the many, many tales of horror which Clarkson noted down for future use. He was neither a credulous nor a gullible man. He would check and countercheck on his witnesses' reputations and characters, and collate one lot of evidence with another from a separate source. The hostility which he had feared when he first saw the city of Bristol on that soft June evening now reared up at him from every side. His health began to suffer, on the nights that were not sleepless he had nightmares about the cruelties on the slave ships. He developed nervous pains in his arms and shoulders. But nothing would deter him. He realized that yet another duty lay before him – that of finding out how the crews of slavers were assembled, and why men worked in them at all.

# IV

Clarkson had repeatedly been told in Bristol, that all seamen 'had an aversion to enter, and that they were inveigled, if not often forced, into this hateful employment'. But, faithful to his system of taking nothing for granted, he wished to prove the truth of these assertions for himself. He therefore became friendly with 'a very intelligent man', Mr Thompson, the land-lord of the *Seven Stars* public house. Thompson was used to putting up sailors during their time on shore, and even to find-ing them new berths. He refused to have anything to do with placing seamen on slave ships since he knew that 'the credit of his house would be ruined, if he were known to send those who put themselves under his care, into it'. This landlord confirmed everything that Clarkson had heard, and agreed to take his earnest new acquaintance round the lowest dives in Marsh Street, which were those frequented by the mates of slaving ships when hunting for crew. Since three or four slaving vessels were just being got ready to sail, Thompson said it was high time to begin their rounds.

These Marsh Street public houses were kept by Irishmen.

They offered music and dancing as well as drink. Clarkson visited Marsh Street nineteen times, reaching a pub at midnight and sometimes staying until three in the morning. This sedate, plump young man, with large protuberant brown eyes would sit, we may imagine, in a corner, studying the Marsh Street scene, which he characterized as 'truly distressing' and which included drunken fights and the normal amount of obscenity and swearing. He soon saw that young seamen, who did not know Bristol, and were 'unacquainted with the nature of the slave trade' were easily tempted by the offer of high wages, enticed into a waiting boat, and rowed on board a slave ship. If some youth did not readily succumb to the blandishments of the mate, he would be plied with drink until intoxicated, 'when a bargain was made over him between the landlord and the mate', and he was carried away insensible. Another trick was for the Marsh Street landlords, who, like Mr Thompson, boarded sailors between voyages, to encourage their guests to run up a large bill just before a slave ship was due to sail. When these men found that they owed more than they could conceivably pay, they were offered the alternative of the debtors' gaol or service on a slaver. Clarkson also discovered that, apart from being ill-treated on a slave ship, seamen were actually cheated. They were forced to sign articles stating that, should they die or be discharged during a slaving voyage, their wages were to be reckoned in the currency of the West Indian island to which their ship was going; and that in any case one half of their wages was to be given them in West Indian currency. The value of this money was considerably lower than that of the pound sterling, so that instead of getting higher wages than seamen in other ships, the crews of slavers were in actual fact paid less. 'The trade' (Clarkson writes in his account of his Marsh Street adventures) 'was, in short, one mass of iniquity from the beginning to the end.'

In one respect Thomas Clarkson was disappointed by his visit to Bristol. He had hoped to persuade a number of retired 'slave-captains' then living there to give him what he termed 'good evidences'. He kept sending these old gentlemen messages – suggesting that if the trade was not in fact as bad as it was reputed to be, they might like to give evidence in its favour; if, on the other hand, it was as atrocious as he believed, 'they had it in their power, by detailing the crimes which attached to it, of making some reparation or atonement for the part they had taken in it'. This Quakerish notion of atonement did not appeal to the retired captains, who refused to recognize Clarkson: 'whenever they met me in the street, they shunned me as if I had been a mad dog.' The reason for their coldness proved to be the fact that some of them, although now retired, held shares in Bristol slaving vessels. We may also presume a natural reluctance to give a stranger from London an affidavit emphasizing that they had spent the best years of their lives in a career which he regarded simply as one of crime.

If Clarkson found Bristol in some ways awkward, Liverpool, which he next visited, became for him positively dangerous. The town talk of Liverpool was, like that of Bristol, mainly about the slave trade. 'Horrible facts concerning it were in everybody's mouth . . . The people, too, at Liverpool seemed to be more hardened, or they related them with more coldness or less feeling.' At Liverpool, Clarkson stayed at the *King's Arms* where, although he had taken a private sitting-room next to his bedroom, he dined daily at the *table d'hôte* downstairs. After he had been there two or three days he noticed how crowded the dining-room was becoming. Mr Dale, the landlord, told him 'in a goodnatured manner' that they were visitors come to look at Clarkson himself. They were, in fact, slave-merchants and slave-captains, who would try to provoke the London visitor by arguing with him, proposing toasts of 'success to the Trade' or talking about him before his face: 'They had heard of a person turned mad, who had conceived the thought of destroying Liverpool and all its glory.' The mounting hostility Clarkson aroused in Liverpool almost ended in his murder by the nine men who tried to hurl him off a pier in a high wind.

While in Liverpool, Clarkson added to his African collections a few purely British articles which he found he had 'entirely overlooked in Bristol'. He would have overlooked them in Liverpool likewise, had they not been displayed in a shop-window. These products of British industrial know-how consisted of iron handcuffs, leg-shackles, thumb-screws and mouth-openers, or *specula oris* which had originally been invented for surgical use in cases of lock-jaw. Armed with this gear, his notes, affidavits and statistics, Clarkson returned to London. He now knew more than anyone in England about the intricacies of the slave trade and the nature of the slave-traders. All he lacked was the first-hand experience of having worked the Middle Passage as commander of a slave ship. This gap in Clarkson's knowledge was soon filled by that famous slaver convert, Wilberforce's friend and spiritual mentor, the Reverend John Newton, rector of St Mary Woolnoth in the city of London. Newton once wrote that a seafaring life afforded 'greater advantages to an awakened mind' than any other career, and was most of all favourable 'for promoting the life of God in the soul'. The command of a Guineaman he had then judged especially conducive to spiritual contemplation, since the size of the crew – double that of ships in other trades – left the captain a great deal of leisure, and even 'the hurry of trade upon the coast' was intermittent. The dangers of slaving could also be turned to good use, for one's faith was quickened and confirmed by the 'evident interpositions of Divine Providence, in any answer to prayer . . . almost every day. I never' (wrote Newton) 'knew sweeter or more frequent hours of divine communion than in my last two voyages to Guinea.'

John Newton entered the slave trade by joining a Guineaman at Madeira in January 1745. By his own account he was the most depraved and foul-mouthed youth on board, specializing in the coinage of blasphemous curses and endeavouring to destroy the vestiges of his companions' religious beliefs. He left the ship in the hope of growing rich by slaving off Sierra Leone. But by a twist of fate Newton himself became the slave of a sadistic Negress in one of the tiny Plantain Islands which lie south of Shilling Point and the Bananas on the old Grain Coast. It was an adventure distinctly unlike others, and one which Newton never forgot. Yet even this distressing episode did not leave him with any automatic sympathy for the victims of the slave trade. Neither as a threadbare starveling planting limes at the order of his employer's African mistress, nor as a sleek slave-captain studying Latin classics in his well-furnished cabin, did John Newton feel any doubts about the trade which he served. The gamut of his African experiences brings us sharply back to the eternal enigma presented by the lives of the slave-traders who form the subject of this book. How was it that cultivated and literate Europeans – professing Christians at that – could totally blind themselves to the foul nature of their profession? John Newton's journals, memoirs and letters provide no answer to this basic question. All the same, since they emphasize it with the greatest clarity, his career on the Guinea Coast is worth consideration. He is the last slave-trader we shall encounter in this book.

# Chapter 15

# Better Late Than Never?

## I

THE PLANTAIN ISLANDS, where John Newton lived out his strange bondage, lie off the territory now known as Sierra Leone, but then loosely termed the Grain Coast. North of them are the Bananas, then the bay of Sierra Leone and the area known to the old traders as the Bulom Shore. To their south is Sherbro Island and the sound of the Sherbro River, where the first trader that we met, Nicholas Owen, gardened, made shell pictures and, in 1759, met his lonely death. In the eighteenth century this region of the Grain Coast was dark with forests, in the depths of which dwelt the Buloms who lived on rice and carved in ivory. 'They have a great many kinds of witchcraft' (Owen wrote of the Buloms) 'which they practise upon one another as they please, notwithstanding severe punishment that's allowed by their laws against it. If they are found out they are obliged to drink a large quantity of poison, commonly called red water, which soon puts an end to their days.' On the Sherbro the fear of drinking red water provided many slaves, for, given the alternative of this test or of being sold, many 'inferior people' were said to prefer the second alternative. 'If a child, for instance, is devoured by one of these animals [leopards],' wrote Zachary Macaulay in his journal for November 1793, 'the King, glad of an opportunity, immediately brings a palaver against the people of the town to which the child belongs. It avails them nothing to protest their innocence or to give assurance of their total ignorance of what became of the child. They are found guilty of making away with the child, on which the whole town, men, women and children are condemned to slavery.' Macaulay, who was sent out by the Sierra Leone Company to be the first Governor of the colony founded by them for freed slaves, also notes a 'strange accusation' against a man alleged to have turned himself into a leopard so as to steal domestic animals. This man was sold into slavery as a witch. African house-boys working in isolated bungalows at no great distance from modern Freetown are still afraid to walk home through the bush at night from a superstitious fear of being made into medicine by leopard-men.

Shilling Point, or Cape Shilling, is a low craggy promontory running out to sea some miles south of Freetown and the Sierra Leone River. Swimming there, or dabbling in the translucent rock-pools on a sunswept morning, you can see the Banana Islands near at hand, and, on the point, the ruins of an old stone wharf at which boats coming to and from the Bananas still put in. Uphill, inland, lurks the village of Kent hidden in trees, with broad sandy streets and old wooden houses. On the upper verandahs of these houses, and in the dark interior of their living-rooms are crudely carved versions of early Victorian chairs and sofas. In the gloaming of such rooms dried-out cigarettes, warm beer and fruit juices are sold by grinning crones.

The Banana Islands, although they lacked a good harbour and were snake-infested, were popular with European slavers, and had several families of black traders, of domineering mulattoes, and of white traders with black mistresses resident upon them. Centres for slaves and ivory, they were covered with fruit trees – plantains, bananas, limes, pineapples and paw-paw. Water-melons and vegetable gardens were cultivated, fowls kept, and life in the little thatched wood-and-wattle houses was not lacking in a certain squalid style. The Bananas were larger and more fertile than the three Plantain Islands. It was on the largest of the Plantains, a low sandy place covered with palm-trees and only two miles in circumference, that John Newton took up residence in 1746, as the assistant, but in reality the unpaid serf, of his master, an English slave-trader named Clow.

Newton had met Clow on board the ship by which he had sailed from Madeira to Sierra Leone, and had realized that this man, once penniless, had managed to make substantial sums trading at Cape Mount. Newton determined to follow his example, and, on condition of entering his service, obtained his discharge from the slave ship. He and his master began to build a house upon the particular Plantain Island which they had selected, and, since the Plantains, unlike the Bananas, produced practically nothing but coco-nuts and rice, they planned to plant a lime-plantation and to raise other crops. 'He was a man,' Newton wrote of Clow, 'with whom I might have lived tolerably well, if he had not soon been influenced against me; but he was much under the direction of a black woman, who lived with him as a wife. She was a person of some consequence in her own country, and he owed his first rise to her interest.' In his account of his experiences in the Plantains, Newton merely alludes to this woman by the initials 'P.I.' – not from any fear of a libel action, but because it was the nearest he could orthographically get to the sound of her name.

Witty and profligate though he may have been in his youth, Newton seems also to have been obtuse and, perhaps, already as sententious as he afterwards became. He could not in the least understand why P.I. loathed him from the start, nor why, once his master was absent, she initiated a programme of deliberate persecution from which the wretched English youth very nearly died. He had contracted some form of fever shortly after his arrival on the island, and could not go on a trading expedition up the Rio Nuna with Mr Clow. Left in P.I.'s ungentle hands, he was given a wooden chest to sleep on, with a log for a pillow. He found it difficult even to get a glass of water, and, when his appetite returned, he was given almost nothing to eat. Occasionally, when 'in the highest good humour', P.I. would send Newton scraps off her own plate, which he 'received with thanks and eagerness, as the most needy beggar does alms'. Once, when ordered to receive her left-overs from her own hands, he was so weak that he dropped the plate, whereupon the woman laughed and refused to give him any more, although her table was covered with dishes, 'for she lived much in the European style'. He was reduced to creeping out after dark to grub up roots in the plantation, eating them raw for fear of detection. While he was still too weak to stand, P.I. would come with her attendants to mock at him, and command him to walk about. She set her slaves on to mimic his hobble, to clap their hands, laugh and pelt him with limes and sometimes with stones. When she was not there the slaves would pity him, and secretly bring him food from their own slender diet. When he complained to Clow, on his return to the island, the man would not believe him.

On his second voyage upriver, Clow took Newton with him. This experiment proved even worse than P.I.'s rule, for, through a misunderstanding with another trader, Clow accused Newton of stealing his trade goods. He locked him up on deck, with only one pint of rice, for forty hours at a time while he himself was trading on shore. It was the rainy season, and Newton's only clothes were an old shirt, a pair of trousers, a roll of cotton stuff and, for his head, a knotted handkerchief. He managed to fish over the side of the boat and would gobble his catch half-raw, while his master sat eating yams and boiled fowl. Returning to the island, he was set to work again planting the limes; his only respite was to study a copy of Barrow's *Euclid* which he had with him, and from which he would draw out diagrams with a stick upon the sand. Mr Clow and his 'wife' sometimes came and watched the lime-planting, passing scathing remarks the while: 'Who knows,' said Mr Clow one day 'who knows but by the time these trees grow up and bear, you may go home to England, obtain the command of a ship and return to reap the fruit of your labours? We see strange things sometimes happen.'

Mr Clow thought he was being sarcastic, but he spoke prophetically, for this same strange thing did happen. In the year 1750 Captain John Newton, commanding the Liverpool slave ship, *Duke of Argyll*, landed at the Plantains, saw his limes fully grown, and bought one boy and one girl slave from Mr Clow and his mistress. When they came on board his ship Newton treated his former tyrant with 'the greatest complaisance and kindness; and if she has any shame in her, I believe I made her sorry for her former ill-treatment of me.' Here Newton was unwittingly following the great precept of Queen Christina of Sweden, who once reminded herself in her *Maxims* that 'beneficence is the best form of revenge'.

P.I.'s peculiar conduct did not deter Newton from the African trade, any more than the generosity to him of her slaves made him in the least unwilling to enslave others. Although it baffled Newton himself, the hatred of P.I. for the sickly English youth is surely quite comprehensible. The recognized, self-important 'wife' of a rich white trader, living in a modified form of the European fashion, she must have been used to her husband's confidence and to being, except for occasional traders, the only person with whom he really talked. A clever young man of Clow's own nation, with whom he could converse on subjects far beyond her ken, and whose command of the English language was so obviously superior to her own, would be calculated to arouse P.I.'s virulent jealousy. We know nothing of this lady's past history, but she would surely have enjoyed getting her own back on a white servant ill with fever.

Saved by what he chose to regard as divine intervention, but which took the rather more mundane form of an urgent message from his father, John Newton finally reached home by making the two last legs of the Middle Passage. When the ship in which he was travelling as a supercargo was almost wrecked in the North Atlantic, the officers and crew treated their passenger as a Jonah. There were even threats to throw him overboard. However, in April 1748, the *Greyhound* entered the quiet mists of Lough Swilly in County Donegal. For a short time Newton led an edifying, church-going life in the austere grey city of Londonderry before returning to England, where after a second African journey, he married the love of his life in a church at Rochester in February 1750. His bride was a childhood sweetheart named Mary Catlett, a gay, religious Kentish girl who had long been, and always remained, his ideal of womanhood. 'It grows late' (he once wrote to her after twenty-four years of marriage when she was away from home):

The maids are gone to bed and I shall soon retire to mine. It is rather lonely at present; but, I thank God, I am a stranger to the remotest wish that it were lawful to me to have any companion but yourself. Since the Lord gave me the desire of my heart in my dearest Mary, the rest of the sex are no more to me than tulips in the garden . . . I have a vile heart, capable of every evil; and, in myself, am as prone to change as a weathercock. But, with respect to you, He has been pleased to keep me fixed as the north-pole, without one minute's variation for twenty-four years, three months, and one day.

## II

Far from feeling the slightest compunction about his African duties, John Newton looked on them with a positive relish. On

Guineamen he found, as we have seen, unsurpassed opportunities to commune with God, and he enjoyed his absolute power over the crew and the slaves – a 'power to restrain gross irregularities in others.' This restraint not only took the form of the use of the cat-o'-nine-tails – 'corrected the carpenter with a cat for having behaved very mutinously in my absence . . . Mem. gave him two dozen stripes' – but also involved setting a religious example to his crew. He told his wife that he devoted Saturday evenings on the Guinea Coast to preparing for a holy Sunday. His actual Sabbath began at four o'clock in the morning, when he sought a blessing for the day and then took what he called 'a serious walk on deck'. After this meditative stroll he read two or three chapters of the Bible and had a silent breakfast followed by prayer. At eleven o'clock the ship's bell summoned his 'little congregation' about him to hear him read the morning service. The bleary seamen were assembled for further prayers later in the day. Tea in the captain's cabin was at four o'clock, followed by a scripture lesson, another walk, and private devotions at six. These religious observances do not seem to have acted as an emollient on his tough crew, for his logs record plans for a mutiny, as well as a considerable amount of punitive lashing.

In one of his frequent letters to his wife, letters filled with devoted affection and studded with references to Divine Providence and to his Master in Heaven, Newton gives a succinct account of the complete power wielded by the captain of an eighteenth-century slave ship. He explains to her how men come and go at his command. If he orders a man to do some specific job, three or four 'will be ambitious of a share in the service'. No man on the ship could eat his dinner without the captain's permission – 'nay, nobody dares to say it is twelve o'clock or eight o'clock, in my hearing, till I think proper to say it first'. He is ushered ceremonially ashore, and a strict watch is kept for his return so that he may be 'received in due form'. No one on board could go to sleep until Newton was back on the ship, no matter how late the hour. He said that he did not value these customs highly for their own sake, but because 'without them, the common sailors would be unmanageable'. Nor did he let his new state lead him to forget his lowly situation as the servant of P.I. on the Plantain Islands.

Few characters are more tedious than the reformed rake. Newton had now abandoned swearing, drank little, and, so soon as his ship touched the coast of Guinea, gave up eating meat so as to avoid sexual temptation. Slaving captains, as we saw at Calabar, would spend long nights carousing in one another's cabins when several ships, anchored in a group, were waiting to be slaved. Newton told his wife that his fellow-captains would mock him for his chastity and his fidelity to herself, calling him 'a slave to one woman' to which he would reply: 'And some of you are slaves to a hundred.' Meanwhile the real slaves would be hustled on board his ship, where the pious Captain Newton would examine them minutely. 'Yellow Will brought me a woman slave, but being long breasted and ill made, refused her and made him take her on shore again, though I am not certain I shall be able to get one in her room,' runs a typical entry in his log. Or: 'Longboat returned with 11 slaves; viz. 3 men, 1 woman, 2 men boys, 1 boy (4 foot), 1 boy and 3 girls undersized which makes our number 26 and likewise about a ton and half of camwood.' 'Sent the steward on shore again in the yawl to purchase a woman slave and he brought her off in the evening, no. 46, she cost 65 bars, though she had a very bad mouth, could have bought her cheaper I think myself.' Or: 'The yawl came off, brought 2 small boys, sent her again with positive orders to buy none under 4 foot, for I think we have little ones enough at the price they now bear.' 'A fine woman slave' died of the flux, and a girl ('no. 92') who had caught it was sent back on shore to die. We may at this point recall the impassioned description of the treatment of African women and girl slaves, which Newton wrote in his abolitionist old age: 'When the women and girls are taken on board a ship, naked, trembling, terrified . . . they are often exposed to the wanton rudeness of white savages . . . In imagination the prey is divided upon the spot and only reserved till opportunity offers.'

Newton's log of the *Duke of Argyll* suggests that, while quite insensible to the actual plight of his slaves, he himself used punishment rarely and only when a plot for insurrection had been unearthed. Then he would clap the men into yokes or iron collars, and use the thumbscrews until their thumbs burst open with their blood. In his *Thoughts upon the African Slave Trade*, which was widely distributed by Clarkson's Committee, and which Hannah More considered 'a sensible, judicious, well-timed and well-tempered pamphlet', Newton wrote of the 'unmerciful whippings' which he had witnessed on slavers. These whippings were 'continued till the poor creatures have not had power to groan under their misery, and hardly a sign of life remained. I have seen them agonizing for hours, I believe for days together, under the torture of the thumbscrews, a dreadful engine, which, if the screw be turned by an unrelenting hand, can give intolerable anguish. There have been instances in which cruelty has proceeded still further'. As an instance of such cruelty he tells his readers of 'a captain, who has long since been dead'. This man would boast of the method by which he had suppressed a slave insurrection on one of his ships, condemning several Africans to death and studying 'with no small attention, how to make death as excruciating as possible'. For his readers' sakes Newton refrained from relating the details of this scene.

Altogether, John Newton spent nine years in the slave trade, and then he only left it in 1754 on the advice of his doctors, after an apoplectic stroke at the modest age of thirty. Newton's change of heart came slowly, but when it came it was complete. From being a profession which enabled a man to develop his spiritual qualities and commune quietly with his God the trade became for him, in his own words, 'a business at which my heart now shudders'. He declared that he could think of no commerce 'so iniquitous, so cruel, so oppressive, so destructive, as the African Slave Trade'. The psychology of conversion is always mysterious. Despite his prolific writings the exact process by which this ardent slave-trader became an ardent abolitionist is not entirely clear. Yet without his first-hand experience of the slave trade, the Reverend John Newton could not have been so useful to the cause of Clarkson and Wilberforce. His is not a specially pleasing personality, and we may leave him with the trite comment, 'better late than never'.

## III

What, then, are we finally to think about the slaving days of John Newton? Or about other slave-traders as cultivated and as

religious as himself? Do we dismiss them as hypocrites? Do we
employ that fashionable label, schizoid, to describe their personalities? Do we take refuge with the old cliché 'the brutality
of the age'? Yet that age is known to history as the Age of
Sensibility, and Newton's love-letters to his wife are sensitive
and affectionate. We must probably conclude that Newton in
his youth and early middle age belonged to that vast and
dangerous multitude of human beings who take the established
order of things for granted, and who lack both the courage and
the time to question every single general assumption – to think,
in fact, for themselves. Newton once described the profession of
captain of a Guineaman as a 'genteel' one. By this he meant the
state in which he lived on board, the power he could exercise
over his crew, the leisure-hours in his cabin translating the love-
poems of Propertius in such a form that they were addressed not
to some 'profane' beauty but to God. A recognized and even a
respected way of making money, the slave trade seemed to
Newton and his colleagues of every nationality a legitimate and
indeed a seemly form of commerce. The dangers it involved
even gave it on occasion an heroic slant. We are told that people
will get used to anything. Recently sickened by the reek of a
Dundalk slaughter-house, in which lambs' heads were lying in
steaming pyramids upon the blood-drenched floor, I reflected
that the merry butcher boys employed there might have been
equally contented organizing the hold of a ship full of slaves.
The evidence Clarkson and his friends collected showed that a
handful of the seamen on Guineamen, like some of the surgeons
and a few of the captains, really did despise their work. That
they were a minority need not surprise us. In life, alas, genuine
sensibility is at a premium, and is unrelated to education or to
class. Heart is rarer than head.

Much has been written about the struggle of Wilberforce and
Clarkson to arouse the national conscience over the slave trade.
Less attention has been given to the attitude to Abolition of the
African slave-traders on the Guinea Coast. These men were
mystified by the Abolition Act of 1807. Captain Crow relates
an interesting conversation with his friend King Pepple of
Bonny upon the subject. Entrenched in his mangrove-swamps
King Pepple had been following Wilberforce's distant cam-
paign with incredulity and with dismay. One day, when Crow

was visiting him, Pepple began asking more than usually searching questions about Europe. He had with him a friend, Calabar Foodra, who was temporarily seeking sanctuary at Bonny after an unsuccessful war with his own chief. Pepple deftly asked Captain Crow to describe to the stranger the nature of European wars. Crow told them of the tens of thousands who were killed in a single day upon the battlefields of Europe, and of the vast numbers who fell wounded. The King of Bonny and his guest expressed surprise. King Pepple then spoke up – and although it is in trade English we may listen to this authentic voice from Africa about 'big man' Wilberforce in the Houses of Parliament. 'What is the matter, Crow' (Pepple inquired) 'that you big man for you gran Palaver-house make all dat noise for we country and we trade? We no kill too much man all same you, and 'spose we black and no sabby book, God A'mighty made we so, and we b'lieve God make we all and make white man sabby book; but you country want for pass all country, and now den stop we trade, and want for pass God A'mighty, but all you big man and all you country nebber can pass God A'mighty.' In King Pepple's view it was better to traffic in human beings than to drive tens of thousands to the slaughter. Why should people in England fuss about the slave trade when they did not fuss about the deaths at Austerlitz? When sober, King Pepple was a man of powerful intelligence, and his arguments here hold a certain validity which seems to have defeated Crow who reports that he 'endeavoured to make some reply to this charge'. Begun in earnest, the conversation ended, however, in a cataract of West African mirth. King Calabar Foodra declared that many men had been killed in the local war which he had just lost and which had turned him into a fugitive. Crow inquired how many men had, in fact, been killed? 'Three men go dead, and too much man lose him foot and him fingers,' was the reply. At this King Pepple fell back upon one of his sofas 'in a roar of laughter' calling his guest a 'poor fool man' for presuming to compare his recent skirmish with the wars on a grand scale of which Crow had been speaking: 'What wo wo palaver* you make!' the senior King of Bonny squealed.

Bonny, as we have noticed, was a species of condominium,

* i.e. what silly talk.

although the second king, King Holiday, had less influence than King Pepple, of whom he stood in nervous awe. King Holiday also had his views on the British abolition of the slave trade, and he told them to Crow in September 1807. It was not only Crow's last voyage to Bonny, it was the last time a Liverpool slaver would ever officially put in there. Crow had command of the *Kitty's Amelia*, a vessel of three hundred tons and carrying eighteen guns, the last ship to be cleared out of the port of Liverpool before the Abolition Act passed into law. King Holiday had learned of this improbable fact from slaving captains who had preceded Crow on the Delta, and so he hastened to pay a visit of ceremony to the *Kitty's Amelia* as soon as she dropped anchor off his town. He reminded Crow how long they had known each other, and that he relied on him to tell him 'true mouth' what was happening in England. All the captains coming to Bonny had said that the King of England was stopping the slave trade. If this were so, what were the people of Bonny to do? As Crow knew, the 'country fash' was to have 'too much wife and too much child', and some of these would inevitably turn out to be great rogues. Now Holiday himself had seen that there were 'bad white men' and he had heard that there were also great rogues in England. God had provided the white man with the gift of book learning and of shipbuilding. Therefore wicked white people could easily be got rid of by being sent to the other side of the world; he also understood that criminals were hanged in England and that a great many people were killed in European wars. 'But God make we black' (here, according to Crow, King Holiday shed tears) 'and we no sabby book, and we no havy head for make ship for sen we bad mans for more country, and we law is, 'spose some of we child go bad and we no can sell 'em, we father must kill dem own child; and 'spose trade be done we force kill too much child same way.' King Holiday added that Bonny people refused to believe that so beneficial a trade could stop, for the ju-ju men had pronounced that Great Britain could never 'pass God A'mighty'.

The good people of Bonny were not alone in regarding the British abolition of the slave trade as hypocritical, or in accusing Great Britain of trying to play God Almighty and to alter the course of nature. During the nineteen years' fight to get the

Abolition Act through both Houses of Parliament one of the opposition's prime arguments had been that Britain would merely be helping the slave trade of the French, the Dutch and other colonial nations which seemed to have no intention of abandoning this lucrative form of commerce. Clarkson had spent a frustrating six months in Paris in 1789. At the outset it seemed as though French abolitionist committees could be formed under the auspices of *Les Amis des Noirs*, and would flourish; but the outbreak of the Revolution not unnaturally diverted the attention of Mirabeau and other sincere sympathizers. Clarkson left Paris in disillusion. In Great Britain the violence of the French Revolution, followed by the Haitian massacres of 1791 gave every radical cause a sharp setback. Opinion veered round against abolishing the slave trade, and it was not, as we know, until 1807 that the long campaign of Clarkson and Wilberforce ended in apparent triumph. It is interesting to note, on the other hand, that the results of the Napoleonic wars persuaded many British West Indian planters to favour abolishing the trade; for they had no wish to see the plantations in the conquered colonies of France once more compete with their own estates, and the best way to avoid this seemed to be to deny the French access to fresh sources of slaves. The self-interest which had originally led these British planters to oppose abolition now worked in Wilberforce's favour and gave him some very unexpected converts and allies.

The Abolition Act of 1807 outlawed the trade in slaves, but, since the penalties were merely pecuniary, a great many contraband slave ships at first continued to ply secretly to Africa and the West Indies. In 1811 these penalties were replaced by transportation for life, and some years later the death penalty (afterwards repealed) was prescribed for those who continued to trade. The threat of transportation effectually ended the British trade. In November 1814, at the Congress of Vienna, Wellington persuaded the continental delegates to sign a declaration that the slave trade must cease. The Dutch officially abolished it in 1814, the French in 1815, and the Portuguese between 1815 and 1830.

I have called the success of the Abolitionists an 'apparent triumph'. It would be satisfying to record that their great campaign once and for all ended the shipment of Africans to transatlantic plantations. It did not.

## IV

'We believe' (wrote the British Commissioners of the Court of Mixed Commission, Sierra Leone, to the Foreign Secretary in London in December 1844):

> That the slave trade is increasing, and that it is conducted perhaps more systematically than it has ever been hitherto. Nearly all the formerly noted slave haunts appear to be still frequented, and notwithstanding the stringent methods adopted by the British Commodore with the powerful force under his command, there can be no question that there has been a very large number of slaves transported both to Cuba and Brazil . . . At Sherbro and Gallinas we regret to state very large numbers of slaves have been collected by the Factors, and in spite of the strictest and most judicious methods adopted in watching different outlets of those places, some Slavers have got clear off with their cargoes.

Wilberforce had been dead eleven years, Clarkson, at the age of eighty-four, was still alive. Two British squadrons were patrolling the African coasts and exercising a limited right of search over all ships suspected of being slavers. The motives for this careful search were economic as well as humanitarian, for now that Great Britain was distinctly out of the slave trade it was vital to prevent other countries profiting by it illicitly. The British frigates, however, were small, old and not sufficiently numerous. American and other slavers carried the flags of nations which had not agreed to Abolition, and could run one of these up at will if chased by a British man-of-war. Horrible tales were told of slave-captains who threw their human cargoes overboard when threatened by a search, and of how the boarding party would find empty holds smelling of Negroes and the iron cauldrons for cooking their food still hot. Conditions in the slave ships became, if anything, much worse, for the necessity to hide the slaves led to their being crammed under casks and coiled ropes, and not let up on deck for air. Wilberforce, who believed human nature to be profoundly and almost irretrievably corrupt, might not have been surprised by his idealism's sinister results. The Abolitionists had under-rated the attractions of the slave trade, and had over-rated the ability of British sea-power to keep it under control.

To patrol the seas was one thing, to patrol the swamps and

the intricate labyrinths of waterways at the mouths of the West
African rivers was quite another. The Gallinas, to the south of
the Banana and the Plantain Islands, remained for decades a
haunt of slavers. In a book published in New York in 1854, the
Gallinas was described by the Italian slave-trader Theodore
Canot as 'a short and sluggish river', oozing out into the
Atlantic. The mouth was 'an interminable mesh of spongy
islands. To one who approaches it from the sea, they look up
from its surface covered with reeds and mangroves, like an
immense field of fungi, betokening the damp and dismal field
which death and slavery have selected for their grand metro-
polis'. At the time of which Canot was writing, the Gallinas
trade was a monopoly in the hands of a 'well-educated mariner
from Malaga' named Don Pedro Blanco. The islets were studded
with slave-factories and barracoons, and guarded by thatched
look-out seats, perched in trees or on poles seventy-five or one
hundred feet from the ground. From these 'the horizon was
constantly swept by telescopes, to announce the approach of
cruisers or slavers'. Don Pedro himself lived in 'a sort of oriental
but semi-barbarous splendour' with an island seraglio in the
depths of the swamp. While Lord Palmerston was Foreign
Secretary, the Gallinas were attacked by a British force from
the sea, and the main slave-factories destroyed. 'The operations
already described were complete as far as they went,' reported
the Commodore in charge, 'still they only checked the Slave
Trade; left there, in one year, it would again break forth with
increased vigour.' The Gallinas were finally reduced by a naval
blockade, and the slave trade in this particular river ended by a
treaty with the Gallinas chiefs. Once again, the value of the
fetish oath could be relied on: 'I have reason to believe' (wrote
Commander Dunlop to the Foreign Office in January 1850)
'that these oaths are seldom broken by the natives, as they
consider that doing so would bring upon them some great misfortune, and they are taken with much solemnity and awe.'
The Gallinas episode is one example of the success of British
diplomacy and the British naval patrol, but detecting and
arresting suspected slavers was not an easy task. The demand
for slaves in the cotton-fields of the United States and in the
coffee plantations in Brazil grew rapidly in the nineteenth
century. The transatlantic slave trade did not end until slavery

itself was abolished in the United States in 1865, and in the Empire of Brazil six years later.

It is thus only three generations ago that traders of European blood ceased to treat African men, women and children as black merchandise.

## V

This has been a deliberately selective study of the Atlantic slave-traders, for a mere catalogue of horrors can prove as repetitious and ineffectual as any other form of mass information. The slave-traders of all countries were individuals. They showed the variations of character which you would find in men engaged in any form of commerce. Their motive, like that of all traders, was to make money. It was the means they coldly chose that condemn them to the execration of posterity.

No writer can foretell the effect his book will have on any reader, but the one certainty he knows is the effect that writing it has had upon himself. Instigated, as I have already said, by the sight of the slave-vaults at Elmina and Cape Coast, as well as by a wish to delve down into the origins of a racial problem that had puzzled me since a happy childhood spent in Washington, DC, I found that my researches and my travels were gradually making me as obsessional as Thomas Clarkson himself. The dimensions of everyday things seemed altered. One was becoming conscious of the evil realities of history which lie behind the façade of much one used to take for granted. My mind seemed filled with pictures of the old Guinea Coast, of the slave ships plunging through Atlantic storms, of human beings sold by *vendue* and by scramble, and of the hideous details of plantation life. These pictures were as vivid as Biard's painting of French and African slave-traders haggling on the Guinea Coast, which is reproduced as an illustration in this book. The friendly face of a Jamaican bus conductor no longer makes me think of rum and calypsos, nor of islands in the sun. The brisk bustle of Bridgetown streets, or the round-eyed Negro children romping in the South End of Boston in the snow now take me back to the shores of Africa in days long past that I have never known. When I read of race riots in America, I think of the dapper slave-merchants of Charleston, and of ships setting out from Liverpool or Nantes or Newport, with manacles and trade-goods in their holds. For these purely personal reasons, I think that we may end with the portrait of a slave ship lying off the Isles de Los on the Windward Coast of Guinea in the summer-time of the year 1773.

This description of *The African,* commanded by a Captain Wilding, is given in the journal of the English botanist, Henry Smeathman, who was spending four years on the Banana Islands collecting specimens of plants for English amateurs. 'Alas!' (he writes) 'what a scene of misery and distress is a full slaved ship in the rains.' He found the clank of fetters, the groans and the stench almost insupportable. Two officers lay delirious in the cabin. Every day two or three slaves dying of the flux, measles or worms, were dropped overboard to the sharks. The sound of the armourer riveting irons on the new arrivals mingled with that of dragging chains, and with the thudding of pestles as the women slaves pounded the rice in mortars. There was the ship's doctor dressing slaves' sores and ulcers, and cramming their mouths with medicines while a seaman stood over the patients with a cat-o'-nine-tails to force them to swallow the draught. Casks, boxes and bales were being hauled on board with creaking tackles, and the carpenter and cooper were hammering away, while others filed and cleaned arms. The barber was shaving slaves' heads, holding his victims by the nose. Goods were being stored everywhere, and the mates would watch over the slaves eating their rice from the little tubs called 'crews' round which six or eight Negroes squatted, using their fingers. Sentinels guarded the barricade which separated the main from the quarter deck. The gangway was choked with black and white seamen from the canoes which were bobbing all round the ship. The galley itself was a scene of 'fire and smoke, chopping, killing, skinning, scalding, boiling, roasting, broiling, frying and scolding. Negroes were using the open latrine near which slave women were washing dirty linen and wiping crockery. Up on the round house, beneath an awning, the captain sat in the shade handing out goods to a dozen traders, while his steward kept the books by his side. Up here under the awning, all was drinking and laughter, lies, blasphemy and rows. There,' concluded Smeathman, 'is a picture for you done from the life.' I am glad to say that it is the last picture of the kind at which I shall ask you to look.

There is, however, one incident with which it seems appropriate to conclude. It occurred on a hot, rainswept night in Benin city, where the houses are set unusually far apart as if everyone were suspicious of his neighbour and where the roads, scarlet with laterite, had turned to purplish mud. I was sitting quietly in a corner of the bar of the Hotel Mogambo, a small, comfortable establishment in which I happened to be spending the night. At a far table a handsome young African chief was seated, wearing fine robes of blue and gold. Beside him was a pretty girl to whom he spoke little. Presently he sent me a message by the steward to say he would like to talk to me. I went over to his table where he introduced me to his companion, whom he remarked was his sister and a dental surgeon – two facts which, when he left us for a moment, she indignantly denied. She said she was bored and tired and waiting for him to take her up to bed. After a short conversation, in which I admitted that I was a writer (although I refrained from saying what I was writing about) he announced that he would like to give me one of his poems as a souvenir. He left the room, his robes richly swirling, and soon came back with a thin printed pamphlet, bound in green paper. It was a poem, he explained, which he had written in hexameters, and it was upon a 'very controversial subject' – the Atlantic slave trade. I took it gratefully and looked at the title. This read:

'*AFRICA FORGIVES. MAY SHE FORGET!*'

# Selective Bibliography

## Printed Sources

*African Non-Fictional Prose in English: Selected Extracts* (University of Ibadan, 1965) to illustrate a paper by Lalage Bown.

Azurara, Gomes Eannes de: *Chronicle of the Discovery and Conquest of Guinea* (translated by C. R. Beazley and E. Prestage; London, Hakluyt Society, 1896, 1897).

Bancroft, Frederic: *Slave Trading in the Old South* (New York, 1931; reprinted 1964).

Barbot, James and Jean: *see* Churchill, John.

Benezet, Anthony: *A Short Account of that part of Africa inhabited by the Negroes, with respect to the Fertility of the Country, the good Disposition of many of the Natives and the Manner by which the Slave Trade is carried on* (Philadelphia, 1762).

Bluett, Thomas: *Some Memoirs of the Life of Job the Son of Solomon* (London, 1734).

Bosman, Willem: *Nauwkeurige Beschryving van de Guinese goud-, tand-, en slave-kust, nevens alle desselfs landen, koningryken en gemenebesten* (Utrecht, 1704). English translation, *A New and Accurate Description of the Coast of Guinea* (London, 1705; reprinted, 1721).

Boswell, James: *The Life of Samuel Johnson* (London, 1791).

Boxer, C. R.: *The Dutch Seaborne Empire 1600–1800* (London, 1965).

Caines, Clement: *History of the General Council and General Assembly of the Leeward Islands . . .* (St Christopher, 1804).

Cash, W. J.: *The Mind of the South* (New York, 1941).

Charleston Junior League (ed.): *Across the Cobblestones: A Charleston Guidebook* (Charleston, S.C., 1965).

Churchill, John: *A Collection of Voyages and Travels* (London, 1732), Vol. V: Barbot, Jean and James: *A Description of the Coasts of North and South Guinea and of Ethiopia Inferior, vulgarly Angola* (first published in French, 1682; translated into English by Jean Barbot).

Churchill, John: *A Collection of Voyages and Travels* (London, 1732), Vol. VI: Phillips, Thomas: *A Journal of a Voyage made in the Hannibal of London, 1693–1694, from England to Cape Monseradoe in Africa . . .*

Clark, Rufus Wheelwright: *The African Slave Trade* (Boston, 1860).

Clarkson, Thomas: *Essay on the Slavery and Commerce of the Human Species . . .* (1786).

# Selective Bibliography

Clarkson, Thomas: *History of the Abolition of the African Slave Trade by the British Parliament* (2 vols., London, 1808).

Clarkson, Thomas: *Strictures on a Life of William Wilberforce* (London, 1838).

Collins, Dr: *Practical Rules for the Management and Medical Treatment of Negro Slaves in the Sugar Colonies, by a Professional Planter* (London, 1803).

Conway, M. D.: *Testimonies concerning Slavery* (London, 1864).

Coupland, Reginald: *Wilberforce* (London, 1923).

Coupland, Reginald: *The British Anti-Slavery Movement* (London, 1933).

Crow, Hugh: *Memoirs* (London, 1830).

Crowder, Michael: *The Story of Nigeria* (London, 1962; revised edition, London, 1966).

Cugoano, Ottobah: *Thoughts and Sentiments on the Evil and Wicked Traffic of the Slavery and Commerce of the Human Species* (London, 1787).

Curtin, Philip D.: *The Image of Africa: British Ideas and Action, 1780–1850* (London, 1965).

Davidson, Basil: *Black Mother: An Inquiry into African History from the Earliest Times of European Discovery till the Eve of Colonial Conquest* (London, 1961).

Davidson, Basil: *Old Africa Rediscovered* (London, 1964).

Davies, K. G.: *The Royal African Company* (London, 1957).

Donnan, Elizabeth: *Documents Illustrative of the History of the Slave Trade to America* (4 vols, Carnegie Institute of Washington, 1935; reprinted in New York, 1965).

Drake, Richard (or Philip): *Revelations of a Slave Smuggler* (ed. Henry Byrd West, New York, 1860).

Duke, Antera: *see* Forde, Daryll C.

Edwards, Bryan: *The History, Civil and Commercial, of the British Colonies in the West Indies* (2 vols, London, 1793).

Equiano, Olaudah: *see* Vassa, Gustavus.

Falconbridge, Alexander: *An Account of the Slave Trade on the Coast of Africa* (London, 1788).

Forde, Daryll C. (ed.): *Efik Traders of Old Calabar* (London, 1956). Containing the *Diary of Antera Duke, an Efik Slave-Trading Chief of the 18th Century*.

Francklyn, Gilbert: *An Answer to the Rev. Mr Clarkson's Essay on the Slavery and Commerce of the Human Species* (London, 1789).

Franklin, John Hope: *From Slavery to Freedom: A History of American Negroes* (New York, 1956; second edition, revised and enlarged, New York, 1964).

Freyre, Gilberto: *Casa-Grande e Senzala* (Rio de Janeiro, 1933).

English translation by Samuel Putnam, *The Masters and the Slaves : A Study in the Development of Brazilian Civilization* (second revised edition, New York, 1956).

Freyre, Gilberto: *Sobrados e Mucambos* (Rio de Janeiro, 1936). English translation by Harriet de Onís, *The Mansions and the Shanties : The Making of Modern Brazil* (New York, 1963).

Fyfe, Christopher: *Sierra Leone Inheritance* (London, 1964).

Gailey, Harry A., Jr: *A History of the Gambia* (London, 1965).

Gaston-Martin: *Nantes au XVIIIe siècle : l'ère des Négriers, 1714–1744* (Paris 1931).

Gaston-Martin: *Histoire de l'Esclavage dans les Colonies Françaises* (Vol. 4 of *Colonies et Empires*. Première série: *Etudes coloniales*). (Paris, 1948.)

Genovese, Eugene D.: *The Political Economy of Slavery : Studies in the Economy and Society of the Slave South* (New York, 1965).

Godwin, Morgan: *The Negro's and Indian's Advocate suing for their Admission into the Churches* (1680).

Greenidge, C. W. W.: *Slavery* (London, 1958).

Jervey, Theodore D.: *The Slave Trade : Slavery and Color* (Columbia, South Carolina, 1926).

Jones, Eldred: *Othello's Countrymen : The African in English Renaissance Drama* (London, 1965).

Jones, G. I.: *The Trading States of the Oil Rivers* (London, 1963).

*Journal of the Commons House of Assembly, Charleston, 1739–1741* (Charleston Museum, South Carolina).

Kingsley, Mary: *Travels in West Africa* (London, 1897, third edition, 1965).

Kingsley, Mary: *West African Studies* (London, 1899, third edition, 1964).

Lander, Richard: *Journal of Richard Lander from Kano to the Coast* (London, 1829).

Laurens, Henry: *A Letter to his Son John Laurens, August 14, 1776* (foreword by Alfred C. Berel; introduction by Richard B. Morrie. Privately printed for Columbia University Libraries, New York, 1964).

Lawrence, A. W.: *Trade Castles and Forts of West Africa* (London, 1963).

Little, Bryan: *The City and County of Bristol* (London, 1954).

Lunan, John: *An Abstract of the Laws of Jamaica relating to Slaves* (Jamaica, 1819).

MacInnes, C. M.: *A Gateway of Empire* (London, 1939).

Mannix, Daniel P. and Cowley, Malcolm: *Black Cargoes : A History of the Atlantic Slave Trade, 1518–1865* (London, 1963).

Martin, Bernard: *John Newton – A Biography* (London, 1950).

Massachusetts Historical Society (ed.): *Commerce of Rhode Island 1726–1800* (Boston, 1914–15).

Massachusetts Historical Society (ed.): *Queries respecting the Slavery and Emancipation of Negroes in Massachusetts, proposed by the Hon. Judge Tucker of Virginia, and answered by the Rev. Dr. Belknap* (Boston, n.d.).

Miller, Henry: *The Air-Conditioned Nightmare* (London edition, 1962).

*Minutes of the Evidence taken before a Committee of the House of Commons . . . to consider of the Circumstances of the Slave Trade, 1790–1791* (4 vols, British Museum, State Papers/Parliamentary/1731–1800/ Accounts & Papers/XXV, XXIX, XXX, XXXIV).

Moore, Francis: *Travels into the Inland Parts of Africa* (London, 1738).

Moore, Samuel: *Biography of Mahammah G. Baquaqua . . . written and revised from his own Words* (Detroit, 1854).

Muir, R.: *History of Liverpool* (Liverpool, 1907).

Newton, John: *Letters and Sermons*, Vol. I (Edinburgh, 1787).

Newton, John: *Posthumous Works: Thoughts upon the African Slave Trade* (London, 1808).

Newton, John: *The Journal of a Slave Trader* (ed. B. Martin and M. Spurrell, London, 1962).

O'Callaghan: *Voyages of the Slavers 'St. John' and 'Arms of Amsterdam', 1659, 1663* (USA, n.d.).

Owen, Nicholas: *Journal of a Slave-Dealer 1754–1759* (ed. Eveline Martin, London, 1930).

Park, Mungo: *Travels in the Interior Districts of Africa 1795–1797* (London, 1799).

Parry, J. H.: *The Spanish Seaborne Empire* (London, 1966).

Phillips, Thomas: *see* Churchill, John.

Phillips, Ulrich B.: *Slavery in America: A Collection of Pamphlets, 1903–1925* (USA, n.d.).

Seeber, Edward Derbyshire: *Anti-Slavery Opinion in France during the Second Half of the 18th Century* (Vol. X of the *John Hopkins Studies in Romance Literatures and Languages*) (London, 1937.)

Sharp, Granville: *Serious Reflections on the Slave Trade and Slavery* (London, 1805).

Sheahan, James Joseph: *History and Description of the Town and Port of Kingston-upon-Hull* (London, 1864).

Snelgrave, William: *A New Account of some Parts of Guinea, and the Slave Trade* (London, 1734).

Society of Friends, Philadelphia: *Epistle of Caution and Advice concerning the Buying and Keeping of Slaves* (Philadelphia, 1754).

*South Carolina Gazette* (Charleston, South Carolina).

Stanfield, James Field: *Observations on a Guinea Voyage* (Seven Letters to Thomas Clarkson) (London, 1788.)

## Selective Bibliography

Taylor, Thomas: *A Biographical Sketch of Thomas Clarkson* (London, 1839).

Unwin, R.: *The Defeat of Sir John Hawkins* (London, 1960).

Vassa, Gustavus: *The Life of Olaudah Equiano or Gustavus Vassa written by Himself* (London, 1790).

Wadström, Carl Bernhard: *Observations on the Slave Trade* (London, 1789).

Wadström, Carl Bernhard: *An Essay on Colonisation particularly applied to the Western Coast of Africa, with some free Thoughts on Cultivation and Commerce; also brief Descriptions of the Colonies already formed, or attempted, in Africa, including those of Sierra Leone and Bulama* (2 vols, London, 1794).

Waterman, Thomas Tileston: *The Mansions of Virginia, 1706–1776* (University of North Carolina, 1946).

Watson, Richard: *A Defence of the Wesleyan Methodist Missions in the West Indies; including a Refutation of the Charges in Mr Marryat's Thoughts on the Abolition of the Slave Trade etc and in other Publications; with Facts and Anecdotes illustrative of the Moral State of the Slaves and of the Missions* (London, 1817).

Williams, Eric: *Capitalism and Slavery* (USA, 1944; reprinted London, 1964).

Williamson, J. A.: *Life of Sir John Hawkins* (London, 1927).

Wish, Harvey (ed.): *Slavery in the South* (New York, 1964).

Wright, Richard: *Black Power* (London, 1956).

Zook, George Frederick: *The Company of Royal Adventurers Trading into Africa* (Lancaster, Pennsylvania, 1919. Reprinted from the *Journal of Negro History*, Vol. IV, No. 2, April 1919).

## Unpublished Sources

Baillie, William: *The Commenda Diary, 1714–1719* (Public Records Office/Treasury/African Companies/T.70/1464).

*Memorandum Book kept at Cape Coast Castle, January 1703 to January 1704* (Public Records Office/Treasury/African Companies/T.70/1463).

Letters to Sir William Codrington from his overseer in Antigua, 1790–1791 (Dodington Park Library).

The Plimpton papers (Special Collections, Butler Library, Columbia University, New York).

The Belknap papers (Massachusetts Historical Society, Boston).

Miscellaneous papers (Massachusetts Historical Society, Boston).

The Peperell papers (Massachusetts Historical Society, Boston).

The Ridley papers (Massachusetts Historical Society, Boston).

# Index

Abolition, 5, 20, 85, 108, 248–62, 271, 274–5, 193n; Act of 1807, 249, 272, 274, 275; African attitude to, 272–4; Committee of House of Commons, 122n, 176, 192, 206, 207; Committee of Privy Council, 122n, 140; in America, 241–5; of slavery, 278

Abolitionists, *see Amis des Noirs;* Brown, Moses; Clarkson, Thomas; Dilwyn, William; Hopkins, Dr Samuel; Lafayette, Mme de; Mirabeau, Honoré; Newton, John; Quakers, the; Ramsay, James; Sewall, Samuel; Sharp, Granville; Wedgwood, Josiah; Wilberforce, William

Accra, Gold Coast, 37, 156; Christiansborg Castle, 32, 53, 186

Adams, Capt. John, 23

African Companies, Brandenburgh Co., 151; *Compagnie du Sénégal,* 151, 198, 206, 207; Company of Adventurers of London, 45; Company of Royal Adventurers of England, 155; Danish Co., 151, 152; Dutch West India Co., 68, 71, 74, 83, 151, 167, 170; English Merchant Adventurers, 151; English Virginia Co., 151; Royal African Co., 37, 89, 150, 151, 152, 155–73, 178, 183, 188; Sierra Leone Co., 264; South Sea Co., 154–5; Swedish West India Co., 151

African forts, garrisons of, 22, 72, 156, 158–60, 163, 190 (*see also* European factors); Christiansborg, *see* Accra; Fort Nassau, *see* Mouri; Fort Orange, *see* Sekondee; Fort Royal, *see* Cape Coast Castle; St Anthony, *see* Axim; St George, *see* Elmina; St Iago, *see* Elmina; St Sebastian, *see* Shama. *See also* Anamabu; Arguin Is.; Bissau; Cacheu; Cape Coast Castle; Commenda; Cormantine; Goree Is.; Gross Friedricksburg; Shama; Takoradi; Winneba; Whydah

African religions, dances, 25–6; European condemnation of, 23, 222; *fetish,* 26, 63–4, 65, 92, 140, 141, 161, 166, 169; funeral sacrifices, 23, 30, 86, 209, 212–3, 221–2; marine deities, 26, 63; *obeah,* 140–143; ritual human sacrifices, 23, 59, 92, 212; *Vodun (Voodoo),* 141–142

Africans in Africa, African/European language barrier, 28, 32; *caboceers,* 172, 173, 179, 181, 182, 187–91, 209; character of, 27, 28, 30; diet, 36; domestic slavery, 85, 88, 175–6, 212–4; Kings' greed for gifts, 62; middlemen, 2, 9, 13, 29, 30, 94, 187; ritual scars, 59; social behaviour of, 27–8, 29; way of life, 27, 28–9; witchcraft, 264. *See also* cannibalism; specific kings.

Agonna, Queen of, 81

Akers & Houston (of St Vincent), 109

Akim, kingdom of, 169, 170

Alcatraz, islands of, 51

# Index

Crowther, Bishop, 23
Cuba, 13, 64, 117, 276; Havanna,
110
Cugoano, Ottobah, 30, 32, 100, 132,
174-5, 194, 195-6
Culshaw, Capt. (*Barbara*), 17
Curaçao, 68, 70, 75
Curtin, Philip D., 59n, 60, 87

Da, Gold Coast, 33
Dahomey, Slave Coast, 89, 94; king
of, 89, 91-5
Danes, 32-3; *see also* African Com-
panies
Dilwyn, William, 250, 252
Dixcove, Gold Coast, 159, 163
Dominica, 52, 108, 122n, 131n;
Roseau, 121
Donnan, Elizabeth, 44
Douglas, Frederick, 228-9
Dove, William, 197-8
Drake, Sir Francis, 49
Drake, Richard, 3-4
Duke, Antera, 209, 212-3, 214, 215-
217, 220
Duke Town, Slave Coast, 216-8
Dutch, at Curaçao, 68, 70, 75;
at Elmina, 65, 69, 70, 71-3, 74,
75, 161, 165, 167, 168; at Suri-
nam, 70, 133; brutality and
callousness, 69, 70; dominant
power on Gold Coast, 74, 155;
first fort, 74; first trade contacts
with Guinea, 68; in Brazil, 68-9,
74, 75; loose interest in Gold
Coast, 74; neglect conversion of
slaves, 70; rivalry with English,
167-70; abolition, 275. *See also,*
African Companies; specific individuals

Ebro, Dick, 203, 204, 209, 254
Edward III of England, 151
Edward IV of England, 41
Edwards, Bryan, 22, 59, 86, 87,
103, 111-2, 113, 114, 122, 137
Efik tribe, 64, 209, 210, 211, 213,
214, 217, 218, 219

Egbo Secret Society, 64, 209, 220-2
Eighty Years War, 65, 68
Elizabeth I of England, 43, 44, 48, 53
Elmina, 5, 22, 33, 42, 43, 53-5, 67-
75, 161, 165, 167, 168, 190, 225,
278; first governor of, 63; building of Castle of St George, 9, 40,
60-1, 62-3; falls to Dutch, 65,
68, 71, 183; sold to English, 74;
St Iago, 68, 72
England, arrival of first negroes, 42.
*See also* Abolition; specific cities
English, at Cape Coast, 150, 156-
173, 178, 187, 189, 235; at Com-
menda, 150, 156, 164, 167;
brutality and callousness of, 69;
buy Elmina from Dutch, 74;
early expeditions to Guinea, 42-
43, 45, 47-53; in West Indies, *see*
Antigua, Barbados, Barbuda,
Dominica, Granada, Jamaica,
Montserrat, Nevis, St Kitts, St
Vincent; rivalry with Dutch,
167-70. *See also* Abolitionists;
African Companies; Plantations;
specific individuals
Equiano, Olaudah, 28-9, 196
European factors, *see* Baillie, Wm;
Barbot, Jean; Bosman, Willem;
Lambe, Capt. Bullfinch; Owen,
Nicholas—13, 19, 22, 78, 82, 83,
157, 163, 167, 178, 179, 188, 189,
190, 276; salaries of, 162
Europeans, condemnation of African religions, 23, 222; effect of
African climate on, 2, 33, 52, 72,
77, 158-60, 163, 186, 190;
European/African language barrier, 28; ignorance of African
history, 38; missionaries, *see* Missionaries; myth of *happy slave*, 21,
86, 114-6, 120, 122, 130-1, 227;
on plantations, *see* Plantations;
patronizing attitude of, 177; views
on Africans, 22, 28, 38, 59-60,
205-6, 207-8, 222. *See also* specific
individuals and nationalities
Exeter, England, 149

# Index

Fabian, William, 41
Falconbridge, Alexander, 4n, 101, 102, 106–7, 187
Fan tribes, 31
Faneuil, Peter, 230
Fernando Po island, 38, 183
Ferdinand and Isabella, 41
Fetu, Gold Coast, 171–2; king's palace, 171; Queen of, 172
Firempong, king of Akyem, 33
Fletcher, Abraham, 142
Freetown, Sierra Leone, 50, 265
French, in West Indies, see Guadaloupe, Haiti, Martinique, Montserrat, St Domingue, St Lucia; merchants, 148–9; early expeditions to Africa, 42, 43; on Goree Island, 206–7; ships, 148–9; *Côde Noir*, 128, 136; abolition, 20, 275; see also African Companies; specific individuals
Fulani tribe, 206

Gabon, Lower Guinea, 38, 81; king of, 80, 81
Gallinas, Grain Coast, 276, 277
Gambia, Senegambia, 40, 45, 104, 225, 233, 238, 239; river, 28, 206
Gaston-Martin, Professor, 148
Genoese, 19n
George I of England, 91, 154
Georgia, 114
Ghana, 34, 35, 73; empire of, 28
Glasgow, 149
Gold Coast, 6, 9, 16, 22, 34, 38, 40, 42, 55, 59, 60–6, 69–74, 155–73; see also specific forts, kingdoms, towns
Gomeno, Lorenzo de, Governor of Bresa, 9, 13n
Gonçalvez, Antam, 8
Goree island, 206, 207
Grain Coast, 1, 2, 38, 262–7; see also specific place names
Grandy, King George, 218–9
Greenidge, C. W. W., 85n
Grenada, 32, 100, 106, 132, 196
Gross Friedrichsburg, Gold Coast, 5

Guadaloupe, 121, 124, 133, 239
Guinea Coast, 2, 8, 9, 35–54, 263, 278; Upper Guinea, 38; Lower Guinea, 38; see also specific regions
Guinea coin, 37
Guinea, Gulf of, 9, 13, 37, 38, 50, 55, 89

Haiti, 64, 141, 142, 275
Hakluyt, Richard, 43, 46, 47, 49, 51
Hakluyt Society, 39n
Hawkins, John, 43, 44, 46, 47–53, 64, 68
Hawkins, William, 46
Hazlitt, William, 250–1
Hemmersam, Michael, 72
Henry the Navigator, 8, 39, 40, 184
Herodotus, 39
Hispaniola, 13, 46, 117
Holiday, king of Bonny, see Bonny
Homer, 85
Hopkins, Dr Samuel, 242, 243

Ibebo tribe, 64
Ibibio tribe, 213n, 214, 220
Ibo (Ebo) tribe, 28–9, 59, 153
Isles de Los, 279
Ivory Coast, 38

Jalof tribe, 52, 206
Jamaica, 13, 59, 87, 96, 103, 107, 108, 110, 111, 112, 124, 140, 142–3, 150, 185, 186, 240, 241; Frontier estate, 142–3; Port Maria, 143; Spanish Town, 121; Trinity estate, 142–3; Worthy Park plantation, 112–3, 124
James I of England, 45
James II of England, 155; as Duke of York, 163
Jaquin, Slave Coast, 89, 91, 94, 95
Jefferson, Thomas, 226
Jeffreys, Sir Jeffrey, 97
Joal, Senegambia, 206
Jobson, Richard, 45
John II of Portugal, 40, 41
Johnson, Dr Samuel, 20–1, 31, 245
Jones, Professor Eldred, 46

# Index

Jones, Capt. James (owner of the *Brookes*), 193n

Kabes, John, 172, 188–91
Kamp, Nicholas, 33
Kings Town, 1
Kingsley, Charles, 49
Kingsley, Mary, 26, 31, 76
Kingston-upon-Hull, 246, 248
Kipling, Rudyard, 50
Knivet, Anthony, 47
Koin, Colonel van, 71
Kumasi, Ashanti, 30, 58, 59, 60
Kwame Ansa, King, 61, 62

Lace, Ambrose, 216
Lafayette, Mme de, 20
Lagos, Slave Coast, 14, 247
Lambe, Capt. Bullfinch, 91, 93–4
Lancaster, England, 149
Laurens, Henry, 223–4, 238, 244
Lawrence, A. W., 32, 36n
Leclerc, Capt., 3
Leopard Society, 220
Little Acron, King of, 81
Liverpool, 12, 76, 110, 145–7, 149–150, 193n, 218, 219, 250, 251, 253, 255, 261, 274, 279; profits from slave trade, 145–6
Lok, John, 42
London, 12, 149
Lopez, Aaron, 226, 234–5, 240–1
Lopez, Abraham, 240
Louisiana, 114

Macaulay, Zachary, Governor of Sierra Leone, 264
Mali, Empire of, 28
Manhattan Island, 74
Mannix, Daniel P., 47n
Martinique, 17, 27, 121, 124, 133
Maryland, 228–9
Mary Tudor, 43
Massachusetts, 231, 233, 237; Historical Society, 226. *See also* Boston; Salem
Maurice, John, of Nassau, 68–9
Meale, Capt. Thomas (*Queen*), 167

Mendes, Abraham Pereira, 240
Merrick, Capt. George (*Africa*), 108–10
Methodists, 131–2
Miller, Henry, 225, 226
Minchinton, Professor Walter, 108n, 149
Mirabeau, Honoré, 193n, 275
Missionaries, 23, 27–8, 33, 40, 67, 70, 131–2, 183, 185, 186
Mississippi river, 114
Montgomery, Alabama, 226
Montserrat, 122n
More, Hannah, 271
Morley, James, 201
Moore, Capt. Samuel, 239
Mouri, Gold Coast, Fort Nassau, 74, 167, 168
Muir, R., 149
Mundingo tribe, 45, 88, 206, 228

Nantes, France, 12, 148, 279
Nevis, 131n
New Amsterdam, *see* New York
New England, 16n, 19, 226, 230–1, 232, 233, 235, 237, 241–3; *see also* specific states and cities
New Orleans, 114
New York, 75, 240
Newport, Rhode Island, 18, 114, 226, 229, 231, 234, 237, 238, 239–241, 242, 279
Newton, Capt. (later Rev.) John (*Duke of Argyll*), 2, 3, 20, 100–1, 104, 111, 150, 175, 235–6, 241, 262, 264–72; enters slave trade, 262; early life in Plantain Islands, 262, 265–7; returns to England, 268; marries, 268; as slave ship captain, 268–71; description of slave ship, 3, 100–1, 269; becomes abolitionist, 271
Niger river, 23, 40, 110, 210
Nigeria, 35, 220
Noble, Capt. Clement (*Brookes*), 197

Oil river, Slave Coast, 165, 200, 208; tribes of, 212

292

# Index

Opie, Mrs Amelia, 123, 124, 125–6
Owen, Nicholas, 1–2, 3, 49, 232, 264

Palmerston, Lord, 277
Papacy, the, 40–1, 43
Park, Mungo, 54
Parke, Capt. (*Canterbury*), 211
Parker, Isaac, 203–4, 214, 254
Parrot Island, Slave Coast, 212
Peace of Aix-la-Chapelle, 154
Pennsylvania, 243
Pensacola Bay, Florida, 3
Pepple, king of Bonny. *See* Bonny
Pepys, Samuel, 155
Pernambuco. *See* Brazil.
Philadelphia, 193n, 229
Philip II of Spain, 48
Phillips, Capt. Thomas (*Hannibal*), 97–9, 150, 178–82
Phillips, Professor Ulrich, 113, 117–120
Pitt, William, 247, 248
Plantain Islands, Grain Coast, 262, 264, 265–7
Plantations, Betty's Hope, Antigua, 105; Farleigh Hill, Barbados, 121; Frontier Estate, Jamaica, 142–3; Providence, Rhode Island, 239, 241; on St Kitts, 121–2; Trinity Estate, Jamaica, 142–3; Worthy Park, Jamaica, 112–3, 124; life on, 104–5, 112–4, 115, 117–44, 229; branding of slaves, 78n; Christianity on, 78n, 128, 131–2; cruelty to slaves, 69–70, 104, 113–4, 127–8, 129, 132, 136–138, 143, 228–9, 270–1; house slaves, 127, 133–4, 139, 228; *maroons*, 136, 139; mortality and sickness, 104–5, 112–3, 126; myth of 'happy slave', 114–6, 120, 122, 125, 131, 227; myth of negro stupidity, 114–5; slave food, 130–1; slave-laws, 111, 128, 136, 228, 244; slave retaliation, 134–6, 139–40, 227; slave revolts, 128, 134, 136, 141, 142–3; slave suicides, 113, 136; sugar cultiva-

tion, 124–7; temperament of slaves, 112, 113–4, 121, 136, 143; treatment of women slaves, 115, 133–4; witchcraft, 136, 139
Plato, 85
Plymouth, England, 149, 254
Porto Bello, 154
Porto Rico, 13n, 117
Portugal, first slaves in, 8–9; Lagos, 9; Lisbon, 9, 12
Portuguese, trading rights of, 9, 41; first reach Guinea, 39; initiate slave trade, 8; kidnap negroes, 39–40; build first fort, 40; sell slaves to Genoese, 13; at Cacheu and Bissau, 183; at Elmina, 5, 9, 22, 33, 40, 60–3, 67–8; at Whydah, 67, 183; in Brazil, 41, 65, 75; in Congo (Angola), 183–186; trade with Benin, 66; attempts to convert Africans, 41–42, 63, 65, 66–7, 184; belief in miscegenation, 63, 184; comparative racial tolerance of, 71, 186–7; in Eighty Years War, 65n; unpopularity with Africans, 41; loose grip on Gold Coast, 65, 68, 183, 186; abolition, 275
Potter, Simeon, 239
Pra River, Gold Coast, 66, 92
Preston, H. W., 232
Price, Robert, 113
Prince, Capt. (*Marlborough*), 168
Providence, Rhode Island, 234, 241; plantation, 239, 241

Quakers, the, 123, 229, 241–3, 248, 250, 252, 256

Ramsay, James, 252
Rhode Island, 234, 249–41, 243. *See also* Bristol; Newport; Providence
Ridley, Matthew, 230
Rio Basso, Windward Coast, 3
Rio de Janeiro, *see* Brazil
Rio Nuna, Grain Coast, 266

# Index